Tony
Nice to see you
last April.
Best

Dear Anthony
Many thanks for your
contribution
Best wishes
Nic C

Educating
Architects

Thames & Hudson

How tomorrow's
practitioners will
learn today

Educating
Architects

EDITED BY

NEIL SPILLER & NIC CLEAR

I would like to thank Rahesh Ram for having the initial idea for this book. Nic Clear, Simon Herron and Mark Garcia for helping hone the choice of schools and the content of the book. Lucas Dietrich and Thames & Hudson for publishing such a fine and important book. Caroline Ellerby for collating, copy-editing and project managing the book – I couldn't have done it without her. Gratitude is also due to the University of Greenwich for providing a new architecture school building by award-winning architects, financial support for this project, and the opportunity to create a world-class school.

I dedicate this book to my two sons Edward and Tom, and to all the people featured in this book, teacher or student. It has been your day-to-day toil and victories that have made this book possible.

Neil Spiller

Drafting chair and table, 2013 (Dino Paxenos / Modern50.com)

First published in the United Kingdom in 2014 by Thames & Hudson Ltd,
181A High Holborn, London WC1V 7QX

Educating Architects: How Tomorrow's Practitioners Will Learn Today
© 2014 University of Greenwich, London

Designed by Michael Lenz, Draught Associates Ltd (draught.co.uk)

British Library Cataloguing-in-Publication Data

A catalogue record for this book is available from the British Library

ISBN 978-0-500-34300-5

Printed in China by Shanghai Offset Printing Products Ltd

To find out about all our publications, please visit
www.thamesandhudson.com. There you can subscribe
to our e-newsletter, browse or download our current catalogue,
and buy any titles that are in print.

Contents

overleaf
Olia Fomina, Frederico Fialho,
Daniel Hambleton, Christoffer
Marsvik, Ana Garcia Puyol,
Varvara Toulkeridou, Ben
Schneiderman, Sarah
Goldfarb and James
Wisniewski, Manta. Smart
Geometry 2012 Studio (tutors:
Guillermo Bernal, Eric
Ameres, Zackery Belanger,
Seth Edwards), School of
Architecture, Rensselaer
Polytechnic Institute, 2012

Paradoxical simultaneities: Architectural education at the edge of the 21st century

- Neil Spiller, Hawksmoor Chair of Architecture and Landscape and Deputy Pro Vice Chancellor, University of Greenwich

This book is about something very valuable indeed. Architectural education is a delicate ecology, but thankfully it is in the hands of deans and directors (call them what you will) who vigorously defend its integrity, right to exist, outputs and students from the vicissitudes and strange economies of academia. These defenders of the faith (many of the most renowned and vivacious are featured in this book) are highly dexterous, often excellent lecturers and public engagers, but above all they are mentors to generations of students who are empowered to go out into the world and change it for the good.

Good architectural education should have the exploration and indulgence of the art school, the technical and pragmatic considerations of the scientific lab, the lawyer's chambers and the builder's hut. Striking this combination of ambiences is very hard; finding the staff to deliver it is equally taxing. We live in a time of eclectic paradox and extreme simultaneities, where very little seems to make sense in relation to

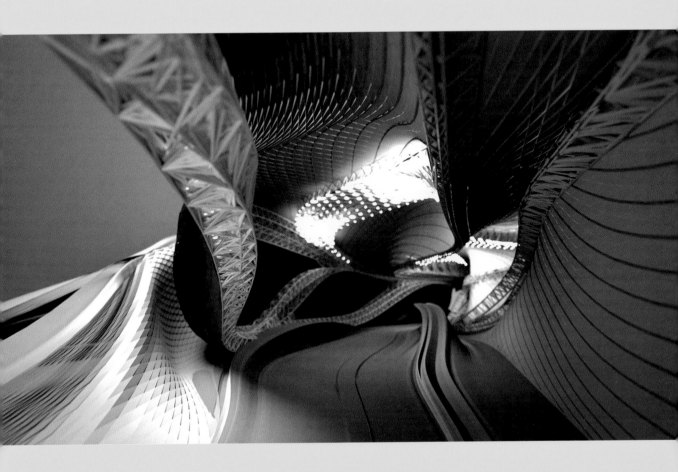

Krisztian Csémy, Jasmina
Frincic and Jakub Klaska,
in-form. Urban Laboratory
London: Studio Zaha Hadid,
University of Applied Arts
Vienna, 2009

economics, politics, social divides, global warming, carbon footprints
and human interaction. Yet despite the sophisms of the everyday,
we are simultaneously becoming aware of our effect on the world,
the limitations of the old bulk-manufactured materials and our integral
interrelationship with all things. In recent years, architectural education
has been presented with numerous creative opportunities to reconsider
itself. These include the great tsunami of technology that has affected
how we work, what we work on, what it is made of and when we work
on it. Materials are changing, models of composite or soft materials
have been developed, and this arena continues to expand.

The emergence of digital fabrication techniques will, of course,
change how our architectures are built, composed and procured. The
old dichotomies between buildings and landscapes are being eroded,
and all terrains are now seen as mutually ecologically synergetic.
We bask in the virtual sun and we can pluck digital fruits from the air.

Tom Smith, Simulating
a Crashed Architecture,
London. Unit 23 (tutors:
Bob Sheil, Emmanuel
Vercruysse), Bartlett School
of Architecture, University
College London, 2011–12

The virtual and the actual are synthesized into a new, ever-growing, smart computational ambience (good or bad). All this, and much more, has brought about the need to discuss, compare and contrast many aspects of architectural education: the buildings it is taught in, the international teaching methodologies employed, the technologies utilized and the histories, theories and futures applied to it, as well as which institutions and people are recognizing the changes, embracing them, baulking at them and subverting them.

The metabolics of architecture school

The best architecture schools are agile, universities are not. The best architecture schools employ iterative teaching methods conducted one to one with students; universities see this as uneconomic. The best architecture schools ensure that nothing is off limits to their students' growing understanding of their world; universities like transcribed learning outcomes, all legislated by politically correct jargon to ensure 'quality', allegedly.

Schools themselves need to be young and vital, but husks can grow around them as staff become set in their ways or complacent or lazy. Once great schools can be handed over to non-visionary custodians, before they intellectually and creatively die, possibly never to be revitalized. This is a process of constant change, as schools are buffeted in the currents of economics, ambition, staff migration, reputation and even fashion, as well as a multitude of other factors. To create a world-class architecture school and maintain it at the cutting edge is a skill few have, and it must be respected at the highest level.

Occasionally a school blossoms with a seismic intensity and becomes a new centre for debate and discourse, its outputs recognized by the architectural cognoscenti. Though this is rare, it disrupts the established order of top architectural institutions, and becomes a catalyst for further change. Those represented in this book are engaged in such battles and ambitions on a daily basis. Their days are full of thoughts about how to inject noise into the system, to precipitate change, and to find new ways of describing and communicating our evolving contemporary spatial conditions and new tactics for creating architectural space within them. A good school forages, consumes, digests, excretes and moves on. It is a creative and thoughtful intellectual nomad, taking joy in offbeat discoveries, delighting in

strange juxtapositions and revelling in new ideas. A good school has an eye to the future through the lens (not the blindfold) of the past. In a good school, *now* is always the first year of something new.

Training architects is becoming more complicated; they need to know more to be able to exist and contribute well in the modern world. It is a unique education that is simultaneously broad and specific, as well as a pedagogic asset the world over. But for all the ambition, excitement and continual search for architectural joy and newness, we must not forget the other side of our existence. As television spouts out decade after decade of global crises, oppression, Armageddon weather patterns, societal unrest and poverty, we have become numb to the implications and forgetful of the pained millions on the face of this little ball of blue, brown and green. Within these pages, Ben Nicholson of the School of the Art Institute of Chicago rightfully reminds us of such myopia (see pp. 236–41), and the huge gulfs of power, influence, resources and respect that architects often reinforce with their puppy-dog optimism and tail-wagging. This is all part of the architectural paradox of the twenty-first century – a matter for students, staff and the profession to ponder over.

Maggie Grady, Nest for a Road Runner Bird, an 'Everything' drawing, Chicago. Creating Home on the Edge of Time studio (tutors: Ben Nicholson, Doug Pancoast, Dan Devening), Department of Architecture, Interior Architecture and Designed Objects, School of the Art Institute of Chicago, 2012

Lessons learned

What have I learned from putting this book together? The first thing is that the world is not in thrall to parametricism, and the nagging fear that it has become a fashionable rash across the world in unfounded. Parametrics are merely another set of tools in the architectural toolbox, and not the harbinger of doom for all other tools. Schools that have propagated parametricism in the past, at the expense of all else, are moving on, and their very powerful PR machines are alighting on other interests and messages.

There is a wide variety of media, intellectual and conceptual context, scale of operation and pragmatic engagement throughout today's architecture schools. I would wager that never before has there been such a fecund diversity of projects – and methods of delivering them – being explored. There is no prevailing orthodoxy, such as the old dogmas and doctrines of Modernism, now happily vanquished. Now, with fewer yardsticks to measure the overall success of a project, much is often left out or seen as secondary to the pre-eminence of form. This varies from school to school and studio to studio, and must be guarded against, as form is merely one element in the deployment of a successful piece of architecture. Another facet of contemporary architectural education is to concentrate on a small part, make it work and test it. While this is often laudable, it can blind students to the wider picture of architecture's social, political and cultural aspects.

One should approach this book as one should approach architectural education: take nothing for granted, view all with a healthy interested intellect, and extrapolate what each word or picture might mean in a wider context. If this book were a cake, it would be one baked by hundreds of chefs, with a variety of mixes and filled with many different kinds of fruits. Some bites will excite more than others, but it is a testament to what we can do. It includes a great number of erudite and knowledgeable authors and teachers; such a selection of views on this subject has never before been put together in book form. Reading each contribution has been a joy for me, as I hope it will be for you.

TTTHub: Tangible Teamwork Table at the Hub. Chief investigators: Flora Salim, Jane Burry, Sarah Pink, Gerda Gemser, Kerry London, Spatial Information Architecture Laboratory, RMIT University, 2013

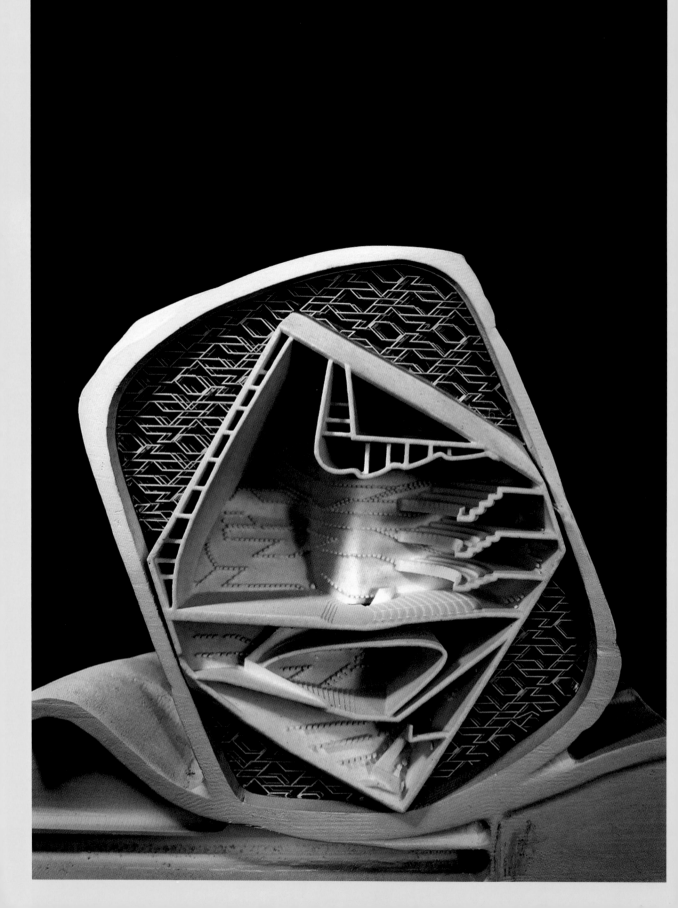

Above all, I can report that, in many places, architectural education is far from dead, resting on its laurels or in retreat. The vanguard are galvanizing it, greasing and deploying it to maximum effect, honing the possibilities for our environments of the near future. As teachers of architects, our genealogy is strong and our architectural experimentation diverse and full of vitality.

Let a million flowers grow.

Timing is everything
... or is it?

– Professor Sir Peter Cook, Emeritus Professor,
Bartlett School of Architecture, University College
London, and Director, CRAB Studio

**Before we start, there is one essential question we must ask, which to
some readers of this book may be an uncomfortable one: What is more
important – architecture or learning? I will not be fobbed off with the
response: 'they're both important'. So I repeat the question: come
on – architecture or learning?**

Cussedly, I find myself quite comfortable with the answer:
architecture!

All through those years from 1964 to 2006, when teaching was my
principal paid activity and my whole universe – friends, enemies, loves,
wife – stemmed from the worlds of the Architectural Association, the
Städelschule in Frankfurt, and Bartlett School of Architecture, University
College London (with a few amusing sorties elsewhere), I described
myself as a 'joke academic', telling myself that I was a working architect
with a bit of teaching on the side. It was only when it was pointed out
that I had revived at least two schools and begat several thousand
architects as part of the machinery of those places that I would admit:
'Well, yes, maybe I'm an academic who dreams of being a joke academic.'
But all the time, of course, I dreamed of becoming an architect.

Now, having built six buildings, I *am* an architect, so maybe
I can relax on that one and begin to realize how much of my response
system is founded in a special particular miasma that invades almost
every school of architecture I know. A certain comfort zone that is fed
by a mixture of tolerance, irritation and mystery, overlaid by mythology,
elitism and escape.

I will explain.

Tolerance

Even the most die-hard schools with the most bombastic of professors and the narrowest of constituencies (one tries to avoid them, but, my God, they still exist), find themselves absorbing deviants, or the odd eccentric. There is the odd study trip, where (like the child in the Hans Christian Andersen story who sees that the king wears no clothes) a student with a wandering eye will notice a building that is not on the prescribed list. Or a lecturer who, by accident, has come along with an original storyline … and the hermetic seal is punctured once and for all.

Opposite to this is the totally soft-centred academy, where not only anything goes, but anyone who reacts vociferously to a position or an architecture is deemed as politically incorrect, as rocking the boat. (One tries to avoid these too, despite their apparent benignancy.)

More subtle is the school that has a territory in which it enjoys indulging. While this may seem strong, such indulgence is usefully mobilized by time, evolving from one identifiable set of fascinations to another. Where the catchment of students deliberately includes jokers in the pack (made more possible if one can eyeball the applicants – a rare luxury). Where the catchment of teachers is manipulated by a director with a good nose, or where the hiring committee – if there has to be one – is wittily constituted. So to some extent, there has to be tolerance, since the mix is potentially (creatively) volatile.

Those in charge of inviting visiting lecturers and critics can, then, also be very subtle: they would be inhuman if they didn't pull in their mates and fellow travellers, but if they pull in their enemies (at least to see the whites of their eyes), and pull in some weirdos, people who happen to be in the district, friends of students or whoever, a very interesting alchemy can set in.

In-house fascinations can then be strengthened from the implicit questioning of the newly exposed alternatives. Students will begin to think for themselves. Faculty architects will regroup. Their architecture might even move forward.

Irritation

Actually, students can be very irritating – how they repeat the obvious, how they see good and bad only in terms of the effects on them personally, how they jump to conclusions, how imitative and annoyingly self-seeking they are. How they butter up to you until they've got all

they need from you, and then hardly give you the time of day in the
street a year later. Similarly, we are all aware how other members of
the faculty can be irritating. I'll bet anybody reading this who teaches
architecture (even in a nice place) has spent at least two hours in any
week groaning about him, her or those who inhibit the programme,
shouldn't have been promoted, pedal crap ideas, have too much
influence with the Dean ... blah, blah, blah. Unfortunately, this seems
to be what makes academic institutions (not) go round.

Capping irritation is a difficult art that requires one to be very
vigilant (tiring), very cynical (dangerous, but useful) or very tolerant
indeed (this can soon lead to a total lack of discrimination). I'll settle for
the middle one: pretend that you haven't noticed how boring the student
is (though I did once go to sleep in a tutorial). One very naughty trick
here is to discuss the work of another student to the first (boring) one;
ten to one, they will not have the wits to notice! The trick with the faculty
bores is to introduce the hate-subject yourself – fast – and before they've
had time to rally, divert the conversation. With luck, they'll melt
(well, maybe).

Mystery

This goes a long way, and can form one of the most enjoyable aspects
of the whole game. After all, the basis of most religions, political systems
and much high culture is based on the unverifiable but tantalizing.
Why should architecture be presumed to be above this? Architecture
is the most engaging, most intangible, most tantalizing bullshit!

How can we prove that one building is better than another?
OK, we can throw around a few statistics and measurements. But
intrinsically better? Really? A step along into justification for method
or mannerism. Why minimal? Why gothic? Why rational? Why spatial?
We're on a slippery slope, but with the elation of the skier who slithers
ever faster and plays 'dare' with the rocks, trees and unexpected crevices.

In parallel, there is surely the mystery of the talented and
imaginative individuals who emerge in the academies. There is
the immense delight of watching someone begin to get the hang of
the designing process, not necessarily by following the rules, but by
stringing together a series of coincident triggers that so often is quite
unique to that person. Surely creativity is one of the greatest mysteries.
Just when things are getting predictable, someone comes up with

THE COOL CHICKS
ALWAYS SEEM TO BE
IN STUDIO 'C'
.... MAYBE I'LL
WORK LATE...?

YEAH! THEY'RE
UNDOUBTEDLY
VERY BRIGHT KIDS

I QUESTION YOUR TERMS OF REFERENCE ... BARBARA

THESE GUYS INSIST THAT ARCHITECTURE _IS_ AN ART FORM

a new take on things. Teaching – or rather the observation of realization – renders you one of its balmy moments.

Mythology

Mythology is surely not the same thing. We should not question the hallowed: building A is beyond criticism, building B is unworthy of discussion. This discussion is relevant: you have to take part in it otherwise you are a fool; you must read the appropriate books, critiques, references, absorb the buzzwords, be able to quote its gurus, otherwise you are a dumbo.

Architecture professors are big on telling you what to (what not to) see, what to (what not to) read, and who to (who not to) listen to, and recent generations of students have developed a great facility for sniffing out who to (and who not to) date, hang out with or be photographed in the company of. We don't need tutors in marketing; in the smarter schools, the kids know well how to market. For some of them, looking at or talking about buildings is seen as bordering on the geeky, but post-theory theory – now that's an impressive line.

Elitism

Probably the most edgy of all on the list. Of course, in my culture it is frowned upon: ethically, socially and psychologically. It is too close for comfort to the shadows of ethnic superiority, privilege and arrogance. Yet on reflection it is the creation of an elite that underpins the advancement of civilization. Culture, in the loose sense of the word, is a form of recognized elitism. The three schools I know best remain elitist and, after a while, play games with the myth of their specialness.

Operationally, I believe in the existence of an elite, but essentially an achievist elite – you can join into it if you have done something very special, or continue to do things that are fairly special. You should not be admitted into the elite just by birthright or dining in smart restaurants, or by being able to quote smart bons mots from others' work (the equivalent of the 'smart restaurant syndrome', actually). By the same token, it is essential that the terms of distinction of the elite should be up for constant revision. Isn't it weird that it takes twenty years to build up a reputation for a school, but forty years to lose it?

One has played it up in order to convince a school that it *is* special, can become *more* special, and those that can't hack it must

get out of the kitchen. Perhaps it is cruel, but the most extraordinary
work can be developed and produced within the hothouse, with some
of it even proving useful to the business of real architecture outside.
Why otherwise does the Foster + Partners office sniff around The Bartlett
with its butterfly net, year after year (and there are innumerable parallels
around New York)?

Nor do I fully take on board the response that, of course, we Brits
just relish the class system. The creepiest instances of rejective elitism
exist around those American architect–academic tables where everybody
is referred to only by first name, and heaven help the child from the
Andersen fable who pipes up, 'But who is Peter?'

Escape

Escape is surely all that is left? Its relevance in the present discussion
is actually two-way. At some time, the majority of architecture school
inmates will escape into reality. Though, of course, a few will blink, find
the air smelly and dart back in again as teachers, comforted by that same
predictability of the students and those same moans of the faculty.

Creative escapism – now that's another take on the issue. At
best, the ideas that are developed via the student experiment, the
really original piece of research, but also, at best, during one of those
extraordinary sequences when two or three critics are really getting
off on the trigger offered by a student project, and are really getting off
on each other's lateral thought/perversity/quaintness/perception –
or whatever. The jazz aficionado will recognize the syndrome, the riff,
the runaway into a momentary sublime.

Thus a school can (just about) exist as a legitimized Temple of
Escape. My carp here (as usual) is that in many cases it is the spirit
of architecture (and not just the mundanities of construction practice)
that is being escaped from. Somehow this detachment, though not
considered polite conversation in academies, has a mysterious, almost
surreptitious, echo in any survey of the landscape of architectural
practice and, to use an archaic word, apprenticeship.

Look carefully at the trajectory of wily Mr X, smooth-operating
Miss Y, or tactically smart Dr Z. Not only their choice of club/bar/pillow/
seminar-group companion will have been judiciously made, but their
movements in and out of school will have been equally deft. Watch not
only who they study with, but when. Watch whose office they attach

NO — I WON'T BE BACK AT
PRINCETON 'TILL THE 18TH

THINGS WEREN'T GOING
SO WELL
THAT NIGHT.....

CRAB Studio (Peter Cook and Gavin Robotham), Soheil Abedian School of Architecture, Bond University, Gold Coast, Queensland, Australia, 2012

themselves to, and when they leave. Since (whatever they say) most of them have access to a bit of family money, when push comes to shove they may even make an uneconomic move.

But now look more carefully still – for there is another syndrome overlaying itself upon this one. Joe went to an unknown school, but got himself into OMA/Herzog & de Meuron/Zaha/BIG/you name it, was good, moved up and moved out with a real credential far better than a Harvard Master's. He is really the player on the scene. Otto went to the AA's Design Research Lab, not to listen to all those funny lectures, but to get a fast run into the Zaha office. Highly marketable. Yale now offers a professoriate of such brilliant contacts that it is irresistible. There is even a new variant: the guy or girl who moves into the big town and goes to every lecture, every gathering and every bar, and then makes a move – school-wards, but probably office-wards. Whereas the seeker for knowledge who plays it strictly through the academic path (Bachelor's/Master's/Doctorate) may well have got caught in the niceties of definition, but will suffer agonies as an underling in Joe's team. Not only that, but Joe might have a few conceptual ideas too: 'Help!' And be able to do more with them: 'Help! Help!' And be able to think faster … dare I go on?

I seriously believe that the academies should take heed. Maybe one day soon the unwritten certification of, say, four years at OMA, Herzog & de Meuron or Zaha Hadid will be recognized as a far more desirable reference than that PhD, or the architecture profession will gradually divide into the categories (to borrow from cricket) of gentlemen and players.

That could be really weird.

This article was first published in *Studioplex, vol. 1: Architecture, a Timely Matter* (Los Angeles, 2012).

250 things an architect should know

- Michael Sorkin, Distinguished Professor
of Architecture, Director of the Graduate Program
in Urban Design, City College of New York,
and Principal, Michael Sorkin Studio

1. The feel of cool marble under bare feet
2. How to live in a small room with five strangers for six months
3. ... with the same strangers in a lifeboat for one week
4. The modulus of rupture
5. The distance a shout carries in the city
6. The distance of a whisper
7. Everything possible about Hatshepsut's temple (try not to see it as 'Modernist', *avant la lettre*)
8. The number of people with rent subsidies in New York City
9. ... in your town (include the rich)
10. The flowering season for azaleas
11. The insulating properties of glass
12. The history of its production and use
13. ... and of its meaning
14. How to lay bricks
15. What Victor Hugo really meant by 'this will kill that'
16. The rate at which the seas are rising
17. Building information modelling
18. How to unclog a rapidograph
19. The Gini coefficient

20. A comfortable tread-to-riser ratio for a six-year-old

21. ... in a wheelchair

22. The energy embodied in aluminium

23. How to turn a corner

24. How to design a corner

25. How to sit in a corner

26. How Antoni Gaudí modelled the Sagrada Família and calculated its structure

27. The proportioning system for the Villa Rotonda

28. The rate at which that carpet you specified off-gasses

29. The relevant sections of the Code of Hammurabi

30. The migratory patterns of warblers and other seasonal travellers

31. The basics of mud construction

32. The direction of prevailing winds

33. Hydrology is destiny

34. Jane Jacobs, in and out

35. Something about feng shui

36. Something about Vastu Shilpa

37. Elementary ergonomics

38. The colour wheel

39. What the client wants

40. What the client thinks it wants

41. What the client needs

42. What the client can afford

43. What the planet can afford

44. The theoretical basis for modernity and a great deal about its factions and inflections

45. What post-Fordism means for the mode of production of building

46. Another language

47. What the brick really wants

48. The difference between Winchester Cathedral and a bicycle shed

49. What went wrong in Fatehpur Sikri

50. What went wrong in Pruitt-Igoe

51. What went wrong with the Tacoma Bridge

52. Where the CCTV cameras are

53. Why Mies really left Germany

54. How people lived in Çatal Hüyük

55. The structural properties of tufa

56. How to calculate the dimensions of brise-soleil
57. The kilowatt costs of photovoltaic cells
58. Vitruvius
59. Walter Benjamin
60. Marshall Berman
61. The secrets of the success of Robert Moses
62. How the dome of the Duomo in Florence was built
63. The reciprocal influences of Chinese and Japanese building
64. The cycle of the Ise Grand Shrine
65. Entasis
66. The history of Soweto
67. What it's like to walk down La Rambla
68. Backup
69. The proper proportions of a gin martini
70. Shear and moment
71. Shakespeare, etc.
72. How the crow flies
73. The difference between a ghetto and a neighbourhood
74. How the pyramids were built
75. ... and why
76. The pleasures of the suburbs
77. ... and the horrors
78. The quality of light passing through ice
79. The meaninglessness of borders
80. The reasons for their tenacity
81. The creativity of the ecotone
82. The need for freaks
83. Accidents must happen
84. It is possible to begin designing anywhere
85. The smell of concrete after rain
86. The angle of the sun at the equinox
87. How to ride a bicycle
88. The depth of the aquifer beneath you
89. The slope of a disability ramp
90. The wages of construction workers
91. Perspective by hand
92. Sentence structure
93. The pleasure of a spritz at sunset at a table by the Grand Canal

94.   The thrill of the ride

95.   Where materials come from

96.   How to get lost

97.   The pattern of artificial light at night, seen from space

98.   What human differences are defensible in practice

99.   Creation is a patient search

100. The debate between Otto Wagner and Camillo Sitte

101. The reasons for the split between architecture and engineering

102. Many ideas about what constitutes utopia

103. The social and formal organization of the villages of the Dogon

104. Brutalism, Bowellism and the Baroque

105. How to *derive*

106. Woodshop safety

107. A great deal about the Gothic

108. The architectural impact of colonialism on the cities
      of Northern Africa

109. A distaste for imperialism

110. The history of Beijing

111. Dutch domestic architecture in the seventeenth century

112. Aristotle's *Politics*

113. His *Poetics*

114. The basics of wattle and daub

115. The origins of the balloon frame

116. The rate at which copper acquires its patina

117. The levels of particulates in the air of Tianjin

118. The capacity of white pine trees to sequester carbon

119. Where else to sink it

120. The fire code

121. The seismic code

122. The health code

123. The Romantics, throughout the arts and philosophy

124. How to listen closely

125. The big danger of working in a single medium (the logjam
      you don't even know you're stuck in will be broken by a shift
      in representation)

126. The exquisite corpse

127. Scissors, stone, paper

128. Good Bordeaux

163. Geomorphology

164. Geography

165. The law of the Andes

166. Cappadocia, first hand

167. The importance of the Amazon

168. How to patch leaks

169. What makes you happy

170. The components of a comfortable environment for sleep

171. The view from the Acropolis

172. The way to Santa Fe

173. The Seven Wonders of the Ancient World

174. Where to eat in Brooklyn

175. Half as much as a London cabbie

176. The Nolli plan

177. The Cerdà plan

178. The Haussmann plan

179. Slope analysis

180. Darkroom procedures and Photoshop

181. Dawn breaking after a bender

182. Styles of genealogy and taxonomy

183. Betty Friedan

184. Guy Debord

185. Ant Farm

186. Archigram

187. Club Med

188. Crepuscule in Dharamshala

189. Solid geometry

190. Strengths of materials (if only intuitively)

191. Ha Long Bay

192. What's been accomplished in Medellín

193. … in Rio

194. … in Calcutta

195. … in Curitiba

196. … in Mumbai

197. Who practices? (It is your duty to secure this space for all who want to)

198. Why you think architecture does any good

199. The depreciation cycle

200.   What rusts

201.   Good model-making techniques in wood and cardboard

202.   How to play a musical instrument

203.   Which way the wind blows

204.   The acoustical properties of trees and shrubs

205.   How to guard a house against floods

206.   The connection between the Suprematists and Zaha

207.   The connection between Oscar Niemeyer and Zaha

208.   Where north (or south) is

209.   How to give directions, efficiently and courteously

210.   *Stadtluft macht frei*

211.   Underneath the pavement, the beach

212.   Underneath the beach, the pavement

213.   The germ theory of disease

214.   The importance of vitamin D

215.   How close is too close

216.   The capacity of a bioswale to recharge the aquifer

217.   The draught of ferries

218.   Bicycle safety and etiquette

219.   The difference between gabions and riprap

220.   The acoustic performance of Boston Symphony Hall

221.   How to open the window

222.   The diameter of the Earth

223.   The number of gallons of water used in a shower

224.   The distance at which you can recognize faces

225.   How and when to bribe public officials (for the greater good)

226.   Concrete finishes

227.   Brick bonds

228.   *The Housing Question*, by Friedrich Engels

229.   The prismatic charms of Greek island towns

230.   The energy potential of wind

231.   The cooling potential of wind, including the use
        of chimneys and the stack effect

232.   Paestum

233.   Straw-bale building technology

234.   Rachel Carson

235.   Freud

236.   The excellence of Michel de Klerk

Alvin's AA: A panorama

– Peter L. Wilson, Bolles + Wilson

Alvin Boyarsky was Chairman of the Architectural Association, in London, from 1971 until his untimely death in 1990. I had the good fortune to land in the first year to graduate under his 'unit' system. Alvin's invention of this teaching method – groups of fifteen to twenty students working intensely with a unit master for the entire year (or perhaps two) – has subsequently been adopted as an academic template worldwide. For this, and the range of experiments and personalities he encouraged, one is tempted to locate Alvin as one of the great architectural figures of the twentieth century, comparable perhaps to Walter Gropius, propagator of the Bauhaus myth.

Alvin's AA was a hothouse of extreme heterogeneity, a warring flotilla of teachers and ideologies, each under his patronage, goading and coaching. Its actors were Archigrammers Ron Herron, Peter Cook (pp. 22–31) and the conceptually astute David Greene; Dalibor Vesely; Bernard Tschumi; Elia Zenghelis; Rem Koolhaas (pp. 177–82; 200–4); a post-Stirling Léon Krier; Jan Kaplický of Future Systems; a pre-RMIT Leon van Schaik; Robin Evans; Paul Shepherd; Daniel Libeskind; Raoul Bunschoten; and Alvin's own products, including Zaha Hadid (pp. 295–300), Nigel Coates (pp. 154–65), Peter Salter, Chris MacDonald and myself. It is not my intention to speak nostalgically of a golden age, but to locate the paradigm shift that Alvin husbanded – a transition from the mechanistic and limited ontology of functionalism to a wider critical, cultural and interdisciplinary reading of architecture.

The emphasis on personality and ideological multivalence propagated at the AA in the 1970s and '80s laid the foundation for the emergence of a later, overheated 'star system'. But architectural myths in those pre-digital days flowed along different channels: insider allegiances and a conspiratorial underground mood (postcards prefigured the email). Alvin's network was international, his relationship to a London architectural establishment antagonistic. He valued this

Ban Shubber, Calais Hypermarket. Diploma Unit 1 (tutor: Peter Wilson), Architectural Association, 1982–3. *Themes 5, Informing the Object*, AA Publications, 1986, p. 67

disconnectedness, the autonomy of the academy. This was not entirely a question of choice. Early in Alvin's chairmanship, Margaret Thatcher, the then Education Minister, had withdrawn government grants for British students at the AA. One of his favourite after-dinner anecdotes involved a quite short Alvin pleading his case, sitting across from Mrs T., who, according to the fashion of the day, was wearing an above-the-knee skirt. There were, he confessed, details of the future prime minister's undergarments that he wished he did not know.

When Alvin took over the AA, the chairman's office was buried in the basement. He was an unknown entity, regarded by the school community (the body that dismissed subsequent chairman, Mohsen Mostafavi [pp. 190–9]) with a certain suspicion. One by one, critical voices disappeared from the horizon – Alvin's Machiavellian side. In the 1975–6 academic year, the chairman's office migrated up to the Bedford Square-facing second floor, to a room that the year before had been the unit space of Léon Krier and his favourite fourth-year student, Zaha Hadid. This I remember well; it was my first year as teaching assistant to Elia Zenghelis in the adjacent room. For my diploma year, Léon had been teaching assistant to Elia – one assumes Alvin had thrown them together while growling something like, 'Well, at least they're all rationalists.' His formula was to serve on his 'well-laid table' (his preferred metaphor for the school) as many exotic courses as possible. The same year that Alvin set himself up in his now-famous office tableau, flanked by bronze busts

Nigel Westbrook, Monastery, Kentish Town Projects. Diploma Unit 1 (tutors: Dalibor Vesely, Mohsen Mostafavi), Architectural Association, 1980–1. *Themes 1, Architecture and Community*, AA Publications, 1982, p. 80

of Wren and Jones (one of which wearing the chairman's pith helmet), Rem Koolhaas returned from New York to join Elia as Diploma Unit 1 unit master. That was Zaha's diploma year, and her conversion to the cult of OMA was almost instantaneous. The twinset and pearls she had worn as Léon's student were replaced by more Constructivist outfits (this was pre-Miyake), reams of patterned silk stapled together. Around midday she would disappear to the ladies' room – staple crisis.

Alvin's well-laid table was also in fact more than just a metaphor; the whole point in teaching under his regime was to be regularly (which often meant weekly) invited to his post-lecture dinners at his favourite Covent Garden restaurant. He often said it reminded him of Chicago, where he had learned never to sit with his back to the window. These dinners were a form of pre-digital networking; as an AA young Turk unit master, one got to know everyone from Austrian Radicals to Arata Isozaki and Toyo Ito. There was apparently much rivalry and jealous gossip regarding this inner-circle status; it was effectively compensation for teaching for an impossibly low financial recompense. Inclusion was also a signal that Alvin approved of what one was teaching. The most positive comment he ever made regarding teaching agendas or individual production was, 'You can do better than that.' He was, in effect, coaching many of us young teachers, and the carrot dangled in front was often an exhibition or another AA publication. This was an invitation to join Alvin and share his hobby, making books.

Kathryn Findlay, Gunton Hall. Diploma Unit 6 (tutors: Peter Cook, Christine Hawley, Ron Herron), Architectural Association, 1977–8. *Themes 2, Spirit and Invention*, AA Publications, 1982, p. 41

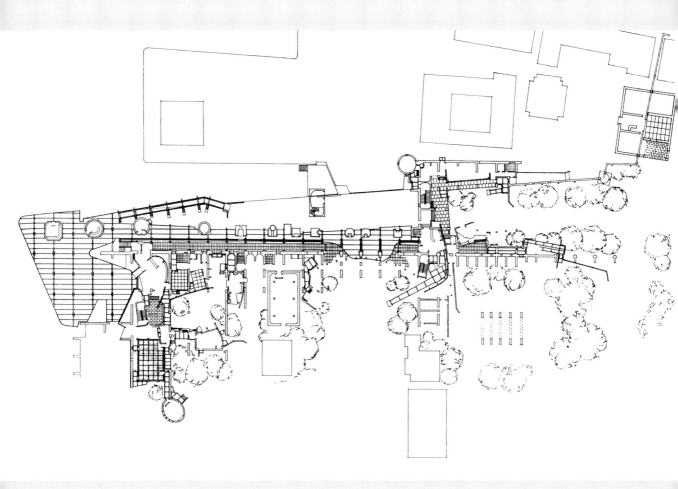

Interviewed by the Design Book Review in 1990, Alvin remarked:

The AA's history and tradition have to do with initiating discussions and propositions which on occasion have been influential throughout the world. Our publications reflect this. We are a small frenetic institution, very much involved with the creative act and if we can capture this in an appropriate form, it could be of some importance to others. Perhaps it is vanity, but we do sell a lot of books in a lot of places and discussion about what we do does take place. A relatively small group of people at one point on the map, working hard and intensely, and with a comprehensive view of what's going on in the rest of the world, can actually make a great difference to the history of ideas.

Jee Seng Heng, The Art Academy, Biennale Gardens, Venice. Diploma Unit 6 (tutors: Peter Cook, Christine Hawley), Architectural Association, 1983–4. *Themes 6, Intuition and Process*, AA Publications, 1989, p. 45

*Our publications are almost handmade. A small group
of us are involved in all of them. Aside from selecting the exhibition
material and the contributions, I'm also involved in the design, the
writing or interviewing, selecting the paper, and so on … the printing
activity stimulates the cycle of students who are attracted to
our school.[1]*

Of Alvin's books, a number stand out as classics in architectural
publishing and are collectors' items today, both for their profound
historic documentation (Christopher Dean's *Housing the Airship*s [1989]
and *Cities of Childhood: Italian Colonie of the 1930s* [1988], compiled
by Stefano de Martino and Alex Wall), and for their corrective trajectory
(*Gunnar Asplund: The Dilemma of Classicism* [1988] and *Sigurd
Lewerentz: The Dilemma of Classicism* [1989]). And from the *Mega*
series, three slim but elegant volumes: Michael Webb's *Temple Island*
(1987), perhaps the most enigmatic architecture book ever published
(there is no beauty that does not have about it a little strangeness);
MacDonald and Salter: Building Projects 1982–1986 (1987), a folio of
exquisite fold-out line drawings; and my own *Western Objects: Eastern
Fields* (1989), for which much experimentation by Denis Crompton
came up with a printing simulation of shoe-polished drawings.

Without doubt the most profound and intellectually grounded
discourse among AA diploma units were Dalibor Vesely and Mohsen
Mostafavi's investigations of architecture as a means of representation
– graphic odes to the iconographic theatre of Renaissance and Baroque
cities. It was an obvious choice for Alvin to initiate the *AA Themes*
books, a formulation and presentation of a number of years' research
by a particular unit, adding up to an in-house manifesto. The first,
Architecture and Continuity, is a dark work, every page laden with heavy
graphite shadow, a graphic mode that did not originate in this studio but
became its signature and leitmotiv, charged with directing us towards
poetic imagination and authentic reality. The first drawing in the book is
by Eric Parry, and beyond that the uniformity of presentation merges the
chiaroscuro plans and sections into multiple fragments of what appears
to be a single, cumulative project. This school of thought subsequently
migrated to Cambridge, where it formed a bastion against the tides
and storms of architectural fashion.

The second publication, *Spirit and Invention,* spotlighted architectural education's long-distance runners: Peter Cook, Ron Herron and Christine Hawley. Their unit spoke out against the rational and postmodern dogmas of the time, advocating instead the intermediate boundary and the architecture of ambiguity, where references are disparate and personal. This intention to blur the edges was taken up by students Kathryn Findlay, Amanda Marshall and Peter Salter. Revisiting the six *Themes* catalogues published in the 1980s is somewhat like visiting a medieval San Gimignano, where each family, suspicious of the others, has set up a tower from which to fire arrows at its neighbours. Inside the towers are armies of defenders (students), some of whom occasionally cross over to a neighbouring tower.

The third catalogue, *The Discourse of Events,* produced by the unit initiated in the early 1970s by Bernard Tschumi and inherited by Nigel Coates, was more concerned with what went on in architecture than with the vessel itself. Here, the precise conceptual moves of Tschumi's teaching evolved between the 1970s and '80s into a graphic tempest of anarchic anti-architecture. To be sure, the scribbled Sturm und Drang graphic style initiated by Ron Arad and brought to grotty perfection by Mark Prizeman was greatly influential both within and outside the AA. This was architecture wearing the clothes of the emerging Punk and New Romantic music and fashion scenes. Its confrontational strategy proved more than successful when external examiner James Stirling failed the entire unit – a problem Alvin got around by inviting a second examiner (Tschumi, as it turned out). This was one of the few AA units connected to the subcultures of London, and it emerged from Bedford Square as a fully formed style, built in countless shops by architectural firm Branson Coates and surviving into the new millennium via Coates's designs and teaching at the Royal College of Art.

In the case of the fourth catalogue, *People in Architecture,* Alvin wrote in the introduction: 'Strangely, the intense and original work emanating from [Michael] Gold's unit has not captured the imagination of his Diploma School colleagues.'[2] This was indeed the case many of us did not want to accept, that such an ostensibly naive and direct automatic process could, through its scrupulous realism, project the drawing of a person, then objects, then an architectural setting outwards until the stage included the city itself. Dalibor Vesely wrote in the catalogue on 'the territory of experience where architecture meets

Mark Prizeman, Giant-Sized
Baby Town's Chemical
Works. Diploma Unit 9
(tutors: Bernard Tschumi,
Nigel Coates), Architectural
Association, 1981–2. *Themes 3,
The Discourse of Events*,
AA Publications, 1983, p. 93

painting',[3] the ambiguity between representation and reality, and Gold
himself generously traced his methodology back to one of my drawings
from life classes he and I had organized in 1978. In retrospect, the
reductive simplicity (both of figures and of plans) and the unashamed
indulgence of these spectacular drawings hold their value as creative
experiments. In 1982, the penultimate year of this studio, Peter St John
rendered a Cecil Beaton photo of Jean Shrimpton metamorphosing,
step by step, into a table and a staircase with reflective surfaces.

The evolution of the *Themes* catalogues charted an increasing
sophistication in AA graphics and printing possibilities. The first two
were entirely black and white, as was that of Coates (except for four
pages of colour), while for Gold's, colour predominates. For *Informing
the Object*, my own diploma unit, fourteen pages of the catalogue were
in colour. Strategies towards the city were here grouped under the rubric
'appropriation and densification'. When dealing with specific objects
or buildings, our dual strategies were the tectonic (making) and the
figurative (signification). Our mode of synthesis often engaged the scale
of landscape and the ordering principles of large-format, laboriously
constructed perspective drawings – these, because within their web of
construction lines, an experienced spatiality cohabited (on the same

Peter St John, Jean
Shrimpton. Diploma Unit
5 (tutor: Michael Gold),
Architectural Association,
1981–2. *Themes 4, People and
Architecture*, AA Publications,
1983, pp. 46–7

page) with generating plans and folded-out sections or elevations. It was
in fact the synthetic graphic rigour engaged in setting up these epic
drawings that characterized our unit's work, a technique that student and
later teaching assistant Neil Porter subsequently used in his spectacular
and much-published perspectives of Tschumi's *Parc de la Villette* follies.
Peter Cook, writing in 2013 on my own designs at this time, describes
'the "devices", the "armatures", the placement of decoys or tantalizing
elements … The first generation of [Wilson's] AA students seized
upon this vocabulary, including – and this is the highest compliment –
students of other people's units.'[4] It was certainly time to move on.

The final *Themes* catalogue, *Intuition and Process*, is a
compendium of projects from various units, produced for the technical
studies department, overseen by Peter Salter. It is again black and white,
with moody reference photos: the brick wall of a Norfolk barn, an island
in the Venetian Lagoon, a currach-maker, Sigurd Lewerentz's flower
kiosk. These atmospheric signposts are interspersed with complex line
drawings, many of which look like sections through wooden boats. Walls
thicken towards the ground, sectional cut rooms are filled with panel
grids. This is the graphic style developed by Salter (in collaboration with
Chris MacDonald). It implies a laborious handcrafted way of building,
bones and skin, buildings with vertebra. It was for some years a cross-
unit style in Bedford Square: manneristically elaborate tectonics, the
Indian summer of the hand-drawn. A few years later the digital eclipsed
the careful graphic experiments that characterized Alvin's AA. Ten years
later it was beneath the intellectual dignity of a unit master to teach
buildings; after Alvin, the word 'building' became a term of derision.

There were many other high points of Alvin's educational construct:
the conceptually astute intermediate studio of David Greene, Zaha's fan-
club unit, Future Systems' spaceships, and those solidly working on the
morphology of the city like Rodrigo Pérez de Arce or Francisco Sanin.
Scanned here is only the tip of Alvin's iceberg.

Architectural anti-realism: The AA School in 2013

– Brett Steele, Director, Architectural Association School of Architecture

The monster I kill every day is the monster of realism.

— Anaïs Nin, *Henry and June* (1986)[1]

Architectural schools have largely surrendered themselves to the forces, habits and conventions of cynical realism, to the ordinary curiosities of the here and now, whose overwhelming contemporary capacity for manufacturing distraction helps account for architecture's recent and dramatic incapacity for believing in a better future, concealed so often these days in their proclaimed 'research' into the present. They no longer devote themselves to speculative realism, to an open-ended experimentation with 'anti', 'partial' or 'alternative' realities, to the urgent invention of those kinds of genuinely visionary projects able to invent new kinds of architectural knowledge through a compelling description of alternative, possible, architectural futures.

This is what important architecture and great experimental architectural schools have always been about, and it is a larger cultural project that schools must now return to after the past several decades of seeing themselves as vocational outposts underpinning the needs of a growing global professionalization of all architectural life. That decidedly twentieth-century project is now, for better or worse, complete. Schools are in a position to lead architectural culture again – this time

right
Architectural Fiction.
Oliver Pershav, Arradial
Bedtime Story for the
Smithsons, King's Cross,
London. Intermediate Unit 2:
Matter & Space (tutors: Ana
Araujo, Takero Shimazaki),
Architectural Association
School of Architecture, 2013

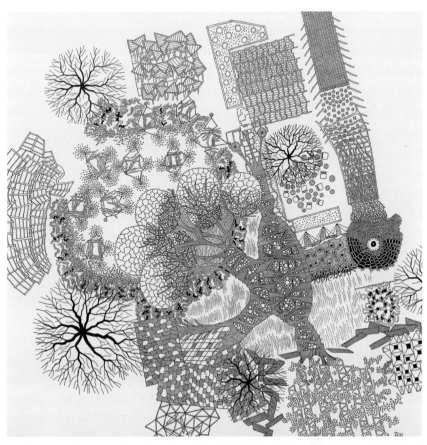

left
Machinic Space.
William Gowland, Off-Grid
Communication Network,
Mexico City. Diploma Unit
6 (tutors: Kate Davies,
Liam Young), Architectural
Association School of
Architecture, 2013

above
Ambient Design.
Soonil Kim, Supernatural
Garden, New York. Diploma
Unit 1 (tutor: Tobias Klein),
Architectural Association
School of Architecture, 2013

in a return of architectural culture understood as a world of ideas and cultural production so great and engaged that it can be seen to provide a context larger than the architectural profession as it is currently understood. The AA School is committed to such a project, to the fabrication of unknown architectural futures (including that of architectural schools themselves) so weird, strange and powerful that they have the capacity to transform architectural life as we know, or imagine, it now.

To a remarkable degree, architectural life is wedded to the future. After all, if the world had no need to alter its built environment, architects would, quite literally, be out of a job. That architects are so dependent upon the necessity of change provides the means to assess the calamitous consequences of architecture's recent loss of nerve regarding future possibilities, given up in exchange for a relentless fascination with the familiar, oversold 'problems' of the world today. The AA School both embodies and promotes a relentless pursuit of new scenarios for alternative forms of practice, whose principal purpose is the envisioning and making of architectural worlds – and careers – that will unfold in the future. To do anything less is to suffer the fate of realists

everywhere who face growing critical irrelevance owing to their embrace of attitudes or practices that simply accept situations for what they already are. To make that mistake today is to mortgage architecture's ability to abstract, speculate or invent architecture tomorrow. As the critic Mark Rakatansky wrote in a recent AA publication: 'Architects don't just make things. *They make things up.*'[2] Too often young architects (like their old schools) forget the second part of the equation – that architectural fabrication involves the stories, scenarios and visions through which they can communicate to a larger audience the arrangement of ideas from which future worlds are assembled.

In these early years of the twenty-first century, architectural schools have allowed a contemporary fascination with the present to become the primary means of explaining (and largely, explaining away) a postmodern loss of architecture's core disciplinary project, which remains the making of previously unimagined, unexpected and untested futures. A century after the invention of the modern experimental architectural school, globalized educational machinery has evolved into an industrialized and fossilized shadow of the original avant-gardist impulses from which it emerged across Europe and North America. Much like the modern professionalization of architecture, alongside which the modern architectural school evolved, the industrialized school of our time pales in comparison to the experimental, frequently eccentric academies that, during the past century, played such an essential role in keeping architectural experimentalism alive.

At such unexpected venues as Henry van de Velde's School of Arts and Crafts in Weimar, a prototype for the Bauhaus; the supremacist faculty at Vkhutemas, founded in the wake of the Soviet revolution; the cool, near-corporate interiors of Max Bill's Ulm School of Design (1953); John Hejduk's renovated workshop floor, sandwiched halfway up the Cooper Union (1975); the unheated daylight studios of Eliel Saarinen's Cranbrook Educational Community (1950s–'80s); and yes, the once-cramped, damp Georgian rooms of the AA School, what is most interesting about the legacy of these alternative architectural academies of the twentieth century is the crucial role they played as provocateurs to the established, professionalizing tendencies of modern architecture. It is a project that schools today must renew so as to avoid the same fate that professional regimentation and standardization has already wrought on so much of architectural life throughout the world.

Amplified Prototyping. Intermediate Unit 2, Driftwood AA Summer Pavilion, Bedford Square, London. Intermediate Unit 2 (tutors: Martin Self, Charles Walker), Architectural Association School of Architecture, 2009

What has changed since the time of schools' Jurassic-era, Modernist forbears is the sheer scale and scope of architecture's own, now fully industrialized and grossly, globally professionalized contemporary forms of practice and learning. This condition must now be internalized into architecture schools' own carefully calibrated critique of themselves, their profession and their audiences. Importantly, this is something to be pursued not only in what and how students work within schools, but also, perhaps even more urgently, in the forms, places and networks through which schools organize themselves – as the architectural realities they inevitably are, as the sites through which new architectural minds, projects and knowledge flow.

Nine unseen architectural realities

My dreams are always criticisms of my action.
— Jean Cocteau, *The Difficulty of Being,* 1947[3]

If the above paragraphs summarize a general horizon of expectations regarding what an architectural school should be aware of today, there are many specific coordinates by which we might start to map an anti-realist resistance to known architectural worlds. The topics, tropes and tribes populating the terrain of a genuinely experimental contemporary architectural school are too many to list in detail here, but a glimpse is given below in examples of the architectural anti-realism now underway at the AA School, aimed mostly at deflecting the more generalizing tendencies of 'reality' and the associated problems of our time.[4]

(1) Machinic space
A detailed exploration of the ways in which technologies of all kinds have subverted the idea of architecture as a fixed, permanent arrangement of dead and inanimate materials. This includes an open-ended exploration of the recent, accelerated embedding of sensors, reconfigurable structural systems and malleable composite materials into everyday architecture, creating today's rapidly evolving, ambient feedback environments. What happens to architecture when the modern concept of space is surpassed by the more modern idea of interface?

(2) Architectural craft and fiction
The making of narratives about the life and circumstances of the

architect and his or her forms of production today, as told via media that cross well beyond the borders of conventional architectural representation. Examples include advanced filmic and digital image-making, animation and hyper-realistic visual simulation deployed alongside outmoded traditional forms of representation. What happens when our goal is to 'blur the line between the imaginary and the real'?

(3) Ambient design platforms

A deliberate loosening up of top–down means of design control through programming and coding of information alongside its visual representation. The embracing of 'self-organizing' and highly advanced

Global Cities.
Yvonne Weng, Forest Canopy
Hanging Settlement, Amazon
Rainforest. Diploma Unit 17
(tutors: Theo Sarantoglou
Lalis, Dora Swejd),
Architectural Association
School of Architecture, 2012

computational technologies aimed at (ironically) the most traditional
(even old-fashioned) of all architectural problems: the problem of form.
What happens when an architect is only one of several 'living' systems
within his or her design world?

(4) Informational cartography

An architectural appropriation and commercial satellite (and other aerial
imagery) for the purposes of rendering such information architectural,
making visible forms the hidden features of cities and their social lives,
including their historical evolution. What happens when plans become
information-rich descriptions of time and chronology, and not just
physical position and arrangement?

(5) Amplified prototyping

An assertive dissolution of boundaries between design and manufacturing
cultures within architecture. New, fabrication-orientated expertise
is emerging in the niche spaces between specific design domains
(i.e., within certain proprietary design software) and the material
assembly of their design guidelines. What happens when architects
go from being distanced designers to embedded makers
of their own projects?

(6) Collaborative studios

The electronic, widely dispersed information space of the contemporary
studio is now a fact of architectural life. Architects and other designers
are working across communications networks of entirely new orders
of simultaneity, making design work infinitely more collaborative and
intensely more accessible and competitive. What happens when the
networked, amplified studio disappears into larger, more accessible,
knowledge networks?

(7) Global cities

Following the unprecedented global urban expansion of the past two
decades – the greatest wave of building in human history – the city is
no longer merely a context for architecture. It is a design project of
its own unique kind, one that upsets the historic relationship between
architecture and the city. What happens when making architecture

encompasses the scale of the city, now realized at speeds greater than the historical making of buildings?

(8) Vengeful histories

For the past twenty years, architectural culture has been dominated by technology, following on from the technological revolutions reconfiguring the architect's own studio and workspace. With the novelty of this revolution beginning to wane, and its own internal histories (even justifications) now widely accessible, how might architecture regain its own historical knowledge, or architectural pasts that might productively inform the future?

(9) Networked knowledge

The history of the modern architectural school is that of distinct, nearly eccentric, geographic locations and cultural eras. The globalization of knowledge acquisition (and not only in the architectural profession) poses new challenges to the making of an international experimental school today. Schools can no longer treat themselves as single destinations or isolated locations. How might schools reconfigure their own internal spaces and external audiences, so that they may be more like their students – rather than the other way around?

The project as prophet

> Tess was awake before dawn — at the marginal minute of the dark when the grove is still mute, save for one prophetic bird who sings with a clear-voiced conviction that he at least knows the correct time of day, the rest preserving silence as if equally convinced that he is mistaken.
>
> — Thomas Hardy, *Tess of the d'Urbervilles*, 1891[5]

Architects have lost track of their capacity to act as Hardy's singular, prophetic bird: a creature capable of singing with clear-voiced conviction while others remain content to look on and follow the flock. Architecture's recent loss of conviction regarding the making of futurist projects has been extraordinary, and has had consequences. Most especially to architectural schools, whose job it remains to create forms of architectural judgment, expressed most clearly in their students' projects, whose collective capacity remains the primary means by which architecture will eventually reach the future – something that happens owing to the very inevitability of our students' future careers.

Hardy himself was a member of the Architectural Association and winner of one of its many well-publicized competitions in the 1870s. This he did early on in his career, before his widespread success as a writer who captured, in compelling ways, the convictions of his generation of artists and architects regarding Modernism's need for inspired, individual clarity and prescience. Hardy wrote at the time of the first great wave of industrialization in England. The ensuing destruction of its towns and landscapes led him, like John Ruskin (another early AA visitor), to imagine a resistance to such forces, which too many architects and others unquestionably embraced as a 'reality' whose interests they chose to serve.

Architectural schools are today in a unique position owing to their capacity to convene new kinds of audiences for and around architecture, in a world whose many complex challenges require, above all, new kinds of speculative realism. For schools to pursue anything less is to admit failure in the worst way possible, through their own, distracted embrace of the here and now. As J. G. Ballard, another great English anti-realist once said: 'Being hyper-realistic about everything is too simple a cop out.'[6] Architectural schools should hope for more – *really* more – in their relentless pursuit of (as yet) unimaginable visions of the future.

A prime meridian

– Nic Clear, Head of the Department of Architecture
and Landscape, University of Greenwich

The University of Greenwich has a long history as one of the UK's few institutions to offer fully integrated and professionally validated Architecture and Landscape Architecture programmes, a tradition that can be traced back to the Hammersmith College of Art and Building (founded in 1881) and Woolwich Polytechnic (1890), which merged in 1970 to form Thames Polytechnic, eventually becoming the University of Greenwich in 1992. Over the years the department has been based in Hammersmith, Woolwich, Dartford and Avery Hill, and these peripheral locations have meant that it has been something of an outsider on London's architecture scene. With the move to new purpose-built studios in 2014, the department will occupy the newest addition to the magnificent buildings that form part of the UNESCO World Heritage site of Maritime Greenwich. Importantly, for the first time since 1981, it has become a true London school again.

In 2010 Neil Spiller arrived as the Dean of the Department of Architecture and Landscape, and a radical transformation ensued. Spiller recruited a number of his former colleagues from the Bartlett School of Architecture, University College London, to form a new team, a new ethos and a new set of expectations and ambitions to complement the move to the new location. No longer content with being a supporting player, the school is taking up the challenge of becoming one of the world's leading departments of architecture and landscape. The programmes at Greenwich aim to address and define new trends and understanding in the fields of architecture and landscape, to posit new aesthetic systems and codes of representation, and to facilitate a body of knowledge, both practical and theoretical, which allows students to develop and refine their own design language, albeit within a rigorous academic framework. Students are encouraged, challenged and inspired in equal measure in an environment where they are able to develop skills

Petya Nikolova, The Two Monasteries, elevation. Unit 6: A Working Spectacle at the Edge of Town (tutors: Rahesh Ram, Melissa Appleton), Department of Architecture and Landscape, University of Greenwich, 2013

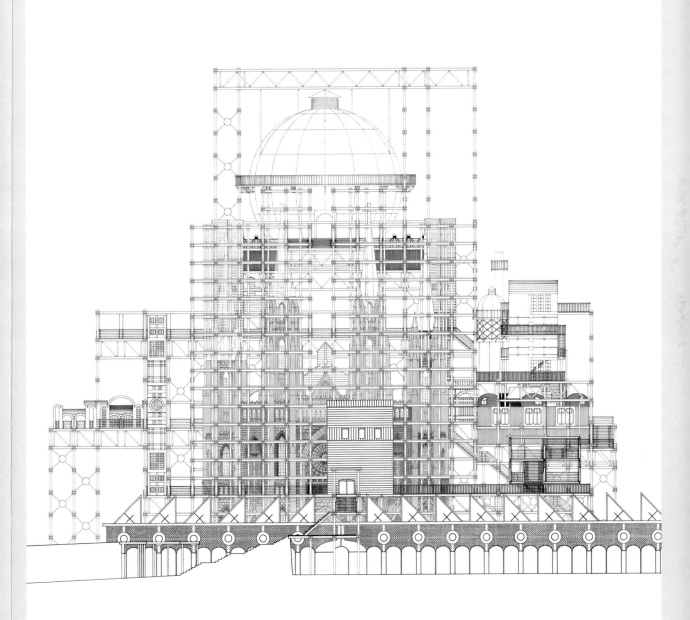

AVATAR, the department has at its disposal world-class expertise in the development of virtual and augmented realities, and in the terrains of synthetic biology, nanotechnology, cybernetics and advanced forms of digital manufacturing – all essential for architecture and landscape in the twenty-first century. Indeed, the way we study history and theory actively engages with the future as much as with the past. We believe we have a responsibility to look forward, to not only deal with what architecture and landscape are and were, but also to set an agenda for what they could be.

It may seem as though the department is trying to square an impossible circle, by combining advanced speculative research with a pragmatic approach to developing skills that will be readily usable and make our students highly employable in a range of industries. In the Project Office, for example, research and practice are combined to allow students to collaborate on 'live' projects in a way that harnesses a variety of new technologies in real situations. Similarly, the Paper House project in 2013 saw members of staff, students and external consultants collaborating on an attempt to construct the largest inflatable paper structure in the world. While the result was not a complete success,

Razna Begum, Grunewald Literary Sanctuary, perspective. Unit 2: Grim Architectures (tutors: Pascal Bronner, Caroline Rabourdin), Department of Architecture and Landscape, University of Greenwich, 2013

Prince Yemoh, Rings of Persephone. Unit 15: Time Machines (tutors: Nic Clear, Mike Aling, Simon Withers), Department of Architecture and Landscape, University of Greenwich, 2013

it sent out a clear signal regarding our ambitions and desire to try what others had not attempted before. In all aspects of our teaching practice, we fuse traditional studio- and practice-based pedagogy with more contemporary approaches that fully exploit the potential of online media, virtual learning environments and social networking.

Architecture and landscape education are currently undergoing some profound changes, and at the University of Greenwich we are making sure that the nature of what we teach and research is flexible and reactive to advances in technology and the expanding global market place. We are educating our students with a toolkit of tactics and strategies to complement a more traditional body of skills, and to have the same passion and drive for their work that we have for our own.

Mohammed Abd Rahman,
The Rothschilds and the
Necromancer of Old London
Bridge, section. Unit 6:
In Every Dream Home a
Heartache (tutors: Adam
Cole, George Thomson),
Department of Architecture
and Landscape, University
of Greenwich, 2013

William Lamburn,
Armillary Sphere. Unit 19:
A Homage to the Golden
Age of Appearances (tutors:
Neil Spiller, Phil Watson,
Elizabeth-Anne Williams,
Rachel Armstrong),
Department of Architecture
and Landscape, University
of Greenwich, 2013

Introduction to the Department of Architecture and Landscape, University of Greenwich diagram

– Mike Aling and Mark Garcia, Senior Lecturers, Department of Architecture and Landscape, University of Greenwich

The diagram of the Department of Architecture and Landscape, University of Greenwich, is a four-dimensional spatialization of some of its histories, theories and futures. It is the first iteration of an ongoing project to continuously, generatively and interactively understand, reflect on and redesign the department's conceptual and actual architectures. Addressing its morphing temporal and theoretical positions in architecture, design and education, the diagram re-describes the explicit and actual, as well as the possible, implicit and latent sources and locations of its innovation, originality, newness and uniqueness.

The diagram blurs the distinctions between tools, models, objects, theories, instruments, researches, histories, questionnaires, networks, maps, inputs, individuals, processes, pedagogies, surveys, origins, ideas, machines, quantities, methods, retrospections, concepts, weaknesses, attractions, predictions, probes, introspections, propositions, groups, participations, devices, compatibilities, creativities, natures, tactics, genealogies, effects, writings, consumptions, indexes, desires, qualities, critiques, catalysts, actions, strengths, accounts, parts, cultures, interviews, prospections, strategies, imaginations, characteristics, synergies, communications, drawings, managements, products, powers, subjects, speculations, socializings, technologies, languages, designs, practices, times and spaces.

The result was built from responses to a questionnaire sent to a representative sample of staff, and analyses more than twenty-five elements, ranging from the personal to the professional, individual research to student projects, and relating to staff histories, theories and futures. This included information about projects, legacies, knowledge, skills, experiences, emotions, influences, education, capabilities, ambitions and desires. It surveyed features such as architects and architecture, books, writings, theories, fiction, media, artworks, artefacts, artists, buildings, designs, engineering and engineers, sciences and scientists, places, cities, organizations and companies, employers, colleges and universities, research fields and questions, expertise, specializations and networks throughout history. This private, previously implicit information was supplemented by research into existing data inputs from public and external sources, and compilations of information such as catalogues, conferences, publications and bureaucratic sources relating to students, visitors, external lecturers and active global networks and interconnections.

The diagram was designed using both hand drawings and CAD softwares, and built primarily on Blender open-source modelling software, and is an associative, parametric/patametric virtual space and data model. The overall form of the diagram and its universe of information constellations, feedback fields and streams has the form of a butterfly nebula, the past and the future exploding from the present at the bottleneck/pinch point at the central core. Containing more than 7,000 separate responses, each its own data point, the diagram identifies, ranks and links individuals through more than 470 points of commonality, interest, synergy, affinity and shared or active research pursuits. These 'nodes' are identified in the centre of the diagram, their spatial positions organized as a mean value located between all staff responses. Their varying and relative sizes indicate the quantity of shared links, indexing the popularity, strength and intensity of common responses/references/interests/concerns. Omitting obvious links and connections such as 'Greenwich', 'architecture', 'landscape', 'design', 'space' and 'time', the top fifty responses that connect the department are listed below, in order of strength and intensity, as a quantity.

Mike Aling and Mark Garcia, Department of Architecture and Landscape, University of Greenwich diagram, 2013-

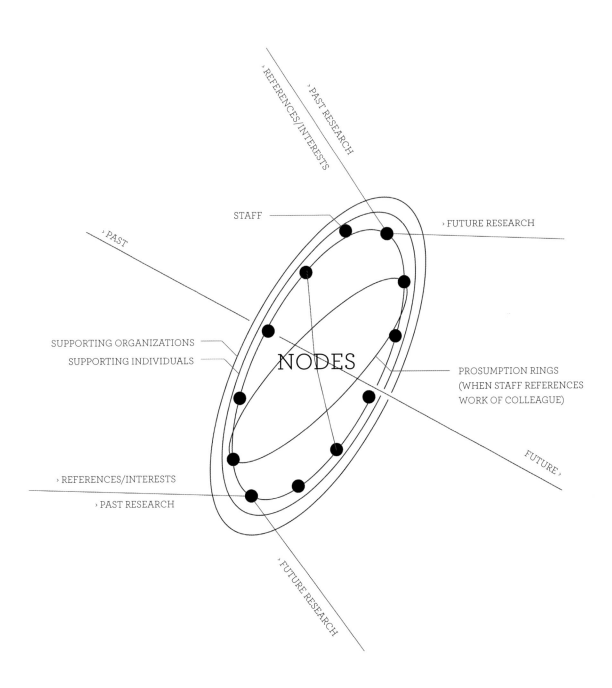

opposite and on p. 72
Mike Aling and Mark Garcia, Department of Architecture and Landscape, University of Greenwich diagram, 2013-

The diagram's multiple and manifold interrelations, scales, complexities, strengths and weaknesses tested the teachers, technologies, processes, products, meanings and lives of the department across actual and theoretical times and spaces. This diagram of the department's universe has already begun to grow and feed back on itself to become a set of real, projective and constructive architectural forces with active, material and physical lives of their own.

Top fifty connections/nodes

Strength and intensity (or quantity) of connections is listed as a number, followed by the content of the connection or node. Where the strength or intensity (as a quantity) of connections is the same, entries are given in alphabetical order.

21: House
14: Venice
13: Drawing
12: Neil Spiller
11: Berlin, Le Corbusier, Tate Modern
10: *AD* magazine, Bernard Tschumi, University College London
9: Apple/Mac, David Lynch, Internet, Robin Evans
8: Barcelona, Ben Nicholson, Cedric Price, college, John Hejduk, Paris, planet, Rem Koolhaas, research
7: The Bartlett, Bill Viola, Daniel Libeskind, Marcel Duchamp, James Turrell, Lebbeus Woods, Mike Webb, OMA, Rome, Temple Island, USA
6: Anti-gravity, BBC, biotechnology/biology, communicating vessels, diagrams, Giorgio de Chirico, Francis Bacon, gravity, Iain Banks, London, Oxford University, Royal Academy, science, science fiction, space station, Zaha Hadid

Contributors: Mike Aling, Mark Garcia, Rachel Armstrong, Nic Clear, Corine Delage, Max Dewdney, Duncan Goodwin, Marko Jobst, Shaun Murray, Luke Olsen, Rahesh Ram, Neil Spiller, Ed Wall, Simon Withers

ROME

PARIS

BARCELONA

LONDON

VENICE

BERLIN   TOKYO

ANDREA POZZO

AMERICA

GIOVANNI BATTISTA

NEW YORK

ROYAL ACADEMY OF ARTS

MARCEL DUCHAMP
SCIENCE FICTION
LE CORBUSIER DELEUZE

ART ARCHITECTURE DESIGN

BERLIN

TATE MODERN

AVATAR RESEARCH

IAIN M. BANKS

Library and Department of Architecture and Landscape, University of Greenwich

– Roísín Heneghan and Shih-Fu Peng,
Heneghan Peng Architects

The pressure to build densely, sustainably and in keeping with the urban character of the Maritime Greenwich World Heritage Site drove the core spatial strategy for the design of the university's new Library and Department of Architecture and Landscape. Located along an approach from the town centre to Greenwich Park, the site – one of the last remaining large plots of land in the area – presented various challenges. Among these was the need to negotiate each of its four edges differently in terms of acoustics, light, sight lines and level changes. Equally challenging was the depth of the site, which demanded a strategic approach to providing maximum daylight for the extensive studio space at the heart of the building – a collection of critique spaces, desk areas, meeting room and display walls that acts as a central horizontal hub.

The plan is based around a series of bands that recall the rhythm of the surrounding terraces of houses and shops. Initially aligned precisely with the terrace of buildings along the east side of the site, these quickly shifted into an A-B-A-B hierarchy, with the wide 'A' bands containing the study, display and administration areas, and the narrow 'B' bands the courtyards and service zones. The 'B' bands are formed as a folding and doubling of the façade, generating voids that increase the façade's surface area without significant disruption to the key spaces within. In order to allow daylight to penetrate all levels of the five-storey structure, the curtain walls are calibrated with reflective aluminium panels on both sides to redirect light deep into the lower levels of the plan. The north–south orientation of the façade's 'folds' leads to an asymmetrical distribution of daylight, which is utilized in the design so that even in the largely light-locked studio, the passage of time relative to orientation can be understood.

Simultaneously, the 'B' bands are designed to house various functions, including ducting, WCs, vertical circulation and aeration for natural ventilation. Akin to gills, their extended length through the entire building assures maximum adjacency to the programmatic 'A' bands. In addition to their basic shared functions, each of the five 'B' bands, or gill lines, fulfils a purpose specific to its location. The first links vertically the various levels of the Library with a series of stairs that act as beams; the second links the Library with the department, while bringing light directly into the basement. The third band provides the primary vertical link through the department via an additional set of beam stairs, the fourth lights the central crit and exhibition space and the fifth terminates the department, establishes a model yard and mediates the building connection back into the existing context. Together, the five bands transform the horizontal studio at the centre into a space at its very edge environmentally, extending its perceptual width within a bounded envelope.

Externally, the building's presence and expression are deliberately varied from different angles. Along its north side, the Library forms a recognizable civic entity and a connection with the Old Royal Naval College, on an adjacent site to the east. A set-back, street-level entrance at the northwest corner provides both a threshold for entry into the building and a space that looks outwards to the early eighteenth-century St Alfege Church, designed by Nicholas Hawksmoor, on the opposite corner. The rest of the Stockwell Street frontage, with café and art galleries at the ground floor, appears from its southern end on Nevada Street as a series of tightly packed volumes that blend into the streetscape; only on rounding the corner do these begin to fragment, revealing the academic activity within.

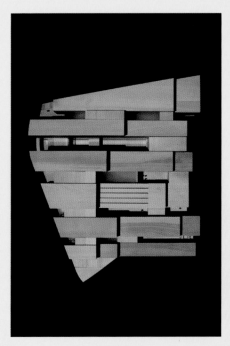

Heneghan Peng Architects,
Library and Department of
Architecture and Landscape,
University of Greenwich,
London, 2014

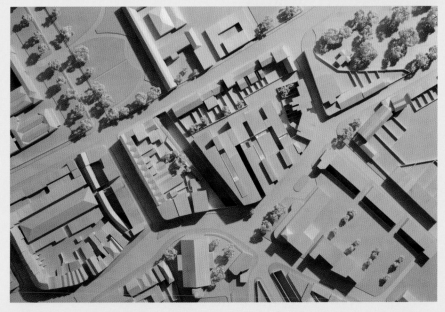

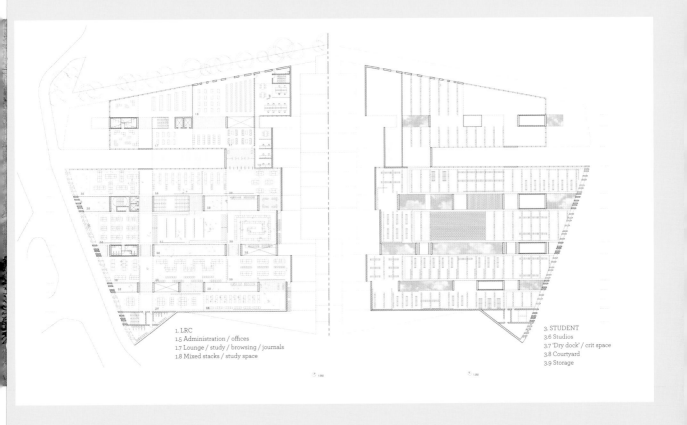

1. LRC
1.5 Administration / offices
1.7 Lounge / study / browsing / journals
1.8 Mixed stacks / study space

3. STUDENT
3.6 Studios
3.7 'Dry dock' / crit space
3.8 Courtyard
3.9 Storage

Heneghan Peng Architects, Library
and Department of Architecture and
Landscape, University of Greenwich,
London, 2014

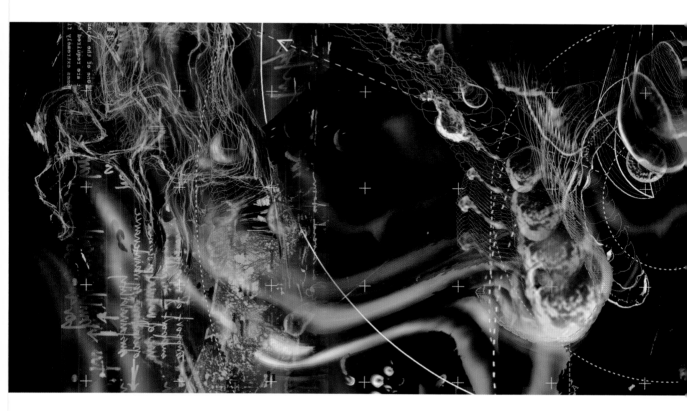

Yet do we all not despise the world as it is? The lies, the hollow rhetoric, the capitalist imperative and vacuous consumerism, the regulations and the bureaucratic mutants that enforce them? Do we still not become unsettled by the uncanny? Do we still peer into the ossuaries of the city and marvel at the bizarre juxtaposition of objects and times that use has deserted? Do we still desire, love and lust? Do we still actively search and thrill for anomaly and rejoice in the delightful swerve of everyday life? We do, and this is Surrealism writ large, aided and abetted by the hyperlinked vicissitudes of contemporary technologies. We must encourage our students to embrace these facts, and open themselves up to the amazing, life-affirming possibilities of these observations. They will not only slake our thirst for architectural difference, but will also prepare our profession for what comes next. This is our task as architectural educators.

Elizabeth-Anne Williams/ AVATAR, Persephone: Expansion of Neptune's Schism. Department of Architecture and Landscape, University of Greenwich, 2013

Bicycles, wormholes, big data and split sights

Surreal means 'on top of' the real. To illustrate this strange terrain, it is useful to conduct a quick foray into some prominent work from the early and mid-twentieth century. The paintings of proto-Surrealist Henri Rousseau, often of bright, multicoloured jungles, exhibit a disquieting realism, which to the contemporary architectural eye might be interpreted as depicting the complex, sometimes technologically enhanced relationships between humans, animals and plants. Indeed, the chimeric nature of much Surrealist work provides many vignettes of this evolving symbiosis. The enigmatic and melancholic piazzas of Giorgio de Chirico, with their contorted perspectives, are similarly analogous to other aspects of our current spatial conditions.

Our contemporary 'spacescape' is not just confined to the anthropocentric realm of Modernism, but is 'ascalar', continually flitting between the virtual and actual, flirting with software, hardware, shareware, freeware and wetware simultaneously. Objects and things drift scale, augmented reality gives us unnatural and surprise perspectives, and the Internet of Things enlivens the mute and gives it a voice. All is not what it seems; perspectives shift and the equivalence of objects is a constant. These spaces of Surrealism are everywhere in the contemporary city. Kurt Schwitters might be considered a founding father of 'big data'; unaided by computers and global-positioning satellites, he collected and preserved some of the vectors of the city – bus tickets, sweet wrappers and newspaper headlines were all grist to his collector's mill. His work gives small and tender glimpses of a city mostly gone now. Yet in the twenty-first century, it is at this scale that modern computer-aided geographical information systems must operate if they are to capture, depict and understand the swerve of the city and our complex linked machinic and natural ecologies.

And so it goes on. The biomorphic landscapes of Yves Tanguy might be seen as comments on the evolving sciences of synthetic biology and our ability to construct environments that are self-determining, bottom-up, reflexive to local conditions and wet. Environments that might bring into question our old-fashioned ideas of construction and the procurement of labour and building materials. Or the paintings of Roberto Matta, who studied as an architect, which, during the 1940s, started to develop what might be described as notations of gravity gradients and spatial 'wormholes' (technologies we are now beginning to create). Or the preoccupation, in later life, of André Breton with creating a mythology of the 'Great Transparents' (a similarity with today's augmented reality, if ever there was one). Or Marcel Duchamp's desiring machines and honorific 'readymades', where everything is not what it seems, machines are sexualized and operate with human imperatives, and the names of our objects have been stolen and rebranded, inappropriately out of context (Windows, Apples, desktops, and so on).

And so it continues: René Magritte's bowler hats grow hair, shoes metamorph into feet and skies are wrapped around bottles, while Salvador Dalí's 'edible beauty' encroaches on urban space daily. The soft, erotic robotics of Hans Bellmer, perhaps best left to the imagination, are not far away. While all this seems full of much architectural possibility, Surrealism also reminds us that there are real issues with ethics for the future of architecture, which will become far more important in architectural discourse in the near future. Francis Bacon's *Three Studies for Figures at the Base of a Crucifixion* (1944) eloquently describes what happens should our biological experiments and medical hubris go wrong. The modern architectural student must ponder on these and many more clues to the future embodied in the Surrealist past. A wide understanding of human culture is important to architects – one can never know too much.

The seven continua

It is this wide variety of spatial possibilities engendered in Surrealism that has caused me to try to describe our contemporary spacescape. The experience of contemporary architects/students is one of positioning their work in relation to seven continua, which are:

Space There is a continuum of space that stretches from 'treacle' space standing in a field – no computer, no mobile phone, no connectivity whatsoever – to full bodily immersion in cyberspace. Along the way, between these two extremes, are all manner of mixed and augmented spaces.

Elizabeth-Anne Williams/ AVATAR, Persephone: Expansion of Neptune's Schism. Department of Architecture and Landscape, University of Greenwich, 2013

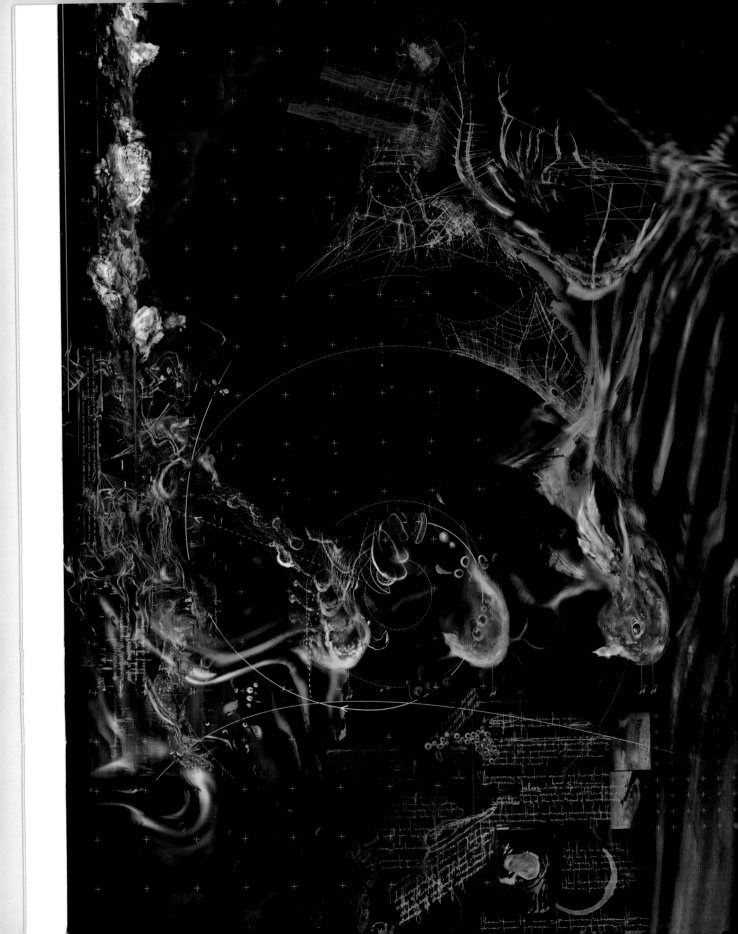

of representation have been used in design and production environments in similar ways to architecture, digital design and manufacture create huge overlaps in the skill bases of a wide range of outcomes. The 3D software that an architect might use to develop or visualize a project is the same used by a filmmaker to create an animation, or a games designer to create a game environment; it might also be the same software used by a graphic, web or product designer (such as the 3D modelling software Rhinoceros). Even within the construction industry, owing to the rise of building information modelling software (BIM), architects, engineers, project managers and surveyors are not only working on the same project with the same software, but also sharing information within the same modelling environment.

Today's generation of designers are defined as much by their software skills as they are by the titles of their professions. The transfer of skills across software is a basic condition of this paradigm. Despite differences in interface design and some of the logistical parameters of the various packages, the majority of available applications are based on similar methodological epistemologies in their structures. The point about software is not that students simply engage with it to represent their projects, but that they understand it as part of a system that enables them to develop a set of skills that are transferable across a wide range of disciplines, utilizing their spatial skills to maximum effect. Because architectural education is still unique in the diversity of knowledge that students are expected to acquire, they are perhaps better placed than students in other design practices.

Students in architecture schools should be encouraged to be just as familiar with film editing and post-production software, games software, scripting and computational coding, and programming cybernetic systems as they are with CAD and BIM software. What is important in encouraging the learning of software skills (I resist the use of the word 'teaching'), is to create an environment in which students can 'play' with a number of applications, preferably in small groups, where they can help and encourage each other to push the tools – and, even if they make mistakes (which they should), use this to begin to understand the core principles of these tools. Once these skills are developed, they can be applied to a wide variety of other packages.

Vipin Dhunnoo, Game Space, pre-production diagram, Greenwich Maritime, London. Unit 15: Time Machines (tutors: Nic Clear, Mike Aling, Simon Withers), Department of Architecture and Landscape, University of Greenwich, 2013

The use of small groups and emphasis on peer support
and collaboration within a version of the 'watch one, do one, teach
one' approach, is often highly preferential to a more formal classroom
scenario, which can render highly uniform and stereotypical outcomes.
Additional support in terms of understanding the broader context of
architecture, from manufacturing processes to historical precedents,
and legislative and legal frameworks to contextual and urban strategies,
still needs to be delivered. But even much of that can be plugged into the
digital design process in the form of 'intuitive models', based on direct
experience.[2] Within the digital design environment, the two activities
of doing and theorizing can take place within the same system.

Chris Kelly, RUBIX:
Impossible Spaces
Augmented Reality
Environment, film still,
Docklands Light Railway,
London. Unit 15: Time
Machines (tutors: Nic Clear,
Mike Aling, Simon Withers),
Department of Architecture
and Landscape, University
of Greenwich, 2013

Hardware

While architecture is to be found everywhere, the profession faces greater uncertainty in its traditional arena of the built environment. Changes in the commissioning and realization of buildings have meant that the architect's role as the head of the building team is no longer standard practice. In many large projects, changes in procurement methods necessitate that project managers and surveyors are in control, and the financial and technical complexity of such endeavours means that buildings are more likely to be valued for their investment qualities than for aesthetic considerations. In some cases, the architecture is simply the clipped-on surface to an otherwise generic product, and the architect is little more than a stylist.

One of the realities of the current state of the profession is that many younger architectural practices have had to embrace the need to branch out into other design areas, utilizing the breadth of the skill base they acquired during their education to its maximum potential. Practices that 'subsidize' their architectural work by designing furniture and products, engaging in rendering or animation, working as art directors or set designers, designing video games, websites or graphics, exhibitions and interactive media are perhaps as common as those who simply design buildings. Multi- and interdisciplinary ways of working provide creative opportunities to question the traditional model of what an architectural student does when he or she leaves college, and open |up the possibility of architecture as 'integrated spatial design', in which the boundaries between disciplines is actively blurred.

If the idea of the architect as lead professional in the designing of buildings is becoming an anachronism, the need for architects to understand how to operate in broader and more collective ways, with the ability to work and support others, must be developed. Architectural education has to embrace these wider possibilities without watering down its core activities for those who wish to become professional architects. But since the traditional role of an architect can vary from a sole practitioner to someone working in a global office as part of a larger team, even then a wide set of possible skills has to be catered for.

Networks

One of the most important aspects of contemporary design culture is the maximizing of the way in which work and ideas are disseminated

through online media, thus providing a public space that links academia and the architectural profession to other disciplines. From the start of their education, students should be encouraged to post and share their work. The main benefit of this is that they begin to feel that their work is part of a dialogue within a wider design community, and to operate in collective, collaborative and supportive ways that will become essential as they move from being students to design practitioners. It is no coincidence that these considerations are the basic principles behind various 'open-source' approaches, which will become increasingly significant within the design community.

The emergence of online resources – whether websites, video hosting, blogging or social media – has given students opportunities to present their work in ways that were unimaginable only a few years ago. Students can be one click away from seeing their work picked up in the mainstream. In recent years, a number of my students, particularly Keiichi Matsuda and Kibwe Tavares, have had their work go 'viral' as a result of their projects being online.[3] Matsuda has gone on to receive international recognition in the field of 'augmented reality', while Tavares's Masters project won both the RIBA Silver

Kibwe Tavares, Robots of Brixton, film still, Brixton, London. Unit 15: Uncertainty (tutor: Nic Clear), Bartlett School of Architecture, University College London, 2011

George Thomson, The Resort, film still. Unit 15: Architectures of the Near Future II (tutor: Nic Clear), Bartlett School of Architecture, University College London, 2009

Medal for best postgraduate architectural student project and a special animation award at the Sundance Film Festival. He has also recently (2013) completed a film, *Jonah*, for Film4. At the same time, blog sites such as BLDGBLOG, Strange Harvest, Architecture and Other Habits and Dezeen cover a wide array of subjects and are useful conduits for speculative and idiosyncratic material – more so than mainstream journals, which tend to be industry focused.

Education

Architecture is a fantastic education; it develops a rich and valuable set of skills. Perhaps one of the problems with much current architectural education is that there is too much of an emphasis on students going into the profession, where those skills can often be unappreciated or completely wasted. The reality is the majority of students entering architectural education will not become professional architects. Architecture schools should not see this as a threat, however, but as an opportunity to capitalize on the growing importance of architectural ideas and skills outside the traditional practice of designing buildings. The profession has much to gain from an expanded sense of

architectural education, and should treasure and encourage the freedom
and speculation of academia, for it is within the spaces of education that
the architectural profession can think and develop new skills and ideas.

Education cannot emulate the profession, nor should it simply
be beholden to it. It has a duty to critically engage with the changing
values, ideas and practices of the profession and set them within
the context of the wider changes of society. This implies the need to
develop political models to address expanding populations, ethical
use of resources and the uneven distribution of wealth and materials –
subjects that the profession often tries to ignore. Architectural education
may have changed greatly in the last 2,000 years, but the challenge
remains the same: to educate students to enable them to generate,
develop, represent and execute spatial ideas – some of which will
become designs for buildings, although many will not. Just as

Neil St John, Augmented
Reality Carnival, film still,
Canary Wharf, London. Unit
15: Time Machines (tutors:
Nic Clear, Mike Aling, Simon
Withers), Department of
Architecture and Landscape,
University of Greenwich, 2013

Vitruvius believed that there were three departments of architecture – the art of building, the making of timepieces, and the construction of machinery – so contemporary architecture should include all disciplines in which architectural skills are clearly demonstrated. Architecture is well placed to capitalize on its rich history and claim its rightful part in the making of all future spaces, whether actual, augmented or virtual.

A good school of architecture develops students who go on to become competent professionals; a great school of architecture develops students who go on to become whatever they want to be.

Keiichi Matsuda, Augmented (hyper)Reality, film still. Unit 15: Year of the Depend Adult Undergarment (tutor: Nic Clear), Bartlett School of Architecture, University College London, 2010

Design animated: Unit 15

– Nic Clear, Head of the Department of Architecture and Landscape, University of Greenwich

After the age of architecture–sculpture, we are now in the time of cinematographic factitiousness; literally, as well as figuratively, from now on architecture is only a movie.

— Paul Virilio, *The Aesthetics of Disappearance*, 1991[1]

I have been exploring the use of the moving image in the construction of new architectural possibilities since 1997, through the work of postgraduate students as part of a design studio called Unit 15. It is not a film unit, but rather an architecture unit that employs the moving image to generate, develop and represent architectural and spatial projects. In my teaching, film, animation and motion-graphics facilitate the creation of new modes of architectural space, representation and practice, and I actively promote a wide variety of techniques, from stop-frame animation to sophisticated computer-generated imagery. The work produced by my students demonstrates a unique approach to content and form, and suggests a whole new series of possibilities for architectural production.

The desire to incorporate the moving image comes out of two main impulses: first as a critique of traditional orthographic projection where the nature of space is largely implied through two-dimensional means; and the second to create architectures that are immersive and time-based. A third imperative is a long-held interest in film, and the

Charlie Barnard, Floating Utopia, pre-production chronogram. Unit 15: Time Machines (tutors: Nic Clear, Mike Aling, Simon Withers), Department of Architecture and Landscape, University of Greenwich, 2013

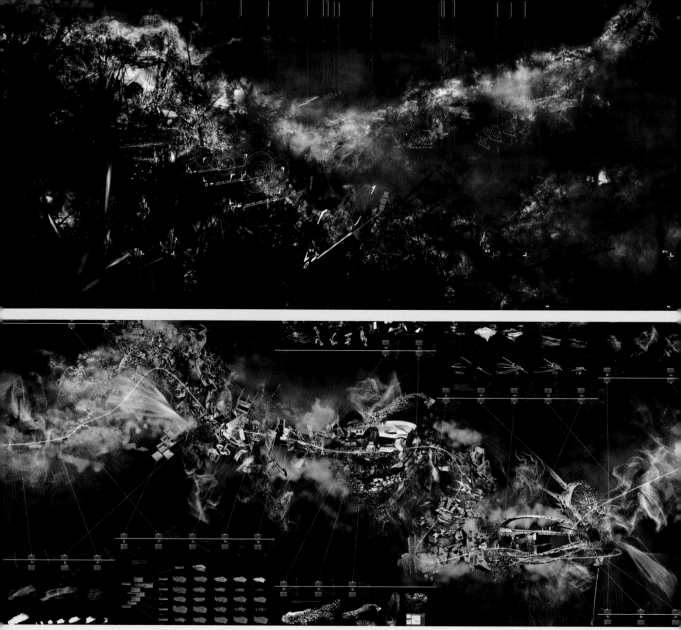

belief that the moving image is the most beneficial way to communicate spatial ideas to a wider audience.

Students in Unit 15 do not make films of their projects; the film *is* the project. But 'film' does not simply mean the linear, narrative-based work of conventional cinema. The moving image can also be integrated within installations and performance-based work, or incorporated into computer games and augmented and virtual-reality environments. There is no standard model; students are expected to use the best means possible to describe their ideas. The development of strategies for deploying time-based work has prompted the generation of innovative techniques, and students must describe the spatial ambitions of their

above
Paul Nicholls, Golden Age – Simulation, chronogram. Unit 15: Uncertainty (tutor: Nic Clear), Bartlett School of Architecture, University College London, 2011

opposite, top
Richard Bevan, Syn
Emergence, meso-scale map,
post-production chronogram.
Unit 15: Architectures of
the Near Future II (tutor:
Nic Clear), Bartlett School
of Architecture, University
College London, 2009

projects, as well as the temporal elements they are utilizing. To do so, they are encouraged to produce hybrid drawings that mix architectural and filmic modes of representation as a way of mapping out their projects. These 'chronograms' have a tripartite function: to develop the narrative; to explain the techniques and methods of construction; and to communicate stylistic and aesthetic concerns.[2]

The methodology of developing moving image-based projects offers students an important insight into the development of complex design projects, for which decisions made at the start carry forward important implications. Unlike with more traditional graphic means, students must attempt to make the project work with the material to hand, rather than simply starting again. The skills they develop in the process are much sought after by architectural offices and transferable across other disciplines, including film, television and web design.

Central to Unit 15's approach is the idea that students are required to engage with a speculative idea of what architecture in the future might be, through an exploration of technologies such as augmented and virtual reality, nanotechnology, synthetic biology, genetic manipulation, robotics and artificial intelligence. Their projects operate on the cusp of technological innovation, and many include what the literary critic Darko Suvin describes as a 'novum', or 'strange newness', where one aspect of the project is created from outside the author's existing scientific paradigm.[3] The overlap between architecture and aspects

below
Dan Farmer, Urban
Plasticity, chronogram.
Unit 15: Architectures of
the Near Future (tutor: Nic
Clear), Bartlett School of
Architecture, University
College London, 2008

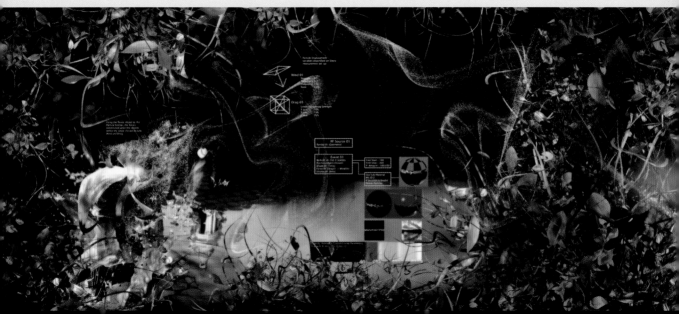

of science fiction is deliberate, with architecture as science fiction a key concept.[4]

The unit draws on a wide range of critical inspirations. Project themes have emanated from novelists such as J. G. Ballard, David Foster Wallace and Iain Banks; theorists including Gilles Deleuze, Félix Guattari, Henry Lefebvre, Paul Virilio, Mike Davis, Manuel De Landa and Constant Nieuwenhuys; and the films of David Lynch, Michel Gondry, Darren Aronofsky, David Fincher, Werner Herzog, Shane Carruth and Wim Wenders. But perhaps the single most important theorist to influence the ideas of Unit 15 has been the work of Fredric Jameson, whose *Postmodernism: The Cultural Logic of Late Capitalism* (1991) has been an important text throughout the unit's history.[5] A later book by Jameson, *Archaeologies of the Future: The Desire Called Utopia and Other Science Fictions* (2005), has become increasingly important as we embraced utopian concepts through the lens of science fiction.[6]

The dissemination of student work is a vital component of my teaching practice. All Unit 15 students are expected to use blogs as a way of documenting the development of their projects and making their work public. The unit has also produced a number of its own publications, and its work has been published in, for example, *Dwell, Architectural Design, Blueprint, Architects' Journal, Building Design, Dazed & Confused* and *Creative Review* magazines, as well as the blog BLDGBLOG. I also regularly curate exhibitions and organize film screenings of student work. The films of Unit 15 students have won numerous awards and been shown at film festivals and exhibitions throughout the world, and students have featured at Onedotzero and Alpha-ville events, as well as the London Design Festival. In 2008, Unit 15 was also the subject of a special screening at the Barbican Centre, London.

Since the move to the University of Greenwich in 2011, Unit 15 has added further depth to its teaching base with the addition of former student Mike Aling (pp. 67–72) and long-term collaborator Simon Withers. The Greenwich iteration is also developing the polemical aspects of Unit 15 through Unitfifteenresearch, a practice-based group that integrates theoretical, speculative and live projects, moving the focus of the unit beyond the confines of academia and seeking to implement some of its ideas through a strategic deployment of new technology.

Richard Hardy, Transcendent City, film still. Unit 15: Year of the Depend Adult Undergarment (tutor: Nic Clear), Bartlett School of Architecture, University College London, 2010

Chris Kelly, RUBIX: Impossible Spaces Augmented Reality Environment, pre-production chronogram, Docklands Light Railway, London. Unit 15: Time Machines (tutors: Nic Clear, Mike Aling, Simon Withers), Department of Architecture and Landscape, University of Greenwich, 2013

Soki So, Hong Kong
Labyrinths, chronogram.
Unit 15: Architectures of
the Near Future II (tutor:
Nic Clear), Bartlett School
of Architecture, University
College London, 2009

A user's guide to the anthropocene (a short passage through a brief moment in time)

– Simon Herron, Academic Leader in Architecture and Unit 16 Postgraduate Design Studio Tutor, Department of Architecture and Landscape, University of Greenwich

This is a present from a small, distant world, a token of our sounds, our science, our images, our music, our thoughts and our feelings. We are attempting to survive our time so we may live into yours.

— President Jimmy Carter, Voyager Golden Record, 1977[1]

On 25 August 2012, NASA's Voyager 1 spacecraft, launched thirty-five years earlier, became the first human-made object to leave our solar system and venture out into the interstellar space of science fiction: a time capsule from our recent technological past, forever trapped in and reliving the sights and sounds of the 1970s, extending our reach beyond our wildest anthropic dreams. Though still somewhat contentious, the margins of the solar system remain an uncertain theoretical zone of experimental astrophysics and fading solar winds – a deep, unimaginable void space littered with a profoundly ancient trace material from the latent death of nearby stars.

The probe, 19 billion km (12 billion miles) from the sun and operating at the outer margins of its capacity, emits only the faintest of binary data streams. It is the size of a small family car, with a decagonal prism at its core, 2m (7 ft) across, housing the central nervous system and equipment bays, with the equivalent circuit complexity of 2,000 colour TVs, continuously recording, sensing, engaging and self-analysing. Carefully conserving energy, powering down its systems while engaging in a reflective, existential dialogue with itself, tirelessly exploring, never bored, reporting back through a deep-space, open-source network, Voyager 1 is HAL 9000 from *2001: A Space Odyssey* without the paranoia.

Alongside the intricate monitoring and communications systems, power supplies and protective shields, a gold-plated phonograph disc – Voyager's 'Golden Record' – provided a calling card to the future from our past. Reflecting on its catalogue of contents, I was struck by the similarities to Stuart Brand's *Whole Earth Catalog*, first published in 1968. Both presented an idealized world view, introducing shelter and land use, industry and craft, communication and community, through ideas of nomadics and learning, and functioned as open-source mechanisms, so that their users might, as the catalogue suggested, 'know better what is worth getting, and where and how to do the getting.' Equally clear and explicit, in both instances, were the demands placed on the imagined user. There was an expectation of cognitive understanding, with a need for reflective self-evaluation and awareness, and the ability to find inspiration and share it: a road map to its maker.

The original mission was conceived in the shadow of Apollo, and in a very different era. The landscape of the early 1970s was one of cultural and political turmoil. The amphetamine-fuelled optimism of the counterculture was long gone, and the new decade was emerging from the hallucinogenic hangover of the 1960s, the Vietnam War and a complete disillusionment with politics, rising oil prices, soaring inflation, social upheaval, industrial decline and failing, bankrupt cities that were sliding into slow decay. In 1977 the Sex Pistols released 'God Save the Queen', an anarchist's anthem; everything that was once stable appeared to have become uncertain. Through the powerful interplay between the forces of nature and technology against those of culture and economics, a strange, distorted, picturesque future was becoming apparent, without any unifying explanation.

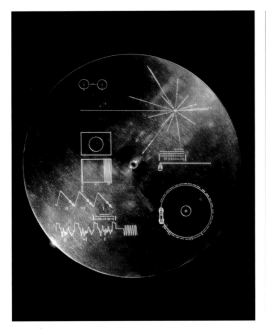

above
Voyager Golden Record, cover

above right
Obelisk historic marker,
White Sands Proving Ground,
New Mexico, 2003

In 2000, realizing that the prevailing cross-disciplinary data no longer fitted the prescriptive model governing the Holocene era, chemist Paul Crutzen and biologist Eugene F. Stoermer coined the term 'anthropocene'. This simple yet extraordinary observation clearly articulated the fundamental shift in planetary systems observed by so many, for so long. The idea of a shift from passive observer of planetary systems and events, to central protagonist and principal driver of planetary change, underpinned the growing argument that we have unwittingly precipitated and crossed into a new geological period. As the thesis gains currency, a central debate has erupted around identifying the exact point of transition from one epoch to the next.[2]

Some have argued that it is the start of the Industrial Revolution, but where is the evidence for this, presented visibly within an identifiable geological layer? Clearly this has been an accumulative, imperceptibly gradual process, which makes a distinct boundary difficult to determine. Stepping aside from climate physics, we might instead reflect upon Buckminster Fuller's examination of the relationship between the chronological rate at which base elements were discovered and of key inventions of science and technology over time. This analysis

Mark Hatter, Fairytale Forensics, reconstruction model. Unit 16: Lost and Found (tutors: Simon Herron, Susanne Isa), Bartlett School of Architecture, University College London, 2001

Wonder Acres, Liquid Gas, 2006

An accidental sea inland empire, 1999

was presented as a graph accompanying Fuller's article 'The Year 2000', published in *Architectural Design* in 1967.[3] By looking closely at the graph, a steep rise can be clearly seen at the outset of the Industrial Revolution, around 1780. A steady upward trend then continues, with plateaus at intervals that broadly align with an economic system of Kondratiev waves (K-waves), which chart a series of fundamental worldwide economic supercycles.[4]

Fuller notes in the same article that in 1932, in the midst of the Great Depression, the ninety-second chemical element (uranium) was isolated, completing the underlying base of the periodic table and marking the start of the age of super-atomics. Prior to this moment there was no direct correlation between the atomic numbers of elements and the order of their discovery. Afterwards, however, elements were discovered sequentially, in rising atomic numbers. This reflected a significant shift in mankind's relationship with and control over nature – a critical moment of rapid technological and industrial acceleration, with 1945 identified as the tipping point and producing a clearly recognizable geological marker.

Trace material with a distinctive radioactive signature can be found in sedimentary material, deposited worldwide, which directly links back to the first atmospheric nuclear event. The first detonation of an atomic weapon occurred at the Trinity nuclear test site in the Jornada del Muerto valley, New Mexico, at 5:29am on 16 July 1945. Standing on the same spot nearly half a century later, in a fenced-off compound, 9m (30 ft) below ground zero, I am aware of the profound emptiness before me. A monolithic basalt construction in a neo-revivalist Spanish aesthetic recalls some classic Western film starring the Duke, and an all-too-familiar haunting image is presented before me, replaying in slow motion in a crazed feedback loop: first the intense flash; followed by an ear-splitting, thunderous crack; then searing heat; and finally a blast shock wave, generating unimaginable pressures and clouds of unforgiving dust.

Looking around, I witness a latter-day techno-pagan ritual, as one devotee after another forms an endless, silent stream of pilgrims paying homage to their god, a new technological divinity. The silence is broken by the firm action click of dozens of shutters, overlaid with the melodic clicks from the mechanical valves of numerous portable oxygen supplies. A confused, mashed-up liturgy – the Techno-Eucharist

– consciously inhales the all-consuming breath of the Anthropocene, at once baptized in the lurid font of the future. A fine-grained, exfoliating dust leaves a deep, penetrative primal residue, occupying every conceivable crevice, exposed or not – an iridescent emerald-green film, liquefying in perspiration, coagulating in nasal mucus. Remember, don't touch the green stuff! Moving north into the sparsely populated, arid wilderness of Nevada's high deserts, I find the archaeological remains of the former national test site and nuclear proving ground: a giant, experimental, open-air vitrine of unprecedented scale and proportion, an unnatural landscape of unparalleled wonder and beauty untroubled by morality, the first true monument to the Anthropocene.

Imagine a journey without a camera, pencil or paper – no physical means of recording. Imaginary maps of absolute emptiness, like maps of antiquity, terra incognita of a vast, unknown land, without scale or points of reference, a landscape subjected to the projective cast of pure imagination, unburdened by history and without resonance to a fixed datum or ground. Of the void space at the centre of the Anthropocene, a vast, 3,500km² (1,351 sq miles) tract of land, only 280km² (108 sq miles) have to date been remarketed as a commercialized space; the rest remains the only one-to-one, real-time, real-world environmental planet modeller, a vast off-the-books landscape with an inbuilt capacity for plausible deniability. Arriving at Mercury, Nevada, a quintessential frontier town an hour's drive northwest of Las Vegas, having passed through camp security, all essentials are catered for: bowling alley, liquor store, movie theatre, cafeteria, general store and RV park. The superficial, surface amenities of any small town – all in an extreme, uncompromising industrial aesthetic of stripped-down sheds.

Moving out of town, along the Mercury Highway, climbing over the valley wall, visitors descend into a strange, unfolding Ballardian landscape, littered with the uncanny detritus from the above-ground nuclear testing. Inexplicable, partially ruptured dome structures, contorted and twisted assemblies of steel, abandoned bank vaults – a Modernist psychotic utopia, or a stripped-down minimalist aesthetic of sunken garages and arrangements of cellular, Donald Judd-like concrete motel units. Further into this wilderness is a disfigured landscape, a 'non-site' formed from an intricate matrix of 828 interwoven ground-implosion events. The largest of these, the Sedan Crater, 390m (1,280 ft) in diameter and 100m (328 ft) deep, viewed from a makeshift

Munitions store and
device assembly bunkers,
Wendover Air Force Base,
Nevada, 1999

Collapsed house,
Nevada, 1999

A domestic scene,
Nevada, 1999

timber platform projecting precariously over the rim, marks a divergence point towards the commercial application of this technology. Here, I am continuously reminded of the extraordinary paradoxical beauty contained within photographer Richard Misrach's *Desert Cantos*, framed by Reyner Banham's treatise 'The Man-Mauled Desert', which guides the untrained eye over this very visceral wilderness, unburdened by any paralysis of virtue.[5]

   I look back over my copy of *Peace Through Strength 1951–1993*, a souvenir edition of the Nevada Test Site newsletter marking the end of atomic testing at the site, complete with a pull-out centrefold: poster pin-ups of atmospheric blasts, a sanitized history documenting the exploits and paraphernalia of industrial weapons development.[6] In the confines of the test site, conventional boundaries between nation state and commercial interests blur. An age of such complexity, faded innocence and dying optimism fuels and reinforces a paranoid urbanism with made-for-TV spin-offs. The short film *House in the Middle* (1954) contains shot after shot of small homes subjected to thermonuclear tests, where the morality of upkeep, tidiness and a fresh lick of paint is presented as a moral duty, with good housekeeping central to national survival.[7] Following the blast, after only a few hours, operatives in normal workwear – slacks and a hard hat – are pictured casually walking over the scene of destruction with apparent disregard for their future health.

above left
Great Overlook, meteor crater, 1994

above right
Target, Wendover Air Force Base, Nevada, 2004

The 'Annie' nuclear weapons test, part of Operation Upshot-Knothole, was shot on 17 March 1953. Scientists built a typical small town on the Nevada Test Site, complete with mannequins, automobiles and a school bus to study the impact of a nuclear blast on an American community. It was the first nationally televised nuclear test shot, dubbed 'Survival City' by the troops and reporters who took part. An unspectacular town laid out like many others with a central strip, Survival City offers a surreal scene of catalogue-living in the age of the atom: an idling car in the driveway, fabrics and soft furnishings from J. C. Penney, a collection of well-maintained homes, along with a school, library, fire station, radio station – nineteen buildings in total.

Before the blast, there was painstaking care and attention to the smallest detail, in a pseudo-forensic manner, in the careful placement of newspapers and the ephemera of everyday life, from pantyhose to bedroom slippers. Documented by a top-secret US Air Force film unit, the scene is captured on 6,500 film reels, shot between 1947 and 1969, of which less than a hundred have been declassified. In Survival City, filmic borders with reality are blurred, and the margins have become confused – a collective amnesia disengages any conventional moral compass. Two weeks after the test shot, J. C. Penney displayed all fifty mannequin survivors, our stand-in heroes from Survival City, with fresh, radiant tans, in its downtown Las Vegas store.[8]

The transformation of a nuclear event into banal, everyday realities was behind the thinking of strategist Herman Kahn, a central figure in the influential RAND Corporation, who imagined an 'evacuation nation' in a perpetual state of alert.[9] Thinking the unthinkable through the application of game theory introduces the idea of a 'Doomsday Machine' as a rhetorical device to support the notion of mutually assured destruction. Kahn and others at RAND pictured a very different scenario, one of survivability and learning to live with radiation, arguing that the effects of fallout were exaggerated. The equally exaggerated figure of Dr Strangelove in Stanley Kubrick's dark satire of the same name (1964) is a combination of Kahn and Wernher von Braun, a wheelchair-bound rocket engineer with a singular-minded prosthesis from another time. Both Kubrick and Kahn drew directly from Peter Bryant's apocalyptic novel *Red Alert* (1958), in which the central protagonists play out the consequences of a flawed maverick general, asking, in the age of the bomb, how safe is safe?

Downwind, east of the test site, beyond Las Vegas and cut into the edge of Mormon Mesa in Moapa Valley, is *Double Negative*, an earthwork sculpture by artist Michael Heizer. As in the work of Robert Smithson, there is an interest in absence, voided space and displacement of matter. For Heizer, the site is matter of fact. Coming from the region, he has a pragmatic relationship with the land – there is no romance for the mythic West – and comprehensively rejects any anthropomorphic reading. The project presents a total, abstracted model of a mathematical argument, questioning the parameters of negation. The location simply provides the space and the material for the work; it is a non-site site.[10]

Double Negative was manufactured with technical precision. Drilling began in 1969 on the 3m (10-ft) rhyolite cap; a full-scale drawing, inscribed directly onto the site, was produced with compression charges. Holes were prepared and exploded in groups of twelve in an array of shots fuelled by Trojan (America's number-one prophylactic) high explosives. The parallels with the earth movements at the Nevada Test Site were abundantly clear: the application of focused charges inducing stress fields with imposed pressure loads radiating out, releasing matter from its cohesive binder. CAT earthmovers redirected 240,000 tons of sandstone, rearticulated into two opposing spill fields. The work initially measured 460m (1,509 ft) in length, 9m (30 ft) wide and 15m (49 ft) deep, but the forces of erosion and decay ensure that it is continually evolving. Visiting requires an acceptance of being lost within the abstracted emptiness of a void space, composed of two impossible negatives.

> *For many of today's artists, this desert is a City of the Future,*
> *made of null structures and surfaces. This 'City' performs no natural*
> *function; it simply exists between mind and matter, detached*
> *from both, representing neither. It is devoid of all classical ideals*
> *of space and process.*
> — Robert Smithson, 'Entropy and the New Monuments', 1966[11]

North of the Nevada Test Site, neighbouring the secretive facility at Groom Lake in the remote Garden Valley, off-road and off-grid, Heizer has since 1973 been developing *City*, an enormous complex artwork of highly engineered earth and concrete structures in various states of completion, which resides somewhere between the ancient structures of the Chichén Itzá, a pre-Columbian city built by the Mayan people

Joerg Majer, Great Overlook
deformation, G.U.L.L.I.V.E.R.
Unit 16: Lost Curiosity
(tutors: Simon Herron,
Susanne Isa), Bartlett School
of Architecture, University
College London, 2004

on the Yucatán peninsula, Mexico, and the Suprematist paintings
of Kazimir Malevich. Rejecting the traditional tools of the artist, opting
instead for the most cutting-edge tools available, Heizer's aim has been
to escape the confines of the local hardware store, the fabrication shop or
traditional steelworkers' yard. In his mind, these traditional institutions
have played too dominant a role in how sculpture has been conceived,
executed and formally expressed. Heizer sought an experimental
sculpture, free from art-historical pressures, which explored the potential
of new materials and processes, engaging with the raw material of the
earth, in the shadow of the atomic bomb.

Seen from the fading shadow of the unmanned space observatory
Gaia, the earth is an object of unparalleled wonder and beauty – and
Voyager an expression of flawed humanity, a work of science and art,

a universal model in synthesis, a gestalt, an object from the end of innocence, driven by technologies of mass destruction and paranoia, sublimated for the collective good.

> *You are right. I understood this myself when I read your novel*
> *The Time Machine. All Human conceptions are on the scale of*
> *our planet. They are based on the pretension that the technical*
> *potential, though it will develop, will never exceed the terrestrial*
> *limit. If we succeed in establishing interplanetary communications,*
> *all our philosophies, moral and social views, will have to be revised.*
> *In this case the technical potential, become limitless, will impose the*
> *end of the role of violence as a means and method of progress.*
> — Vladimir Ilyich Lenin, in Adam Roberts, *Yellow Blue Tibia* (2010)[12]

The salon of lost content (the refuge of misfits): Unit 16

– Simon Herron, Academic Leader in Architecture and Unit 16 Postgraduate Design Studio Tutor, and Susanne Isa, Year One Coordinator and Senior Admissions Tutor, and Unit 16 Postgraduate Design Studio Tutor, Department of Architecture and Landscape, University of Greenwich

The collection of works illustrated here represents a small sample of a considerable body of student work produced under the umbrella of Unit 16, initially based at the Bartlett School of Architecture, University College London, and now at the Department of Architecture and Landscape, University of Greenwich.

Consider this

Have you ever had that curious and unsettling feeling that we are all unwitting subcontractors for Google or Facebook? With every reflex captured through the interstitial surface of a keyboard, our smallest, most unconscious nuances filtered through an unimaginably complex array of algorithms and neural processes? Increasingly, we are living vicariously through the encrypted pseudo-personalities of our onscreen micro-personas, drifting through hypertext paradigms, switching through various mediated, context-specific selves, instant messaging, twittering, and making ourselves up as we go along.

Mashing of context, enacting genres, adopting alternate personalities, outsourcing our emotions while exhibiting those of others – whose personality is this anyhow? With such an interrelated set of experiences – the 'global village' of the twenty-first century – the

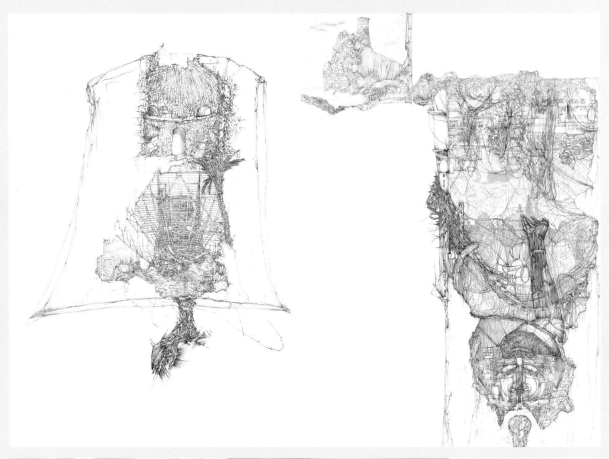

left
Adis Dobardzic, United
Nations, Stratford City,
London. Unit 16: Nostalgia
for the Future (tutors: Simon
Herron, Susanne Isa),
Department of Architecture
and Landscape, University of
Greenwich, 2012

opposite, left
Adam Bell, Lampshade, The
Restored Commonwealth
Club. Unit 16: Restoration
(tutors: Simon Herron,
Susanne Isa, Jonathan
Hagos), Department of
Architecture and Landscape,
University of Greenwich,
2013

opposite, right
Adam Bell, The Restored
Commonwealth Club. Unit
16: Restoration (tutors:
Simon Herron, Susanne
Isa, Jonathan Hagos),
Department of Architecture
and Landscape, University of
Greenwich, 2013

self becomes shapeless and ever-more difficult to pin down. Physical boundaries, language and ideologies have traditionally defined the geographical limits of the tribe. The machines and technologies of mass observation and communication blur and dissolve these former Cartesian certainties. So what happens to the total social construct? What remains of the physical self? What are the social and hardware needs of the near future?

Programmes

Reflecting on this uncertain world, Unit 16 programmes act as catalytic devices, uncovering architectural possibilities by embracing uncertainty and strangeness, redefining how we live. The immediate past and the conformative rhetoric of the present are rejected in favour of an uncertain speculative space, which challenges the preconceptions and inevitability of things. Tactically, this sense of imposed amnesia provides a distancing agent, an insulated operational zone outside the stylistic orthodoxies of the time. The programmes are intentionally structured to undermine any predictive response, presenting instead a dysfunctional set of questions and challenging students to hold a critical mirror to themselves and the world around them.

Drawing

Drawings are seen as spaces for constructive mischievous play – combinations of architectural and non-architectural components, scales and notation systems, twisted and distorted, paradoxical, collapsing in time and space, creating new thoughts and meanings for subject, object, and constructed events imagined alike. Inconvenient rules of gravity and strictures of Euclidean geometry have been replaced with mathematical recipes of uncertainty. Drawings produced within this active real-time dynamic field work as filters, with both real and perceived mass and density, collating and testing unexpected relationships.

The building site is part paper, part digital immersive layers of multidimensional code, made of transferred suspended references; an elaborate interwoven fluid matrix shifting through time and space, conflating hard conditioned facts with half-truths and myths. In this way, drawings become transformative tools, evolving surfaces in flux, containing the traces and histories of their manufacturer. The design unit's primary function must remain a central component of the architectural discourse nervous system, providing the essential polemic fuel, an emotionally charged vapour agitating complex generative structures into being. Ultimately, it is a catalytic incubator of architectural thought and practice, a shapeless pressure vessel, a reaction chamber generating a critical mass, a space of complete distraction and unburdened imagination.

Adam Bell, Mirror View, The Restored Commonwealth Club. Unit 16: Restoration (tutors: Simon Herron, Susanne Isa, Jonathan Hagos), Department of Architecture and Landscape, University of Greenwich, 2013

right
Joerg Majer, Finger
Evidence, G.U.L.L.I.V.E.R.
Unit 16: Lost Curiosity
(tutors: Simon Herron,
Susanne Isa), Bartlett School
of Architecture, University
College London, 2004

below
Jinhyuk Ko, The Ship
of Fools. Unit 16: New
Common-Wealth (tutors:
Simon Herron, Susanne
Isa), Bartlett School of
Architecture, University
College London, 2010

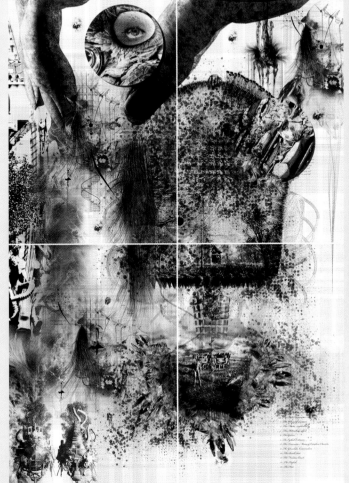

above
Kevin Yu Bai, Aerial
View, The Cathedral,
Mount Olympus. Unit 16:
Experimental Station (tutors:
Simon Herron, Susanne
Isa), Bartlett School of
Architecture, University
College London, 2009

Working the realities of landscape

– Ed Wall, Academic Leader for Landscape, Department of Architecture and Landscape, University of Greenwich

Landscape practice is a series of intricate and interwoven operations that are social and spatial. As landscape architecture, it is informed by physical sites, constituted by a convergence of processes. In her essay 'Site Citations', Elizabeth Meyer suggests that the design of sites has been 'central to establishing landscape architecture as a discipline.'[1] Despite the associations it has had with art, architecture, engineering and horticulture, she claims, landscape architecture is differentiated from other disciplines by its relentless engagement with site throughout the design process. By reading sites as social and spatial entities, it is becoming a design practice that is essential to addressing contemporary circumstances: environmental damage, economic uncertainty and social inequality.

Rising tides, storm surges, earthquakes, landslides, mass migration, summer holidays, urban farming, accelerated supply chains, waste management, industrial pollution, urban growth, rural neglect, global media events, constant surveillance, police presence, cultural diversity, intangible land values and cloned new towns: these are the everyday processes and forms of our landscape. They are not extreme occurrences against a background of balanced ecologies, just societies and shared lives – the daily experiences and spaces of a landscape in constant change. They are the frequently dirty and sometimes delightful realities of landscape that are the focus of landscape architecture.

Previously constrained by its embrace as a scenographic medium, landscape has in the past represented the unreal. In *The Production of Space* (1991), Henri Lefebvre claims that a landscape that 'offers an already clarified picture' is a 'mirage'.[2] He is concerned that as

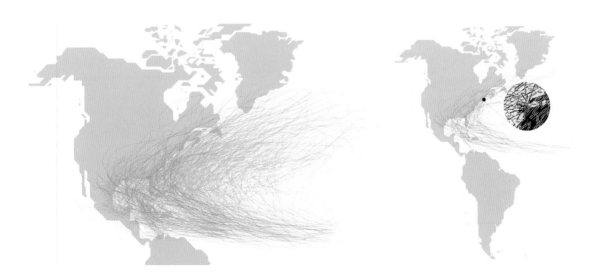

above
Guy Nordenson, Catherine
Seavitt and Adam Yarinsky,
Mapping of Hurricane
Patterns, New York, 2010

above right
Guy Nordenson, Catherine
Seavitt and Adam Yarinsky,
Multi-scalar Ecologies of
Hurricanes, New York, 2010

a representation of space, it falsely claims a transparency to real life
that is misleading. But this illusion, which James Corner also recognizes
in *Recovering Landscapes* (1999), is never permanent.[3] Corner sees it
as a 'veil of pretence', unable to conceal the 'erring realities of life'. For
him, this narrow definition of landscape as scenic interrupts its ability
to engage with the urgencies of contemporary life. Instead, by focusing
on understanding sites as tangible forms and processes, landscape
architecture is able to advance as an inventive social and spatial practice.

Realities

The London landscape has many competing realities, but the Thames
and its surrounding river basin are among its most prominent – a context
that has for centuries framed both the everyday and the extraordinary.
There are fewer more dramatic events than the Thames flood of 1928
and the North Sea flood of 1953, which transformed the relationship of
the city with its river. The overwhelming combination of surging tides
and heavy storms provided grounds for the construction of the Thames
Barrier, which opened in 1983, and flood defences around the North Sea,
and continue to motivate a discourse about the effect of flooding on the
city's infrastructures in the context of a desire for further urban growth.

Everyday events also unfold at the scale of individuals. The direct
action of Trenton Oldfield, a lone protester who waded into the Thames
in 2012 to disrupt the annual boat race and the elitism it represented,
offers a contrast to these regional floods. The protest was a fleeting

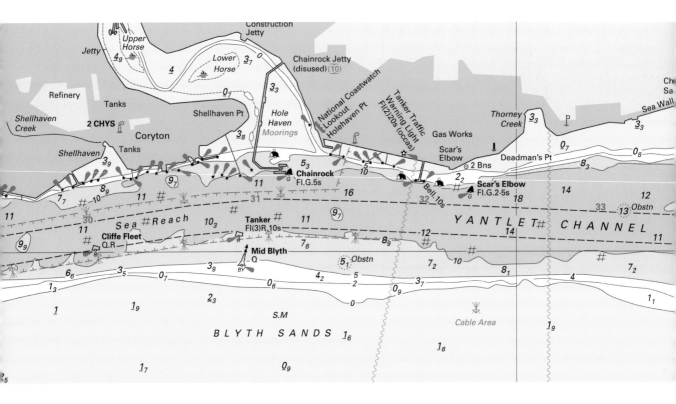

moment of interruption, which has since drawn a lengthy political reaction. This single action opened up questions of education, migration and the legitimacy of protest itself, and highlighted a landscape indivisible from the social constructs from which it is made. Other acts of resistance, for example at Taksim Gezi Park, Istanbul, in 2013, and Zuccotti Park, the temporary home of Occupy Wall Street protestors, two years earlier, highlight how the presence of people comes to define these landscapes. They also reveal the significance of less tangible regulatory contexts, which are not immediately evident to the observer in constructing the lived reality of these places.

But behind these occurrences are clues to their composition and what they mean to design practice. What exist are processes rich in information. For landscape practice, the task is to translate this site knowledge creatively, interpret social actions spatially and understand dynamic ecologies effectively. These realities of landscape are embedded with an abundance of data that is both immediate and

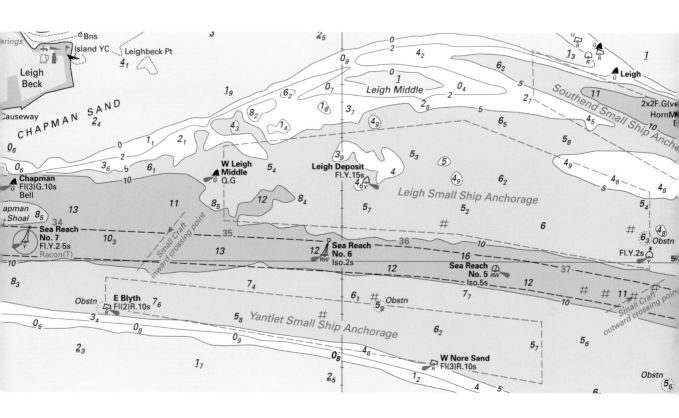

Imray Laurie Norie & Wilson,
Measures of the Thames,
London, 2010

concealed; to uncover this and work the information imaginatively
offers landscape architects exceptional grounds for their practice.

Designs

The Thames environment provides many contexts for landscape
practice in London, and is the geography from which the *All London
Green Grid* emerged – a strategic open-space and green infrastructure
framework, initiated by the Greater London Authority, which grew from
the initial *East London Green Grid* plan.[4] The two strategies recognize
that green and open-space networks should be read, as Peter Beard
describes in the *East London Green Grid Primer*, 'as infrastructures
in themselves'.[5] This metropolitan-scale mapping quantifies the
contribution of existing and potential open spaces. Beard further
observes that these green and open spaces are 'placed as deliberately
as their engineered counterparts with their own rational contribution.'
This embraces an approach to landscape based on spaces and processes,

rather than objects, and one that designers can engage with through the layers of evidence as they are revealed.

Working with landscape as an infrastructure also offers a scale of operation necessary to understand this vast geography. Even the term 'grid', adopted for London's open-space and green infrastructure strategy, implies what Corner describes as 'a vast surface for flexible and changing development over time.'[6] Although the *All London Green Grid* is not an orthogonal structure, the sense of order and exacting dimensions that would be expected from an engineered approach offers, Corner continues, 'autonomy and individuality of each part' within it.

As the grid is realized through built projects, the distinctness of local discourses, regional politics and global trends, economies and climates are likely to be more closely felt. Work with the manageable elements of landscape, which Beard recognizes as contributing in a 'measurable and quantifiable way to the functional hardware of the city', needs to be carefully mediated with the unplanned.[7] How the instability of climatic events can be engaged with will require hybrid solutions that are social, technological and ecological. The aim of the *All London Green*

Greater London Authority, Opportunities Across the All London Green Grid, London, 2012

Grid to increase access to open space will necessitate a generosity
as to what is permitted in these spaces, as well as who is allowed in.

Working with water and preventing flooding is central to the grid's
framework. Addressing the increasing development of green spaces
and the subsequent inundation of drainage networks has also been the
focus of much landscape architecture practice. Area frameworks that
were prepared from the *East London Green Grid* considered directly the
absorption of rainwater by the landscape, creating conditions that allow
communities to adapt to climate change. The Thames Barrier represents
a harder infrastructural approach to flooding than the *All London Green
Grid*. After the North Sea flood in 1953, when thousands of people were
killed, a barrier in the river was considered necessary to protect London.
But in the Netherlands, the flood led to a national strategy, transforming
the country's relationship with the sea. The Dutch have a long history
of managing the threat from water, and the Delta Works system was built
along the coastline as the latest of a series of flood defences that have
defined the population's relationship with its environment.

These challenging conditions have significantly informed the
work of Adriaan Geuze of landscape architecture firm West 8. As a
highly engineered environment, the landscape of the Netherlands is
a frequent setting for his projects. Geuze takes an inventive approach
to site information by opening it up through the design process. His
portfolio of work, which presents the conceptually abstract alongside
rigorous site research, demonstrates an ability to recognize the dramatic,
as well as the ordinary conditions of landscapes. For the 1990 Prix de
Rome-winning project located between the Dutch towns of Breukelen
and Vinkeveen, Geuze investigated a landscape of transportation
infrastructure, landfill waste and water bodies. Principal to the design
is a 5km (3-mile) terminal that simultaneously facilitates a centralized
water-management system, a national waste and recycling treatment on
which a new city could emerge. But importantly, and in contrast to Field
Operations' masterplan for the Staten Island landfill site Fresh Kills
(2006),[8] Geuze embraces the unsightly processes of the landscape,
openly working with the unseemly juxtaposition.

West 8's design for the Eastern Scheldt Storm Surge Barrier
(1992) also accepts the exposure of the Dutch polder landscape,
recognizing its position in the migration patterns of a number of bird

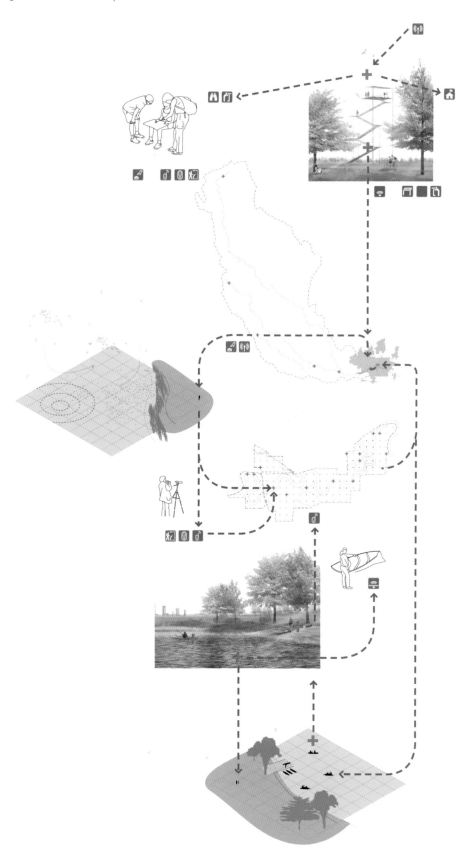

Project Studio, Water Works
Park, Des Moines, Iowa, 2011

'illusion of transparency' that accepts space as neutral forms.[10] What is proposed here, however, is accepting the immediately accessible and interrogating what is not. It advocates understanding the political interrelations that have formed these spaces, and requires the designer to recognize the incompleteness of knowledge and anticipate when it has been obscured. It also requires designers to interrogate the partiality of all site information, understand the sources of secondary data and question how any new data generated by a design will be used.

The challenge is then to work with this data spatially. To be useful in material practice, rather than just points on a map, the collected data must be translated into spatial form. New techniques must be developed to expose these sites and methods, and enhanced to develop them as designs. This does not negate the significance of traditional methods and established techniques of drawing, but rather highlights the need for specific approaches to each encountered landscape. Site investigations are defining innovative designed landscapes. Rather than abstract approaches based on the individuality of the designer, working with the realities of the landscape offers greater potential for inventive designers to engage with the immediate and difficult relations with our environment. These ways of working landscapes reveal what Corner describes as 'alternative sets of possibility' through creatively engaging with site conditions.[11] They are embracing sites that can be understood spatially, opening up landscape practice as a speculative and transformative process that can work in new and fascinating ways.

The digital generation

– Bob Sheil, Director, Bartlett School of Architecture,
University College London

The typical undergraduate beginning an architecture course today was six years old at the turn of the millennium, born in the same year as the Apple QuickTake, the first commercially available digital camera. They took their first steps as the World Wide Web entered our homes, and by the time they were ten, Facebook had launched and Concorde had made its last flight. In their teens, the digitalization of the information age was in full flow, 3D printing was mainstream and the construction and design industries were exchanging protocols on manufacturing processes. By the time our freshers were accessing their first university podcast lecture, they were simultaneously downloading a plug-in upgrade and uploading their own latest applet development.

These students of today, the architects of tomorrow, are the first generation entirely raised in a digital culture, shaped by a period of profound and dynamic change and entirely familiar with technologies that are always new. In terms of digital skills, a large proportion of what they learn is self-taught and informed through their peers. The relationship they have with the institution is radically different to that of previous generations, and certainly different to that of their tutors when they embarked on the same journey decades ago. The industry, too, is increasingly global, diversified and connected. Once it was a fairly straightforward task to describe what an architect did and how education related to it – now it is far from straightforward. By necessity, the architectural school has become a testing ground for what architecture could be, and what architects could do. This is a profoundly liberating and positive condition, and a forward-looking

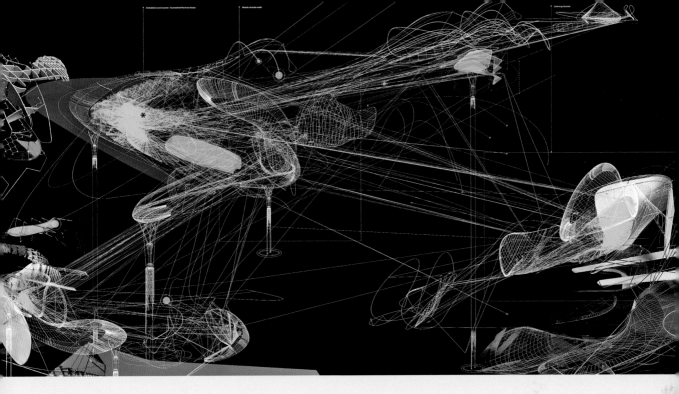

Emma-Kate Matthews,
Spaces of Uncertainty: The
Augmented Instrumentalist,
Moses Barrier, Venice. Unit 23
(tutors: Bob Sheil, Emmanuel
Vercruysse), Bartlett School
of Architecture, University
College London, 2010–11

and progressive educational environment can offer opportunities and rewards that far outweigh the stagnation imposed by certainty.

In this regard, the most progressive schools of architecture must define their own priorities by setting and evolving ambitious agendas for discourse, knowledge, practice and research. They must generate questions, and questions within questions. They must look at old questions and see that they can be asked again. They must interrogate human strife in all its forms, ask what it is and what it could be. They must set out their stalls skilfully, tactically and knowingly, and ply their trade through seduction, temptation, allure and the promise of fulfilment. They must operate as sanctuaries and laboratories, workshops and networks, families and rivalries, and both archives and publishing houses of fact and fiction. They must nurture ambition, talent, aspiration, expertise and skill, and establish way points of origin, departure and return for young navigators. They must construct realities, defend the vulnerability of embryonic ideas and devote valuable time to play, experiment and failure.

To stay progressive, schools must take risks, be prepared to reinvent themselves, shun stagnation and inbreeding, challenge all the other great institutions, including those of industry and practice, and stay lean and fit, rather than hierarchical and unwieldy. In short, schools of architecture today must continually relearn how to educate the architects of tomorrow, and in this endeavour they must establish

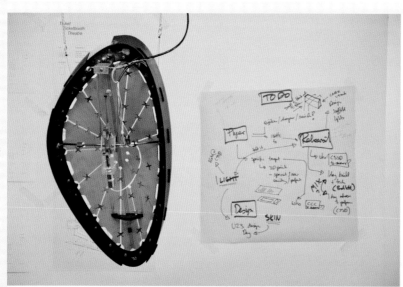

Maria Knutsson-Hall, Slothball, São Paulo. Unit 20 (tutors: Marcos Cruz, Hannes Mayer, Marjan Colletti), Bartlett School of Architecture, University College London, 2011–12

Misha Smith, Prototype for a Spatialized Instrument. Unit 23 (tutors: Bob Sheil, Emmanuel Vercruysse), Bartlett School of Architecture, University College London, 2009–10

what the architects of the next fifty years need to know, while giving them the tools and confidence to adapt as the decades unfold.

Standing before this generation is the ever-expanding question of how architecture relates to emerging technology, and particularly to those technologies connected to the production of buildings. For centuries, the construction of prototypes, artefacts, buildings and structures has operated on a rolling tradition of visual and verbal communication between designers, consultants, makers, clients, users, regulatory bodies and contractors. In making buildings, roles were defined in which individuals and disciplines were located on a chain from concept to execution. All were reliant on its links being successfully forged, not only to achieve results, but also to underpin their status within their respective professions and trades. Prevailing over the entire process was the design, an assemblage of cross-referenced visualizations, specifications and quantities that formed the templates and instructions for making.

Over the past decade, key relationships between design and making have been thoroughly redefined by integrated and automated digital technologies. The exchange of information between design and fabrication is no longer a slow chain of vulnerable links, but a rapid flow of data in which design and making can be a simultaneous process. A vast expansion of the remit, scope and potential of the designer has subsequently been released, allowing for their direct engagement and control of the fabrication processes. Some designers, who are equally adept at representation as they are with putting things together, grab this opportunity to redefine their role as hybrid disciplinarians. Others remain within the realm of making information for making buildings, but they too are adapting to the consequences of being directly connected to the processes and procedures of how their work is made.

Within this context, one of the central predicaments facing the education of architects today is to define the designer's expertise in relation to an industry in revolution. Clearly there is a need to access new technology, to become familiar with it, establish a critical position in relation to it and, finally, claim authority and credibility in this new domain. In response to this paradigm shift, and across many of the leading architectural institutions in the world, unprecedented investment in equipment and resources is presently underway. Many of the most ambitious schools of architecture are expanding their estates to include advanced fabrication laboratories to house tools previously only associated with advanced industrial environments, and these are run by staff with multidisciplinary skills in manufacturing, design, craft, programming and materials. A new relationship between teaching, research, industry and practice is emerging, one that is adaptive and collaborative, nonlinear and mutually dependent. Underpinning its future is the digital generation, unleashed and not like anything we have seen before.

Tom Svilians, The Bradbury Transcripts, Bradbury Building, Los Angeles. Unit 23 (tutors: Bob Sheil, Kate Davies, Emmanuel Vercruysse), Bartlett School of Architecture, University College London, 2012–13

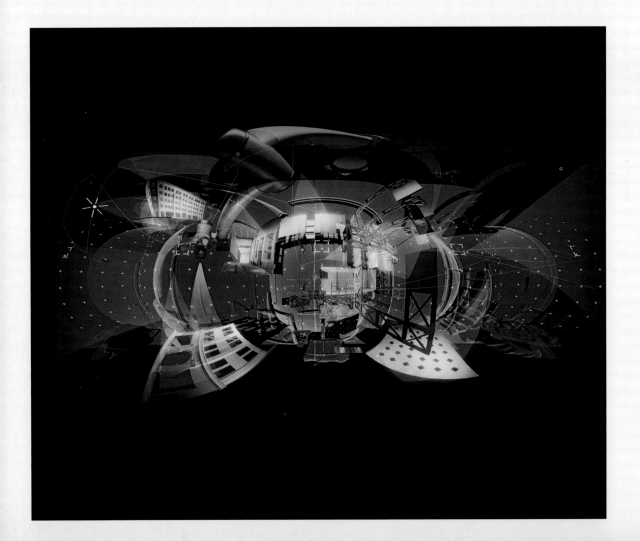

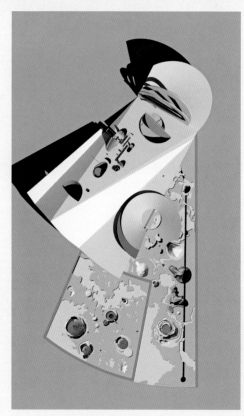

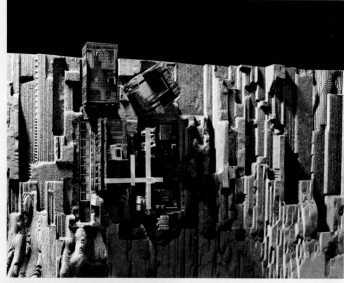

Sonila Kadilliari, Pre-Ecopoiesis Mars Yard, Florida. Unit 11 (tutors: Laura Allen, Mark Smout, Kyle Buchanan), Bartlett School of Architecture, University College London, 2012–13

Tamsin Hanke, Magnitogorsk, Chelyabinsk, Russia. Unit 17 (tutors: Yeoryia Manolopoulou, Niall McLaughlin, Michiko Sumi), Bartlett School of Architecture, University College London, 2012–13

Ollie Palmer, Mind Control in Architecture. PhD (tutors: Stephen Gage, Ruairi Glynn), Bartlett School of Architecture, University College London, 2013–

The imaginarium of urban futures

– C. J. Lim, Professor of Architecture and Urbanism and Vice-Dean, Bartlett School of Architecture, University College London

Logic will get you from A to B. Imagination will take you everywhere.

— Albert Einstein[1]

Ned Scott, The War Rooms: New St James's Park, London. Unit 10 (tutors: C. J. Lim, Bernd Felsinger), Bartlett School of Architecture, University College London, 2012

Recently, my architectural pedagogy has been more concerned with how the city of the twenty-first century might adapt if we are serious about living sustainably, and with the potential of speculative spatial occupation, rather than of individual physical buildings. Today, utopian ideals are met with incredulous admiration or lofty condescension, or sometimes both; an overview of professional journals from the past decade reveals a marked shift away from fantastic propositions in favour of constructed reality. The floating, walking and flying propositions of Buckminster Fuller, Archigram, the Metabolists, et al, have all but floated, walked or flown away.

This is not so much due to narrow-mindedness on the part of our current crop of architects, but more a sign of the times. Just as science fiction can only be a doppelgänger for the present, architectural vision is chained to the presiding zeitgeist. Only in the aftermath of such great upheavals as the First World War would a scrupulously practical man like Walter Gropius, in his 1917 manifesto for the Workers Council for Art, call for architects to 'engrave their ideas onto naked walls and build in fantasy without regard for technical difficulties. To have the gift of imagination is more important than all technology, which always adapts itself to man's creative will.'[2] Gropius went on to predict that the architects of the future would make 'gardens of the desert' and 'heap wonders to the sky'.[3]

Our unit at the Bartlett School of Architecture, University College London, represents an emerging architectural voice in the discourse of environmental and social urban sustainability – a long-overdue treatment of the subject from an architectural perspective that is speculative, design propositional and critical-theory focused. Current discourse on sustainability appears to concentrate either on the technical aspects of ecological design at the scale of individual buildings, or establishes the general principles for planning urban environments. Unit 10 attempts to address what the spatial and phenomenological implications are when sustainable design is applied to a city, what new hybrid typologies of programme and landscape are birthed and the role that we as citizens will play in the production of a relevant social space.

Simultaneously inventive, poetic and credible, the unit's projects all posit a divergent status quo, taking speculative and sometimes impossible ideas to their logical conclusions. Technical exposition and environmental science underlie much of the use of poetics and fictional narrative (often science fiction) to stimulate strategies for ecological symbiosis between nature and the built form to address climate change. In *The Eternal Autumnal Micro-Climate*, for example, Martin Tang 'paints' the city of Kyoto, forever golden with the warm smells of autumn, by way of engaging in serious technical and environmental research into a carbon-neutral, self-sustainable energy system.

Science fiction is prophetic – its utopian visions have predicted the future as much as representing a past that was never possible. Although adopted by the defence and food-technology industries, science fiction is often treated with wariness in respect to urban design, leading to accusations of utopianism. This has not always been the case. Sir Ebenezer Howard's 'garden city', described in his *Garden Cities of To-morrow* (1898), was itself inspired by Edward Bellamy's utopian novel *Looking Backward: 2000–1887* of ten years earlier, a bestseller that immediately spawned a political mass movement and several communities adopting its ideals. Letchworth and Welwyn Garden Cities in the UK were based on Howard's concentric plan of open space, parkland and radial boulevards, which integrated housing, agriculture and industry, and are two of the few remaining realizations of utopia.

C. J. Lim, The Hunting Exchange of Maribor: The heavenly gardens of food sustainablitiy, Maribor, Slovenia, C. J. Lim/Studio 8 Architects, 2012

C. J. Lim, The Hunting Exchange of Maribor: 'Open season' shopping for local produce, Maribor, Slovenia, C. J. Lim/Studio 8 Architects, 2012

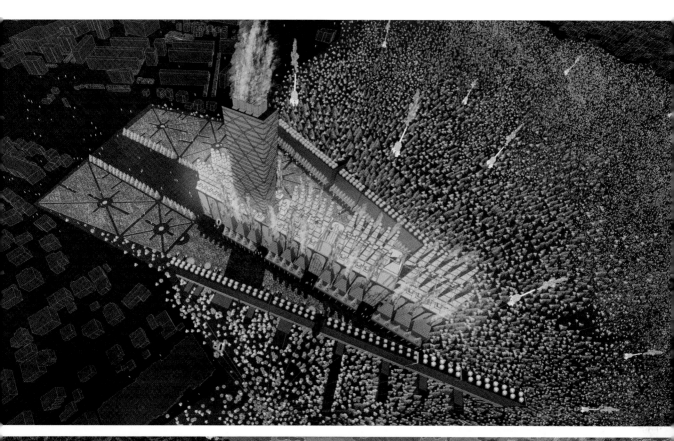

above
Martin Tang, The Eternal
Autumnal Micro-climate:
A thousand origami cranes
float, shield and cultivate a
single season, Kyoto. Unit
10 (tutors: C. J. Lim, Bernd
Felsinger), Bartlett School
of Architecture, University
College London, 2012

opposite
Martin Tang, The Eternal
Autumnal Micro-climate:
The lake is dyed orange in
colour by the mass migration
of salmon, Kyoto. Unit 10
(tutors: C. J. Lim, Bernd
Felsinger), Bartlett School
of Architecture, University
College London, 2012

Inspired by Howard, the science-fictional scenario and proposed
urban strategies presented by Unit 10's Ned Scott in *The War Rooms*
address the challenges the UK faces regarding energy security and
fuel poverty, and speculate on the hypothetical consequences of a
future in which the many risks associated with the country's long-term
energy strategy come to bear. Science fiction always holds a mirror to
the present; the discourse of Unit 10 often takes the notion 'what if …'
as its starting point. The projects question how humanity adapts – and
no process of change threatens us more radically than what we are
doing now to the natural environment we so depend on. Nevertheless,
Steven McCloy's *European Union: The Gardens of Fantastica* is an
imagined past that causes us to look back in regret at the development
of the twentieth century, and parodies the seemingly surreal political,
economic and infrastructural landscape of twenty-first-century cities.

In the last decade, there has been continual statistical abstraction
of scientific proof exposing the global emergency of climate change
and the detrimental effects on our environment. But facts and figures
are poor tools for stimulating debate – compelling visual narratives

of the built environment are more conducive to engaging the public imagination. The storytelling nature of the unit's work has a role in the eco-war efforts for humanity. Thandi Loewenson's *City of Melencolia* is a psycho-topography existing in a state of extreme solipsism in the mind of a failed fictional explorer, Diego Vasquez, which tackles urban ecological alienation across the environmental, economic and political spheres of the city.

J. G. Ballard wrote that the psychological realm of science fiction is most valuable in its predictive function, projecting emotion into the future.[4] Speculative visions of the built environment, whether or not they are accepted, are reflections of society and have a powerful influence on the public consciousness. An architect's greatest influence lies in the visualization of an alternative reality, the aesthetics of which can capture the public imagination in negotiating issues that transform our cities in the face of climate change.

opposite
Thandi Loewenson, City of
Melencolia: The landscape
of super-ego and urban
governance. Unit 10
(tutors: C. J. Lim, Bernd
Felsinger), Bartlett School
of Architecture, University
College London, 2013

Steven McCloy, European
Union: The Gardens of
Fantastica – The Garden of
Anaerobic Digesters, Paris.
Unit 10 (tutors: C. J. Lim,
Bernd Felsinger), Bartlett
School of Architecture,
University College London,
2013

above
Thandi Loewenson, City
of Melencolia: The failed
explorer, Diego Vasquez,
implores an uninterested
Queen Isabella to invest
in his quest for a new
world of instinctual urban
infrastructure of heat, light,
water and energy. Unit 10
(tutors: C. J. Lim, Bernd
Felsinger), Bartlett School
of Architecture, University
College London 2013

Audacious encounters

– Nigel Coates, Professor Emeritus,
Royal College of Art

Seven years of plenty, or seven years of famine? In the time
of the Book of Genesis, seven years would have seemed a lifetime.
In the modern era, seven years is longer than most marriages,
and for anybody would be a very long time to study. School leavers
contemplating a career in architecture must prepare for the hardship
and endurance of this proverbial eternity – not just for the protracted
commitment, but for ramping strain on their finances (or their
parents') and their attention. Few secondary schools introduce
it into their curriculum, so for the builders of tomorrow,
studying architecture is a leap of faith.

But architecture students are attracted by the prospect of making a
difference to their surroundings. Once into their studies, most acquire an
existential thirst for the subject; they are on a path that, for the brightest,
leads to a lifetime of passion and learning. In my own experience as
a student of architecture (1968–74), the BA years at a provincial school
were reasonable preparation for taking up a place at the Architectural
Association in London. The AA had seemed unreachable – a private
school with high standards and high costs. But having discovered that
one could qualify for a grant to study there (I was one of the last), the
best school in the country was not as out of reach as I had thought.

Under the legendary leadership of Alvin Boyarsky (see pp. 40–9),
the AA had blossomed into a culture zone that, in contrast to the
miserable economics of the UK, attracted not only ambitious students,
but also some ultra-smart tutors. Alvin used to refer to London as his
'landing strip', and invited prominent exponents of radical architecture
from around the world to take part in his revitalized iteration of the
school. The freewheeling approach of the 1960s stabilized into an
encyclopaedic mix of all the contemporary strands, from community
action to utopian idealism. All of these approaches were tried and
tested by staff and students and had one thing in common – they

had no intention of teaching people to build. Instead, architecture was held up as existential truth, a culture rather than a skill; it could shape a philosophy, as well as a way of being. As an architect, one would be an artist, a sadhu. With building as a by-product of one's learning, the real reason for becoming an architect was to channel ideas into the 'project'. Indeed, when eventually I did build, particularly in Japan and the UK, I never gave up the project, and opted for an ongoing 'research', as this project-based work became euphemistically known in academic jargon.

Divisible cities

In our final year at the AA, one book had more impact than all the tomes on architecture my fellows and I had thus far devoured. *Invisible Cities* (1972) by Italo Calvino captured our imagination like no other, and put any lingering fascination with Aldo Rossi in the shade. Despite the lack of illustrations, the book's systematic variation succeeded in evoking the true spirit of the urban condition. Each chapter identified a city with a luscious female name ('Fedora', 'Smeraldina', 'Ottavia'), and unravelled how a beguiling impression could boil down to precise architectural characteristics that tallied with the behaviour of its inhabitants.

The sum of these chapters/cities comprised a lexicon that divided one city into many: 'Thin Cities', 'Cities and Signs', 'Cities and Eyes'. Together they seemed to capture our own broadening understanding of what architecture could encompass. One of these, 'Continuous Cities', was very close to the title of a key Superstudio project of the time, Continuous Monument (1969), a gridded structure that eclipsed all existing architecture in its drive to extend, highway-like and uniformly, all around the globe. In their infinite variety of poetic tropes, Calvino's cities are born from the contrast between the idealized and the materially real. These opposites need not so much to resolve their differences in dialectical exchange, as to fuse into one as they do in any city – London or Venice, Calvino's stereotype included.

The AA Diploma school had assumed a similar post-structuralist mode. When Alvin introduced the 'unit' system, he cast the die that would influence the best architecture schools around the world. Only in hindsight did we realize what was so special about this system. How did it improve on the tried-and-tested year structure that had served schools so well before? Fellow students Zaha Hadid (pp. 295–300), Peter L. Wilson (pp. 40–9) and I were mentored by the likes of Bernard Tschumi,

Rem Koolhaas of OMA (pp. 177–82; 200–4) and Peter Cook (pp. 22–31).
Whether students or staff, the rivalry and identity of each unit helped
drive everyone forward, heightening competition and getting results.
If you performed well as a teacher, you would be rewarded with a show
in the AA Gallery or publication by the AA's new imprint.

In Calvino's concluding chapter, Kublai Khan asks: 'Towards which
of these futures the favouring winds are driving us?' Marco Polo replies:
'For these ports I could not draw a route on the map or set a date for the
landing. At times all I need is a brief glimpse, an opening in the midst of
an incongruous landscape, a glint of lights in the fog, the dialogue of two
passers-by meeting in the crowd, and I think that, setting out from there,
I will put together, piece by piece, the perfect city, made of fragments
mixed with the rest, of instants separated by intervals, of signals one
sends out, not knowing who receives them.'[1] Superstudio's Continuous
Monument seemed somehow simplistic and empty by comparison.

NATO manoeuvres

As a young tutor in the run-up to what became the architecture group
NATO, I developed a framework with the students, which concentrated
on one area of London. For a whole year we would examine every aspect
under a microscope, perform various exercises on it and cut sections
through it. We would begin by making domestic objects that reflected a
theme; one year it was 'work and home'; another, 'art and science'. Using
the primitive equipment of the time, each student would make a video
about their object, communicating its use and spirit. These micro-films
would be dissected in post-production storyboards, which in turn were
used as a tool to examine the chosen part of the city. The projects had
individual authorship, otherwise how could they be assessed? But each
unit member also worked with the group to weave their individual
projects into one morphing bricolage.

I would guide the process, but never fully direct it. I undertook
projects myself, nudging students forward, as well as testing my
directives. Some students would soon be way ahead of me. They found
ways to put the post-punk irony of the time into their work. Consciously
or otherwise, we were taking part in a laying-on of hands; teacher and
student were alternating roles. Needless to say, the outcome of this
student–teacher love-in was too much for the external examiners. In
1983 James Stirling famously rejected the work of the entire unit as

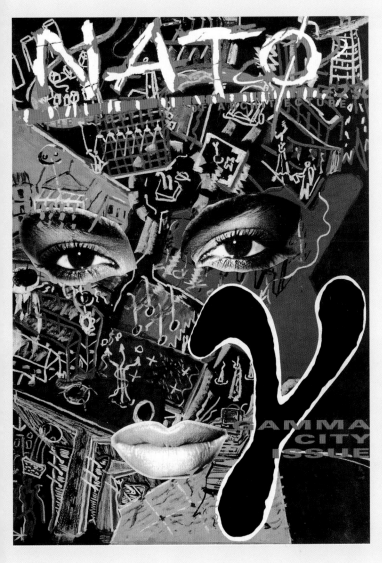

Cover of *NATO3*,
'Gamma City' issue, 1985

Unit 10 brochure,
Architectural Association
Projects Review, 1983

little more than scribbles. But, encouraged by Alvin, we fought back, and the NATO group was born with nine members, including myself, and graduates from the graduating groups of 1982 and 1983.[2] With its eponymous magazine, NATO made an instinctive media *putsch*, and managed to step outside the institution. Several exhibitions in important public galleries tied in nicely with each new issue. Back at the AA, the technique for creating vivid urban scenarios, what Brian Hatton called 'mighlihoods', set the bar for many other AA units.[3]

Like all young teachers, I learned by teaching others, and in that period I had the good fortune of a particularly talented bunch who wanted to go beyond the expedience of many of their fellows. I encouraged them to be subversive in their approach to design. They would make use of what they found, including both London's 'ruins' and otherwise discarded moments of architectural heroism. Remaindered books on Konstantin Melnikov and the Festival of Britain provided material for advanced workshops that involved their dismembering. I would invest in vast amounts of electronic components for collective,

NATO, *Gamma City*,
Air Gallery, London, 1985

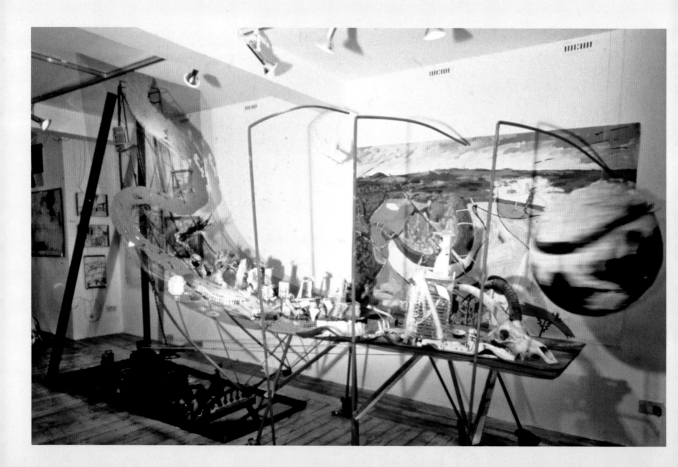

rambling city models. We could easily build a whole stretch of London in an afternoon. As well as conceiving buildings, imagining events ran rife, a strategy developed from the Tschumi discourse on 'architecture and events'. Existing buildings were reinvented with dizzy new programmes that linked into the social history of the locality. A project could be built into a true reality; the dozen or so members of the unit were standing in for a real population. If you published the results and said they were true, then they were true: how was the reader to argue?

Unlike the kind of architectural expression that arises from a theory (such as 'folding' or 'parametricism'), this strategy fabricated a total world – not a utopian or an ideal world, but a gritty one that was a plausible paradigm of what actually existed. It captured that imaginative increment that goes hand in hand with the act of design. The scenario – indeed, the 'narrative' – helped build the students' work into a deliberately fictional reality. Rather than being confined to 'paper', we created a blueprint for acting as an architect in a real-life situation.

Royal College of Art,
Architecture Annual,
1996–2011

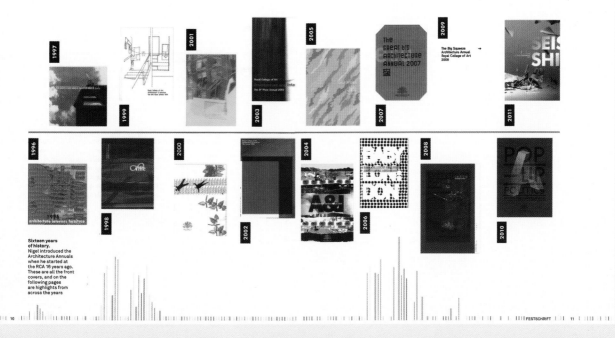

SWEET SIXTEEN

Over the last 16 years, Nigel Coates has led the creation of a unique architectural culture at the RCA. To mark his departure, we publish this *festschrift* of recollections and reflections from some of those who've shared the journey along the way.

Sixteen years of history.
Nigel introduced the Architecture Annuals when he started at the RCA 16 years ago. These are all the front covers, and on the following pages are highlights from across the years

Many of the graduates from that period knew exactly how to bridge their studies with their professional work.[4]

Elite excellence

When I was studying at the AA, students at the Royal College of Art were designing perfect white villas in a secessionist idiom. We were not looking for this kind of refinement, and sneered. I had a counterculture taste for radical and artistic ideas, and believed (and still do) in the latent heroism of every student and that to be a good architect you need to lean hard against the system. In 1995 I became Head of Architecture (and Interiors) at the RCA. I was told to organize the department as I would my office; the experiment would be to add more structure to a tiny department that until then had flattered students with their postgraduate MA status. In reality, they had inhabited a laissez-faire environment at the top of the building, and had been given little guidance or critical encouragement.

I set about expanding the relatively autonomous territory of the architecture department into an entity with its own dynamics and culture. Teachers and students would operate in the protected confines of an elite institution. The lack of funds was obviously a disadvantage, but other advantages abounded. Like Zaha Hadid, I saw my office as a mini-atelier in the style of the AA unit, and so it followed that I would apply the same framework here. I exploited its pocket scale (there was an average of fifty students on the MA course during my tenure), yet it had to feel like an academy ten times its size. Told that it would never work in the pseudo-sophisticated, rarefied context of the RCA, I nonetheless decided to set up three architectural design studios. Each would be led by two tutors who, ideally, had not worked or taught together. I wanted raw edges and lively differences. The last thing we needed was for students to follow a formula, or think the tutor was always right.

The department soon became a viable alternative to larger schools, and bathed in the critical potential of a rich spread of alternative approaches. The college's many disciplines and associated laboratories were the cherry on the cake. Students were thinking and doing. I foresaw their education evolving naturally into multidisciplinary practice. Rather than rehearsing for the real world, students were encouraged to capture an alternative reality with precarious scenarios, which were

Nicola Koller, This Sceptred Isle, outer suburbs of North London. Thesis project, Architectural Design Studio 4 (tutors: Gerrard O'Carroll, Fiona Raby), Royal College of Art, 2003

Tomas Klassnik, Desktopolis, Aldgate, London. Thesis project, Architectural Design Studio 1 (tutors: Roberto Bottazzi, Payam Sharifi), Royal College of Art, 2006

part prediction, part based in a radically evolving technological and multicultural world.

At the turn of the millennium, London was engulfed by momentous changes – an entrepreneurial building fever, an increasingly multicultural society, a revolution in digital communication, the fear of terrorism, an unstable future, all of which were colluding to transform the city. My students were keen to engage these tendencies, and see where they could lead in terms of architecture. It was not such a leap to imagine a mosque coupled with an artificial Halal meat-manufacturing plant, or housing that overstated the need for security, post-9/11. One project took on the absurd lust for investment characterized by the City of London, and proposed building over the spires of the fifty-five churches that nestle among the glowering office towers crammed into the square mile – it would only be a matter of time (and technology) before these air rights would be exploited by developers. Experiments of this kind wrestle with the power of architecture, or indeed with its lack of it. It certainly was not an innocent language, subject only to matters of style or a materiality. Students could find the contradictions and opportunities in the contemporary urban condition.

Thesis projects produced over this period combined imagination, wit, politics and a futurology with an iconic sting in its tail. Beyond the classic architect's dream, they were paradigms of the real world, and enabled all of us to come face to face with the real interface between society and our profession. Ideas ricocheted between tutor and student; we were using fiction to grasp reality. A small department was attracting the most talented students and, once graduated, they were snapped up by the best offices in town for their combination of chutzpah and imagination. In line with the school's open agenda, some became critics,

Mark Prizeman, Wolf Housing, Bermondsey, London. Graduation project, Diploma Unit 10 (tutor: Nigel Coates), Architectural Association School of Architecture, 1983

some became teachers, and many formed their own practices, rather than signing up to a life of fodder in those of others.[5]

My own style of teaching combines protection and provocation: carrot and stick. Students need to work hard and win the interest of their teachers; equally, they must be driven by their own critical judgment and not accept what others deem acceptable. Above all, one needs to be able to judge for oneself and reach that bit further. Little by little, year on year, we edged up standards at the RCA, and won respect from within and without. The college seemed happy enough if the Royal Institute of British Architects gave us flying colours. While students from other courses saw how architecture as we practised it was relevant to them, the college administration became preoccupied with its own preservation. In 2011 the RCA embarked on a policy of radical expansion while charging (at the time of writing) the maximum fee of £9,000 per year. Perhaps there was a need to rethink the school of architecture.

Nigel Coates, Royal Mint Square Housing Competition, Shadwell, London. Graduation project, Diploma Unit 10 (tutor: Bernard Tschumi), Architectural Association School of Architecture, 1974

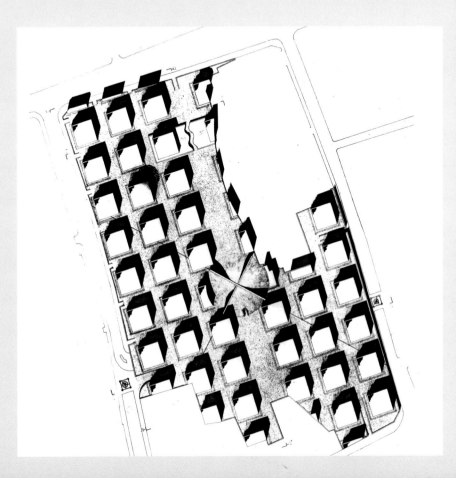

Audacious alternatives

Currently, the state education system frames a paucity of support for any study even vaguely related to the arts. Luminaries – Lord Rogers and Grayson Perry among them – have called for an arts strand in the revised secondary school curriculum to no avail. This squeeze on arts education has also forced universities into short-term gains, with a larger proportion of places offered to high-paying overseas students than to those from Europe or the UK. Our higher-education system appears to be in danger of degenerating into a paradigm for the demise of Europe, and its inverse – the rise of the Asian economic tiger. Lumped in with the arts, architecture has fallen foul of the government's borrowed wisdom on promoting sciences, which is odd given the economic benefits of the UK's position as one of the top architectural providers in the world. Today's students frequently complain of poor value for money.

Architectural education is often polarized into two opposing camps: one sustained by ideas; the other practical and technical. I signed up to the former from the beginning, the side that sees the beauty in reconfiguration and resistance. But in reality, architecture must bridge the two and can only choose between one or other of these extremes. In my experience, invention comes from exploring the cracks between reality and ideas, and their resolution must team context and function with narrative. The story, the plain of the illusory and make-believe that captures human experience, serves to emphasize an overlap between the imaginary and the real. Rather than a merely practice-based approach, a school needs to make room for architecture as a culture, and should allow its students to soar in ways they will never match in the future.

Haiwei Xie, B.R.I.C. House, Chelsea Barracks, London. Thesis project, Architectural Design Studio 4 (tutors: Nicola Koller, Rosy Head, Tom Greenhall), Royal College of Art, 2012

Since stepping off the academic travelator, I have joined a small group with a common interest in architectural education, 'without the institution'.[6] We signed up to this experiment because we believe it can reinstate core values. A new school is in the making: the audaciously named London School of Architecture. It will subscribe to an open-ended framework charged with possibility, but with low fees and without the encumbrance of prestigious buildings, rectors, libraries and IT departments. Today's computer-savvy students can find all the information they need online. In the emerging blueprint, the school occupies borrowed buildings, collaborates with architectural practices and favours a new kind of apprenticeship that cross-pollinates designing for others with designing for oneself. With the best teachers and the best students swapping their insights and skills, exchange is the key, and at half the price of their predecessors.

As university education tips towards crisis, raises fees and cuts spending beyond either reach or relevance for any truly creative young designer, non-state higher education emerges as a viable and attractive alternative. My hunch is that alternative schools will eventually become the norm, and university courses a quaint throwback to the twentieth century. London deserves a school that sees architecture as an all-encompassing and all-listening art that reflects the rapidly changing world of communication overload and multivarious identities. It will be a school built on frisson, on the pleasure of becoming an architect.

School of thought

– Mark Morris, Associate Professor and Thesis
Coordinator, Department of Architecture,
Cornell University

And you America,
Cast you the real reckoning for your present?
The lights and shadows of your future,
good or evil?
To girlhood, boyhood look, the teacher
and the school.

– Walt Whitman, 'An Old Man's School of Thought', 1874

Sweeping changes came to architecture curricula in the late 1950s,
'60s and '70s, moving schools kicking and screaming from the
Beaux Arts-inspired teaching habits established since their founding.
This was largely due to a burst of postwar recruitment of young baby-
boomers. Nowhere was the old guard versus new guard tension felt
more keenly than at the University of Texas, where, in 1952, the new
architecture dean, Harwell Hamilton Harris, sought to reinvigorate
this programme by hiring a group of young teachers that included
Colin Rowe, Bernhard Hoesli, John Hejduk, John Shaw, Lee Hodgden,
Lee Hirsche and Werner Seligmann.

In his book, *The Texas Rangers: Notes from an Architectural
Underground* (1995), Alexander Caragonne, a student of Rowe's at
both Texas and Cornell University, reviewed the group's trajectory:

In the years immediately following the Second World War,
the faculty and curriculum of the College of Architecture at the
University of Texas, as in other provincial architecture schools

A 'school of thought' might be defined as a collection of people sharing a point of view or set of opinions, usually in regard to a philosophy, social or cultural movement. The term is also used to define the currency of such values, the juxtaposition of old or new schools typically used to describe paradigm shifts.

scattered about the country, precisely mirrored the three principal ideas animating the course of architecture throughout the early half of the century. Two predominantly European educational models – the rigorous but rapidly receding École des Beaux-Arts model of the American academy, and Walter Gropius's assimilated version of the Bauhaus programme – were uncomfortably lodged alongside that of a third, homegrown American school, a blend of regionalism and pragmatism. In the best circumstances, this odd combination might resemble a kind of carefully balanced American Shinto; in the worst cases, it would display symptoms of an advanced state of academic schizophrenia.'[1]

The US GI Bill (1944) provided a glut of architecture students to coincide with these pedagogic shifts. Indeed, the unprecedented swelling of the postwar student population was often the excuse given to overhauling many architecture programmes in the name of efficiency, if not ideology. The reconfiguring of foundation courses and studios along Bauhaus lines offered a more accessible first phase of design education

Father Mowbray in *Brideshead Revisited* (1945) lamented: 'The trouble with modern education is you never know how ignorant people are. With anyone over fifty you can be fairly confident what's been taught and what's been left out. But these young people have such an intelligent, knowledgeable surface, and then the crust suddenly breaks and you look down into depths of confusion you didn't know existed.'

In 2013, Ann Ju wrote in the *Cornell Chronicle*: 'By joining edX, Cornell has formalized its commitment to help faculty start offering MOOCs, which are burgeoning in popularity and have been called the democratization of education … The details of exactly how Cornell will proceed to offer [them], including questions of administration, intellectual property, faculty support and course selection, will be guided by recommendations from an ad-hoc committee.'

Milstein Hall, Cornell University

– OMA

Milstein Hall is a new addition to the existing buildings of Cornell's renowned College of Architecture, Art and Planning. Sited between the historic Arts Quad and Falls Creek Gorge, the new structure redefines the entrance at the northern end of the campus. The existing AAP was housed in four separate buildings, distinct in architectural style and programmatic use, but similar in typology. Rather than creating a new freestanding structure, the architects chose to create a unified complex, 4,366m² (47,000 sq ft), with continuous levels of indoor and outdoor interconnected spaces, housing studios, a gallery and crit space, and a 253-seat auditorium.

To provide studio space with panoramic views, a large, horizontal plate was lifted off the ground and connected to the second levels of Sibley Hall and Rand Hall. Enclosed by floor-to-ceiling glass and a green roof with forty-one skylights, it cantilevers almost 15m (49 ft) above University Avenue to establish a relationship with the Foundry, another existing facility. The wide-open expanse of the plate – structurally supported by a hybrid-truss system – stimulates interaction and will allow flexible use over time.

The exposed hybrid trusses were designed to balance structural efficiency and circulation within the open plan of the design. Custom-designed lights and beams were carefully coordinated, using normally hidden elements to define the ceiling plane. The lighting is programmed by a highly efficient Lutron control system, connected to daylight sensors to maintain constant light levels, while chilled beams provide cooling by utilizing lake-sourced water, reducing the need for cumbersome HVAC mechanical systems. Heating is distributed via a concrete radiant heated slab, and high-performance insulated glass units were used on all the exterior glass walls, ensuring efficient mechanical systems and an abundance of natural daylight.

The cantilevered area is a unique space within the upper plate, owing to its visibility from the pedestrian walkways below and transparent views from East Avenue, approximately the same elevation as the studio floor. Given the southern and eastern exposure, a solution for moderating daylight was required. The architects looked to Petra Blaisse of landscape architecture firm Inside Outside to design a custom curtain to preserve the views out to the Arts Quad, maintain natural daylight while reducing glare and present a striking façade at the northeast entrance to the Quad. Blaisse's concept for the curtain was considered together with the design for the auditorium curtain, using drawings by the sixteenth-century architect Hans Vredeman de Vries to suggest another space outside Milstein Hall. The enlarged perspectival drawings were digitally printed onto white vinyl mesh and perforated with holes along the perspective lines.

The green roof is punctuated by a cluster of north-facing skylights, which gradually increase in size towards the centre of the plate. Two different types of sedum create a gradient pattern of dots, which transition from small, articulated circles near the Arts Quad at the south, to a larger, dense pattern of dots at the northern end, towards the natural landscape of the gorge. Above and below the continuous strip of glass, 3.6m (12-ft) long, two thin bands of Turkish marble define the extents of the upper plate. This marble veining was important in achieving the horizontal bands of stone, which emphasize the floating nature of the plate. The naturally striated marble had a direct influence on architecture firm 2by4's design of the ID building, located on the south cantilever's east façade. The building's name is engraved on marble panels in vertical bands, resembling a barcode of lettering while at the same time appearing to dissolve into the stone.

Underneath the upper plate, a ceiling of custom-stamped perforated aluminium panels extends through the interior and exterior spaces, de-emphasizing the boundary between them. This echo of the stamped metal ceilings found in New York creates a room-like space below the upper plate, surrounded by the existing façades of Rand Hall, Sibley Hall and the Foundry. Above the grid of panels, acoustic blankets tune specific zones, such as the area overlooking the road to absorb noise from passing cars, the auditorium to improve auditory

OMA, Milstein Hall, Cornell
University, Ithaca, New York,
2006

performance and the covered plaza to reduce noise from the adjacent offices, classrooms and auditorium.

The 465m² (5,005 sq ft) critique space sits beneath a dome of double-layered concrete. The exposed underside is a cast-in-place structural slab, which spans the main space below. The dome was formed using two layers of plywood, and the concrete was poured in a single twelve-hour period. Strip-light pockets were cast together with electrical and sprinkler systems, forming a clearly defined central space out of a complex construction process. Above the structural dome slab, a concrete topping slab forms the exterior surface. The dome serves multiple functions, supporting the raked auditorium seating, and forming both the stairs leading up to the studio plate and the artificial ground for exterior seating pods, custom-made by Fabrice Covelli of Fproduct. From the main entrance, a concrete bridge spanning the space draws students into the auditorium or brings them down the sculptural stairs to the lower level. The bridge's structural concrete truss railing and stair allow it to span the dome without columns. A vertical 'moving room', fabricated by the firms Global Tardif and Schindler from plywood panels, serves as the lift, connecting the three levels. Large enough to move models and materials between the studios and crit space, it can also accommodate a chair and reading lamp. The moving room was fully assembled near Quebec City, dismantled and reassembled on site.

Milstein Hall provides the department with its first auditorium and large-scale lecture hall within its own facilities. The auditorium, designed to provide maximum flexibility for a multiplicity of programmes and functions, is divided into two areas: fixed seats on the raked section of the dome, and loose seats on the level floor. When the auditorium is not used at full capacity (it can hold 3,000 people), the lower level can be used for studio critiques and smaller meetings. Both fixed and loose seats were custom-designed by the architects, and manufactured by Finnish office furniture company Martela Oy. The design reinforces the flexibility of the auditorium, as the cantilevered seat backs fold down to form a continuous bench to accommodate higher-capacity seating. The bench configuration can also be used for exhibition and display, or to create a side table out of an unoccupied adjacent seat. The simple, rectangular form of the loose seats with their seat backs folded flat and grouped together can serve as tables for display or exhibitions.

OMA, Milstein Hall, Cornell University, Ithaca, New York, 2006

The auditorium can be further transformed into a boardroom, assembled at the touch of a button, which automatically raises sixty-one seats from below the level floor section. The architects custom-designed this method of integrating the boardroom with the auditorium, and it was manufactured by Figueras International Seating, based in Barcelona. Furnished with electricity, an oversized tablet and storage bin, each of the seats can be raised or lowered independently, and is attached to a post that allows 360° rotation with locking positions every 7.5°. When privacy or blackout is required, a custom-designed curtain, digitally printed on both sides with Hans Vredeman de Vries prints unfurls from the balcony in one continuous motion.

The insertion of Milstein Hall into the existing AAP campus forms a new gateway to the northern end of Cornell's campus. Together with the recently completed addition to the Herbert F. Johnson Museum of Art, the architects' design transforms an under-utilized area into a new corridor for the arts, planning and design.

BLENDscapes:
In support of a new era of transdisciplinary exchange in architecture

– Evan Douglis, Dean, School of Architecture, Rensselaer Polytechnic Institute

Any great school of architecture is faced with reconciling two seemingly competing desires in the context of developing the identity and ethos of its programme: the necessity to pursue a more speculative agenda of novelty and surprise, so important to the development of an elastic mind entering the discipline of architecture, and the ethical mandate confronting successive generations of our profession to respond in creative and innovative ways to a complex planet undergoing continuous change. Often seen as oppositional and ideologically at odds, this classical dialectic, still so prevalent in many of our institutions today, unfortunately perpetuates an antiquated model of disciplinary silos that are unproductive in an era of multiplicity, complexity and new hybridized forms of engagement.

From the content of our curricula to the organizational distribution of our faculty, there lies a hardened stratification reaffirming an accepted delineation between theory and practice, art and science, the real and the imaginary, and the experimental world of academia in relation to the hyper-pragmatic expectations of the profession beyond. However effective these categorical juxtapositions may have been in the past, in terms of facilitating a cohesive management of knowledge, given the extent of challenges specific to the twenty-first century requiring interdisciplinary collaboration to effectively respond to the complexity at hand, it is imperative that the educational model for the study of architecture be thoroughly reconceptualized. Transdisciplinarity for

Evan Douglis Studio,
Caviar 3000, Lanzhou Urban
Planning Exhibition Centre,
Lanzhou, China, 2012

architecture represents a radical departure from collective singularities in favour of a more bottom-up, integrative approach. A series of strategic linkages are established from the beginning, based on the premise that a more expansive coalition of partners will produce a body of new and unexpected ideas. These discoveries, in turn, offer a new space for ingenuity and innovation, capable of reimagining the world in novel and unexpected ways.

At Rensselaer Polytechnic, the oldest technological institute in the US, the School of Architecture is ideally situated to draw upon the extraordinary breadth of science and engineering resources currently in place. In support of the fusion between art and science, which is often unobtainable in most architecture schools given the traditional separation between disciplines, we have been fortunate to take advantage of this unique educational and research setting by reconfiguring many of our professional and research programmes as nimble, non-hierarchical and inherently collaborative arenas of speculative engagement. Astronaut Mae Jemison, who believes, as I do, that art and science are inextricably linked, noted in her 2002 TED lecture that the two are simply 'manifestations of the same thing', and 'avatars of human creativity', and should therefore be embraced as an interdependent school of thought.[1]

One such programme that exemplifies this significant paradigm shift is Rensselaer's Center for Architecture Science and Ecology (CASE), located in the offices of Skidmore, Owings & Merrill on Wall Street. Conceived as one of the first academic and industry collaborative partnerships and committed to the development of next-generation building systems, this internationally acclaimed educational and research laboratory attracts students, faculty and experts in the disciplines of architectural design, aerodynamics, bioinformatics, molecular biology, civil engineering, computational and ecological economics, urban planning, games and simulation, material science and building physics. From the start, there was an explicit desire to bring together a broad spectrum of minds in order to reassess the future of architecture as a complex ecology of interests in which quantitative and qualitative thinking were pursued as a holistic project. No longer bound by the constraints of convention, this larger conversation represents a new era of disciplinary engagement so important to reimagining the world.

In contrast to the accepted model of sustainability in architecture, which simply focuses on maximizing building-energy performance based solely on the utilization of current technology, CASE proposes a radical reassessment of the very building blocks manufactured today. Taking clues from NASA, the belief is that any next-generation building system should manifest, from unit to whole, the most advanced collective intelligence available at the time. When one considers the extraordinary global challenges facing the architecture profession today – energy depletion, global warming, rising coastal waters, antiquated buildings and infrastructure, and rapid globalization – there is a compelling reason to embrace transdisciplinarity not only as a more effective collaborative model in support of shared knowledge, but also, perhaps more importantly, as a call for action.

Reaffirming its strategic value for architecture, director Anna Dyson says: 'The larger goal of CASE is to facilitate a revolution in the building design and construction industry, which is the sector responsible for the largest proportion of toxic emissions, as well as nonrenewable waste and energy consumption, within our contemporary context. CASE researchers are already developing innovative approaches to environmental challenges, which transform buildings and infrastructure into living systems that restore biodiversity with a compatible relationship with natural ecosystems. Systems that allow cities to viably harness wind power atop aerodynamically shaped buildings; new solar technologies for façades that track the position of the sun and convert its light and diverted heat into storable energy, which can be used for on-site water purification, heating, cooling and lighting buildings.'[2]

While listing only a few examples of their current research, there is a powerful sense that a new era of manufactured nature in architecture is beginning to emerge, capable of responding in real time to a complex world. This is precisely the paradigm shift we envisioned for architecture and through the collective efforts of many dedicated to a project of conjoined ideation. There are countless discoveries for our profession still yet to come.

Evan Douglis Studio,
Moon Jelly, Choice Bakery,
Brooklyn, New York, 2009

opposite, top
Paul Chan, Excavate Penn
Station. Affective Machines:
Re-envisioning Penn Station
Studio (tutor: Casey Rehm),
School of Architecture,
Rensselaer Polytechnic
Institute, 2013

opposite, bottom
Graham Billings, Normative
Fluidity. Re-envisioning
MiSci Studio (tutor: Andrew
Saunders), School of
Architecture, Rensselaer
Polytechnic Institute, 2013

above
Evan Douglis Studio,
POP[up]^ structures, 2012

Instigations: Reimagining better futures

– Mohsen Mostafavi, Dean, Graduate School of Design, Harvard University

It is the responsibility of a design academy such as Harvard's Graduate School of Design to imagine, to think of possibilities – potentials that may one day become reality. This wishful, optimistic mode of working lies at the core of our design disciplines. The architectural imagination is not solely based on the intuitive capacities of individuals. One of the tasks of design education is to help provide the tools, techniques and methods that enhance constructed imagination. In contemporary practice, we often witness examples of formal projects without a clear connection to the specific traditions of design, or social projects without due attention to the formal and aesthetic qualities of a discipline. The modes and practices of design need to confront the challenges of our contemporary societies. This relationship between knowledge and societal impact is central to contemporary design pedagogy at the GSD.

The Architecture and Landscape Architecture departments already existed at Harvard (both among the first programmes of their kind in the country), when Joseph Hudnut, as Dean, created the umbrella of the School of Design in 1936 as a means of bringing the disciplines together. The Bauhaus provided the closest example of the kind of unity of the design fields Hudnut was seeking. Himself a recent appointment, he hired Walter Gropius, the founding director of the Bauhaus, which had closed its doors in 1933 under pressure from the Nazi regime, to chair the Department of Architecture. Hudnut and Gropius set about their complex task of transforming the school. Their alliance, uneasy at times,

Arthur Liu, Nicholas Croft and William Quattlebaum, Real and Imaginary Variables, National Art Museum, Oslo. Real and Imaginary Variables option studio (tutor: George Legendre), Graduate School of Design, Harvard University, 2012

Lucas Correa Sevilla, The City Under One Roof and the Vertical Hutong: Transforming Beijing's Dominant Types. Dominant Types and the Idea of the City option studio (tutor: Christopher Lee), Graduate School of Design, Harvard University, 2011

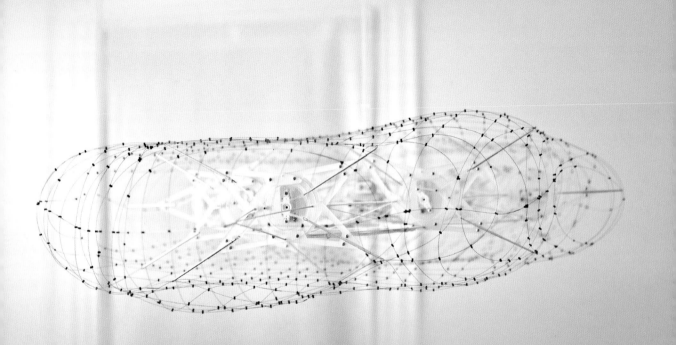

Yarinda Bunnag and Mark Rukamathu, Endeavourism, Los Angeles. House of Endeavour option studio (tutor: Wes Jones), Graduate School of Design, Harvard University, 2011

and the all-encompassing idea of a design school, made the agenda of the GSD distinct from its peer institutions.

Its pedagogic aspirations and diversity of its faculty meant that the school quickly became not just an American institution, but one with a strongly international outlook. The intellectual programme of the GSD as a truly global school, addressing issues at varied scales around the world, has continued to flourish ever since. The introduction of the Urban Design programme by Josep Lluís Sert in 1960 moved the school explicitly towards a focus on urbanization, which was particularly critical after the Second World War, given the need to rebuild cities across the globe. This early commitment to societal impact has remained an identifiable part of the school's mission throughout its history.

At the centre of the school's mission are the three departments of Architecture, Landscape Architecture and Urban Planning and Design, each committed to being the leader in its own discipline. In the Department of Architecture, the core programmes prepare students by giving them disciplinary knowledge, mediated through drawings, models, renderings – techniques. It is the students' understanding of projective geometry, however, that brings to the fore the procedural methods for architecture's formal characteristics and potentials. The combining of methodological and thematic issues throughout the four semesters of core studios, and the subsequent 'option' studios, introduces students to materials, construction, structure, environmental systems, economics, clients, the city, history and a host of other subjects – at times integrated into the studio sequence, and at others taught independently as thesis work. This tripartite structure – core, option, thesis – allows the devising of unique architectures at multiple scales for different locations and needs.

James Leng, Point Cloud. Quantitative Aesthetics seminar (tutor: Panagiotis Michalatos), Graduate School of Design, Harvard University, 2012

The Department of Landscape Architecture occupies a commanding intellectual position, in part because of the changing role of the discipline, transcending the design of gardens, parks and other forms of public space. Landscape architecture today negotiates an increasingly important zone between architecture and urbanization. This is particularly noticeable in terms of the methodological and procedural offerings of landscape architecture in relation to alternative modes of planning and urban design. It is imperative for landscape architecture, while remaining focused on the themes connected to its core subject matter, to also develop innovative theoretical and practical responses to larger-scale

territory. The Department of Urban Planning and Design has led the investigation into alternative modes of urbanization, which has been an explicit area of recent research and pedagogy at the GSD. The school is continually seeking new ways of exploring urbanization: distinct yet complementary approaches include landscape urbanism, infrastructural urbanism, extreme urbanism, critical ecologies and new geographies. These investigations have been the subject of lectures, seminars, conferences, studios and the Urban Theory Lab, making the school the centre of contemporary discussions on urbanization and urban issues.

The diversity of academic backgrounds of GSD students makes it imperative for us to be able to constantly articulate the conceptual framework and purpose of our pedagogic ideas. Teaching intertwines the knowledge of a particular field with a series of arguments and conversations that establish a collaborative rapport between teacher and student, which enhances the educational experience. The explicitness of pedagogic aims can provide a more coherent and visible road map. This distinguishes our efforts from the apprenticeship models of learning. While learning through doing – or, more appropriately, learning through making – remains a cornerstone of our pedagogy at the GSD, the questioning method of our approach constructs a more explicitly projective mode of practice.

But how can one both learn and project? Learning through projecting ideas is at the heart of the speculative education promoted at the school. Speculative learning must lie at the heart of our pedagogy and practice, rather than considered only when some foundational learning has already occurred. At the same time, we need concrete methods through which such ideas are construed and brought into reality. This orientation explains the school's emphasis on the importance of different types of drawing as catalysts for imagination and projection. Combining an understanding and knowledge of both digital tools and hand-drawing has helped our students and faculty explore issues of the utmost significance for the disciplines today. Drawings, in this sense, transcend know-how; they are the necessary means for constructing new forms of imagination. It is the interface between the constructed imagination and the knowledge of a particular discipline that leads to disciplinary advancement.

Peter Zuroweste and Nicholas Potts, The Culture of Liberated Congestion: A Manual for the Proliferation of Land Value. Neokoolhisms option studio (tutor: Ciro Najle), Graduate School of Design, Harvard University, 2012

Jeremy Jih, Babel. Graduate thesis (tutor: Mariana Ibañez), Graduate School of Design, Harvard University, 2012

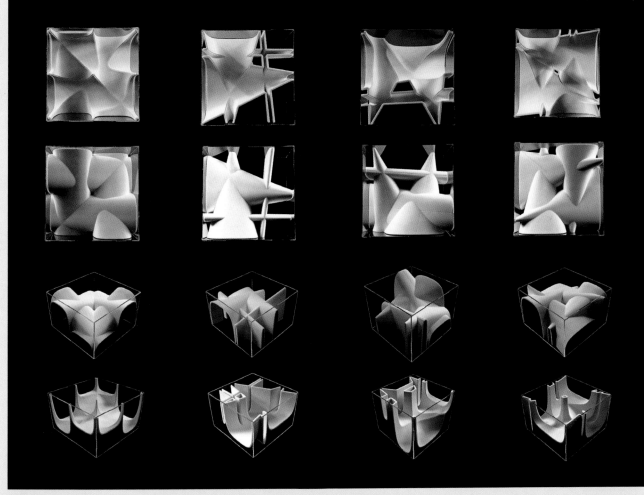

McCormick Tribune Campus Center, Illinois Institute of Technology

– OMA

The McCormick Tribune Campus Center at the Illinois Institute of Technology, in Chicago, was the first building designed by Rem Koolhaas of OMA in the US. It was begun in 1997, and completed in 2003. The aim of the project was to reinvigorate the urbanism inherent – but long since neglected – in architect Mies van der Rohe's 1940 masterplan for the school. The architects' design for a new large, single-storey centre provides a focal point for the previously separated halves of the campus. It features a noise-absorbing steel tube that covers the elevated subway train, which passes overhead, and, inside, a dense mosaic of programmes that include a bookstore, food court, café, auditorium, computer centre and meeting spaces.

OMA, McCormick Tribune Campus Center, Illinois Institute of Technology, Chicago, 2003

The design sought to energize a campus whose student population has halved since the 1940s, but whose footprint is now double its original size. For the architects, the challenge was to create a building that re-urbanizes the largest possible area while using the least amount of built substance. To create a new point of density for the campus, the building was located at the heart of the Institute – a large rectangle that sits between S. State Street, S. Wabash Avenue, E. 32nd Street and E. 33rd Street – and directly underneath the 'L' train, the artery that connects the

campus to the rest of Chicago. By enclosing the tracks above the campus in a muffling cylinder of stainless steel, a formerly deafening no-man's-land becomes not only tolerable, but also a magnetic environment. The encircled track, known by students and locals as the 'Tube' – becomes a crucial part of the new building's image.

Rather than stacking activities in a multistorey building, the architects opted to arrange each programmatic element of the campus centre in a dense, single plane. To achieve this, they carried out a study in 1997 to map the 'desire lines' of student foot traffic across the campus. These intersecting diagonal paths were maintained inside the centre itself, linking the multiplicity of activities via a network of interior streets, plazas and urban islands, which together form 'neighbourhoods': twenty-four-hour, commercial, entertainment, academic, recreation and other urban elements in microcosm.

The unifying element of the campus centre is the roof: a sloping concrete slab that protects against noise from the 'L' train, while

OMA, McCormick Tribune Campus Center, Illinois Institute of Technology, Chicago, 2003

encompassing the heterogeneous programmes below. Where the roof ducks beneath the 'L', the underside of the Tube juts through the concrete as a reminder of what is above. The long overhang of the roof embraces the adjacent Commons Hall, Mies's student centre, designed in 1953. The original perimeter and interior wooden partitions have been preserved, and now function as a food court.

OMA, McCormick Tribune
Campus Center, Illinois
Institute of Technology,
Chicago, 2003

Just about enough

– Perry Kulper, Associate Professor of Architecture, Taubman College of Architecture and Urban Planning, University of Michigan

Architecture students today can enjoy a fifty- to sixty-year productive life cycle in architecture. Given the title of this book, this observation should not go unnoticed. Relating the multiple educations of young architects to the history of ideas enables a generative contextualization of the work of education, its various organizational models, curricular logics and disciplinary positioning. These areas can be discussed in relation to the values and continuities of cultural production, both architectural and not, thus locating and promoting education to a participatory medium, rather than relegating it to the status of an indifferent bystander. Equally, understanding the relationships of the constituent parts that comprise architectural education, the roles they play and how they are structured, requires continuous reappraisal and transformation as societal motivations and spatial demands change over time.

As cultural agents, first and foremost – provocateurs, let us say – architects need to be dexterous thinkers and versatile designers; at minimum, an agile species. They should be well versed in visualization and production techniques of all kinds, keen on implementing diverse design methods in different situations and masters at broadening the conceptions by which we imagine architecture to be possible.

To be in the eye of cultural and discursive storms, educating architects must revel in significant political, economic, material and technological changes, not to mention needed educational transformations. Importantly, education needs to lead the assault – to be out front, provoking and seducing our imaginations, sneaking up our cultural and spatial shirtsleeves. Relational thinking that considers the types, durations and strength of relations is required above all else. This approach should be embroidered across the assertions above and the phrases below, triggering connections where others might not notice

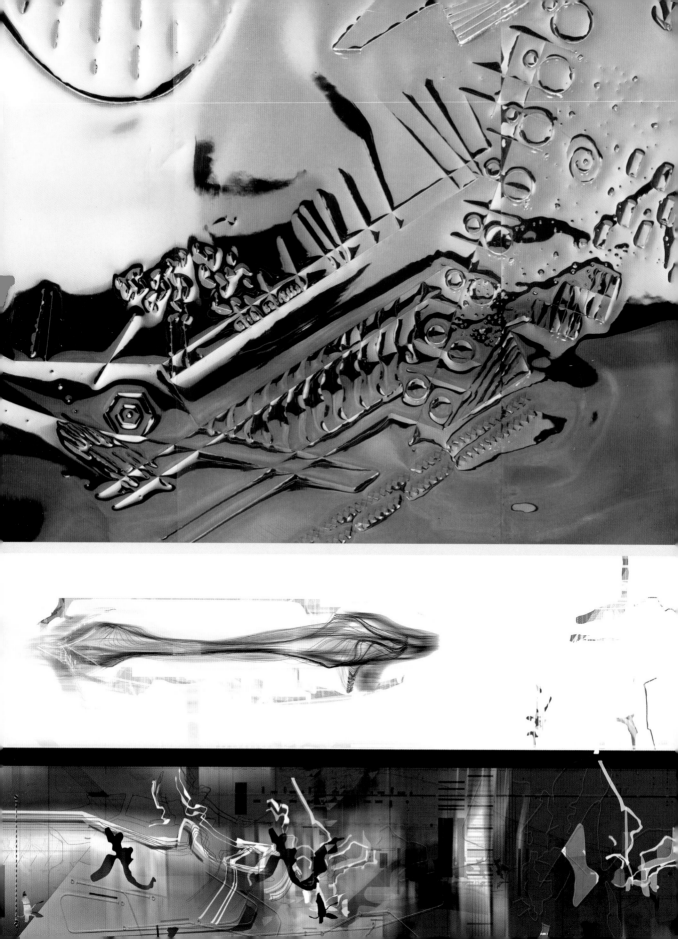

Paul Holmquist, Zooø,
Site/Self-reflective Plan:
Mimetic Feints and
Eructations 'with Sacrifice',
Los Angeles Zoo, California.
Thesis studio (tutor: Perry
Kulper), Southern California
Institute of Architecture, 1999

them, optimistically motivating the cultural agency of architecture
and everything it entails: now, then and almost.

1. Architectural education should be pithy, contentious; its head
    always on the chopping block, like it or not.

2. I like thinking about Van Gogh's lone, white iris, Lady Gaga
    and nanotechnology – all in the same spatial sweep.

3. There are substantial differences between building, architecture
    and spatiality – a simple observation with game-changing
    consequences, like what is in and what is not.

4. I like thinking about the abandonment of typological obligations
    in favour of ecological provocations. This approach invites
    contingent and unpredictable practices, rather than confirming
    what is already known. This kind of thinking breeds as yet
    unimagined spatial species.

5. Using pre-spatial language prompts can trigger inventive
    programmatic thinking. Imagine germinal objects, verdant
    programmes, fallow surfaces, knotted thresholds, all subject
    to change at the flip of a phase shift, just like that.

6. I like thinking about Wallace Stevens's Thirteen Ways of Looking
    at a Blackbird as a template or DNA for developing critical skill
    sets, capable of gathering heterogeneous characters in search
    of a strangely familiar, yet just out of reach, whole.

7. Probing questions should infectiously populate the educational
    terrain of architecture. For example, when is the time of rendering?
    Could architecture be schizophrenic, delusional and paranoid,
    simultaneously? Might a plan be made here and the section made
    over there, both suddenly morphing into a transitory landscape,
    or something like that?

Brian Foster, Unbiased
Operations: Experimental
Authorship, Double House
roof plan. Thesis studio (tutor:
Perry Kulper), Taubman
College of Architecture and
Urban Planning, University of
Michigan, 2007

8. I like thinking about the contemporary architect being many
    architects, a hybrid species, agile and skilled at occupying

contested edges and dusty perimeters, yet capable of turning on a dime.

9. Twenty-first-century architects might speculate on split temporalities and split topographies. Imagine architectural propositions that scan data surfaces of now, then and sometime sites, morphing at warp speed while hijacking our expectations and suddenly disappearing, just about like that.

10. I like thinking about promiscuous conceptions of architecture in the twenty-first century: spatial ventriloquism; architecture that behaves like a fast-change artist; red; three houses in one.

11. Unlike the language of architecture, the language of representation positions materiality as conceptual, temporality as malleable and gravity as negotiable, akin to alchemy, just a bit like that.

12. I like thinking about developing digital software that could simultaneously embroider metaphorical impulses, narrative twists, statistical mutants and the consequences of a psychological whim, spatially, without batting an eye.

13. Arguably, architectural education should be grounded in the history of ideas. Equally, it needs to be a high risk-taker, a tightrope walker, a contemporary hybrid of Harry Houdini and Evel Knievel. I like thinking about this, too.

14. I like thinking about the daytime façade of a home-improvement centre reconfiguring itself to become a nocturnal agricultural surface, changing land values as it morphs from one form to another. Or, what about duplicating a domestic interior, sending the clone into the neighbourhood at night to commingle with other domestic environs? Or, I like thinking about suburban backyards that regenerate themselves, becoming a collection of fish markets by dawn and a luminescent electromagnetic field by night.

15. Analogous thinking – this looks like that, this behaves like that – can increase an architect's formal and material imagination and

You Ling Lim, The Schizophrenic Motel Lifts its Skirt in Fear of the Shadows of Water, Java-eiland, Amsterdam. Spatial Outlaws Studio (tutor: Perry Kulper), Taubman College of Architecture and Urban Planning, University of Michigan, 2006

Sen Liu, Fitness Center, Regenerating: Version 1+2, Camp Lonely Landfill, Nuiqsut, Alaska. Refined Form Studio (tutor: Perry Kulper), Taubman College of Architecture and Urban Planning, University of Michigan, 2008

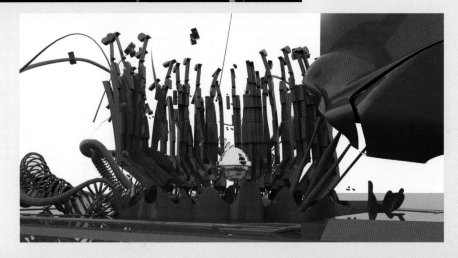

Vittorio Lovato, A Roadside Motel: Rooms, Lobby, Sign and Pool, Analogic Design Method. Occupations Studio (tutor: Perry Kulper), Taubman College of Architecture and Urban Planning, University of Michigan, 2012

The Arrival of Hope
Formation of airships approaching Detroit City
with their own coordinate system deployed and targets aimed

architectural range instantly; a hundredfold in a snap of the fingers, just like *that*.

16. I like thinking about the use of generative history and progressive theory with big, lush and fidgety velvet-cushioned chairs at the table of twenty-first-century architectural education.

17. Marcel Duchamp's Three Standard Stoppages might be a metric for the construction of architectural education, transforming accepted norms, twisting as they might, approximately like that.

18. I like thinking about an architectural proposition formally structured, like paired cuckoo clocks wearing hip waders. The architectural surfaces might be tattooed like an embroidered, sequinned pair of Western boots, and the landscape for the architecture might be organized like the Chinese game of 'Go', crossed with calligraphic utterances. Analogues work like that.

19. Once an inviolate part of the socially and subjectively constructed figure of the architect, the architectural drawing is an increasingly complex affair – a tricky business, to say the least. I like thinking about that, I guess.

Chi Song, Skeleton of Redemption: Arrival of Hope, Detroit. Thesis studio (tutor: Perry Kulper), Taubman College of Architecture and Urban Planning, University of Michigan, 2009

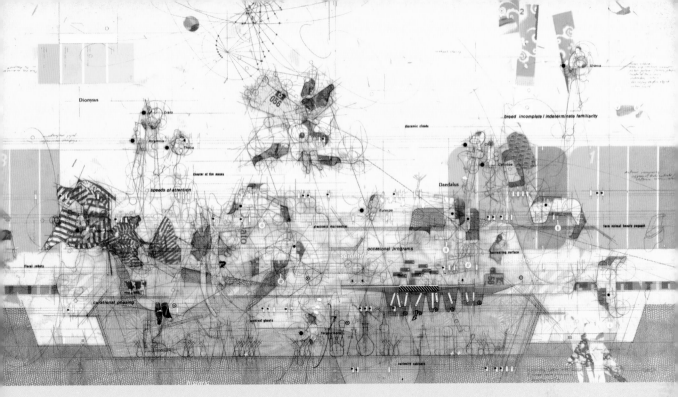

Perry Kulper, Central
California History Museum:
Aspectival Drawing, 2012

20. I like thinking about an educational model in which it matters
less what you work on, and more how intensely you work on it.

21. A new city proposition for China might require different design
methods in relation to hybridizing biomorphic interests and
geographic data-splicing. Diverse and highly varied design
methods might allow us to work with different circumstances
like that.

22. I like thinking about architecture that might materialize the space
of a building's construction, rather than the building itself. Or what
about motivating erasure as an architectural activity? It is entirely
possible to think about these things.

23. The education of twenty-first-century architects should not aim
to prove the profession. Rather, I like thinking about significant
points of contact and critical points of difference between
professional training and disciplinary positioning.

24. I like thinking about what the twenty-first-century architect might
think about.

Some thoughts on pedagogy

– Nanako Umemoto and Jesse Reiser,
Reiser + Umemoto/RUR Architecture

Throughout our careers as architects, and over twenty years of teaching, we have maintained a clear sense of the complementary relationship between research and practice. This derives from our conviction that in any endeavour, theory and practice – with their unique limits and demands – are mutually informing. Indeed, our work, both professional and pedagogical, is structured around the model of a laboratory in which theory and practice combine to imbue buildings with critical force and to frame pedagogy around precise architectural concepts.

From the beginning, we have participated in an ongoing inquiry into connectivity between architecture, landscape architecture, engineering and urban design, along with theatre, film, computation and fabrication. Our experience has been that truly innovative projects are not solitary productions, but the result of collaborations among the disciplines, each contributing its own expertise. This does not mean that architecture alone cannot drive the discourse, rather that it can have resonance with other disciplines by probing its own boundaries. This relationship holds true both for practice and in education.

Our students explore an expansive assortment of topics, including the misreading of spatial and structural logics (Misprision); typological mixtures (Megachurch); and urban infrastructure, from the macro to the micro. Rather than developing an entirely top-down strategy or developing solely bottom-up logics, the studios attempt to establish each project as a dialectic between top-down and bottom-up, having separate systems for separate work, producing an intricate, productive yet cohesive result. In order to create a sustainable and robust whole, multiple models of the local are employed in such a way that they are flexible, can feed back on one another and create diverse locales.

Reiser + Umemoto,
O-14, Dubai, 2011

Reiser + Umemoto/
RUR Architecture, Kaohsiung
Port Terminal, Taiwan, 2014

The current infatuation with scripting is in pursuit of an architecture that will be, at long last, more fully intentional, tractable and rigorous. Scripting is a useful addition to the digital toolbox when used to explore well-defined design concepts, but it can become a substitute for active judgement. Inertia takes over and architects fool themselves into thinking that repetition – whether simple or complex – is a form of rational thought. There are many aspects and applications of computational design and analysis that are common today; the risk is that the seduction of these tools creates an illusion of rigour, which obscures the role of active critical assessment. The challenge for the future development of computation in architecture is to know when and how it should be applied to design.

In broad terms, our architectural design research explores the potential of experimental, and often counterintuitive, design methods to expand the repertoire of functional, effective and reflective experiences a building might engender. Confident in the skills of established design methods to serve the needs and desires of the client, our research entails three distinctions that deviate from such received methods: a broader conception of the beneficiaries of architectural experience (individual and collective, immediate and mediated); a methodical bracketing of expectations in building performance in order to discover new effects; and an ongoing social, political and philosophical reflection through critical discourse on the changes in contemporary life that might nominate new potentialities as salient and beneficial.

Reiser + Umemoto/
RUR Architecture, Taipei Pop
Music Centre, Taiwan, due for
completion 2017

Since the publication of our book *Atlas of Novel Tectonics* (2006), our research has been aimed at correcting, modifying and enlarging upon those arguments, and, with the opportunities afforded by our own practice, testing their applicability in a wider range of scales and more complex cultural contexts. For the last twenty-five years, our practice has been characterized by a sustained involvement in competitions, both public and private. Competitions are the perfect vehicle for practices with speculative ambitions, because they allow for a high degree of experimentation within the constraints of site, programme, deadline, and so on. They become an occasion to develop and refine one's theoretical stance, while at the same time working through the formal and organizational problems that define the arc of the overall project in the discipline. Our first large-scale commission came about as the result of a competition – which also included proposals from

Rem Koolhaas of OMA (pp. 177–82; 200–4), Zaha Hadid (pp. 295–300) and Thom Mayne – for an eighty-four-storey mixed-use tower in Dubai. Although we didn't win the competition, the developer who ran it on behalf of a local real-estate company commissioned us to design a twenty-two-storey office high rise in the city.

In many respects, O-14 embodies the concepts developed in the *Atlas of Novel Tectonics*. But the 'reality' of building at this scale inevitably involves forces that, however rehearsed in discourse, still exceed one's capacity to imagine. One would think, for example, that the experience of completing a large-scale project would result in a more tempered pragmatism. If anything, we found the opposite to be true, leading to a re-evaluation of our theoretical stance. While we still maintain an approach to design that focuses on issues of materials and organization, we have increasingly come to appreciate the cultural, social and political forces that have always been in play. These insights have significantly affected the form and content of the studios and design seminars we offer. Our most recent book, *O-14: Projection and Reception* (2012), also addresses this expanded constellation of influences on contemporary architectural practice.

We believe that our recent success in international competitions – the Taipei Pop Music Centre and the Kaohsiung Port Terminal – came about because the designs and our rhetoric engaged a wider range of issues than many of our more strictly materially driven projects. Because of their scale, complexity and urban demands, it is clear that these two projects cannot help but significantly impact our thinking on the nature and role of experimental design processes. It is our intention, upon their completion, to consolidate the insights gained during their realization into a second volume of critical reflection – to amend, develop and expand upon the essays of the *Atlas of Novel Tectonics* and continued academic participation.

Insuk Shin, Misprision, Convention Hall, New York. Graduate studio (tutor: Nanako Umemoto), Graduate School of Architecture, Planning and Preservation, Columbia University, 2012

Hilary Simon, Megachurch, Garden Grove, California. Graduate studio (tutors: Nanako Umemoto, Jesse Reiser), Graduate School of Architecture, Planning and Preservation, Columbia University, 2009

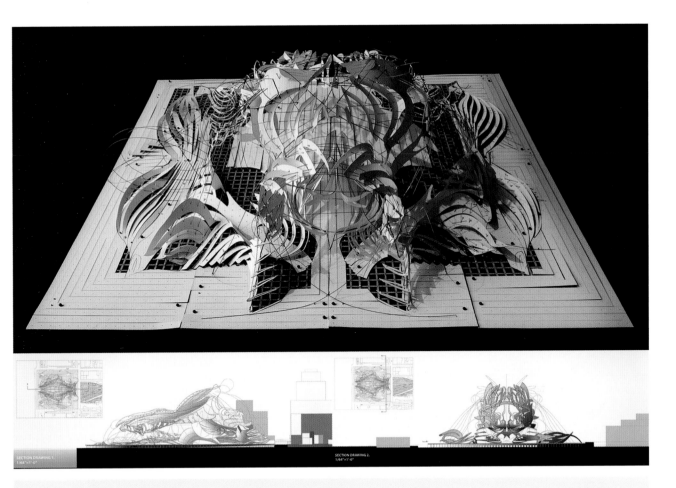

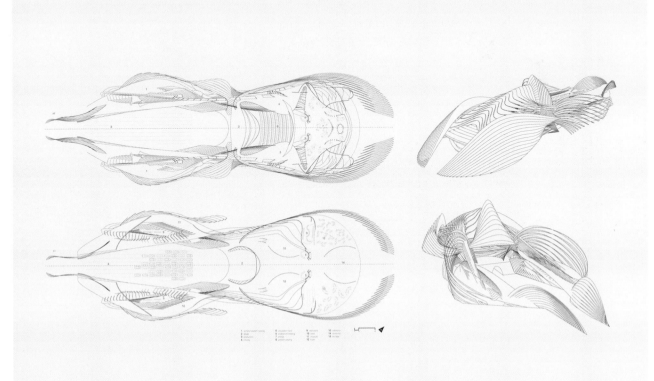

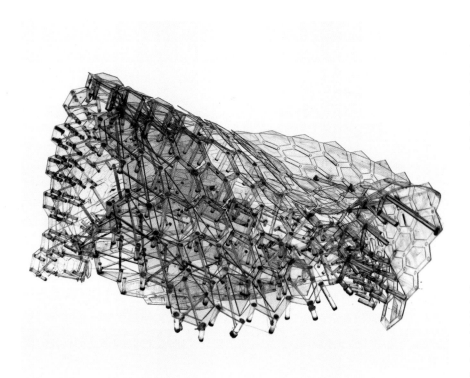

left
Yun Shi and Wenyu Jiang,
Misprision, Convention
Hall, New York. Graduate
studio (tutor: Nanako
Umemoto), Graduate School
of Architecture, Planning
and Preservation, Columbia
University, 2012

below
Alex Levian and Ziba
Esmaeilian Baboukani,
Megachurch, Garden Grove,
California. Vertical studio
(tutors: Nanako Umemoto,
Jesse Reiser), Southern
California Institute of
Architecture, 2012

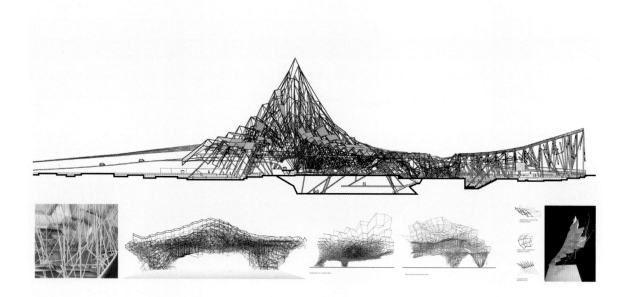

right

Ng Yee Chung and Kong Man Fung, Misprision, Convention Hall, Chicago. Graduate studio (tutor: Nanako Umemoto), Department of Architecture, University of Hong Kong, 2010

below

Yang Dai, Megastructural Landscapes, Linear City, Tokyo Bay. Graduate studio (tutors: Nanako Umemoto, Neil Cook), Department of Landscape Architecture, School of Design, University of Pennsylvania, 2010

EXPLODED AXONOMETRIC

3D truss
Structural system

Connection
from Parkway 41
to drop-off area
+20.00

Drop-off area
+0.00

Ground
Public Landscape
Piazza

External layer
Diagonal grid
Structural frame

Structural rod

Internal layer
Diagonal grid
Structural frame

Enclosure
Convention Hall and
Theatre

Metal and glass panels

Circulation
and related
programmes

Truck road
from ground to
loading dock
Basement car park

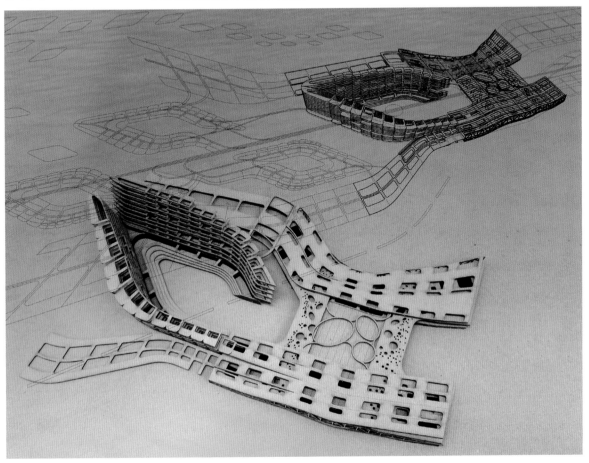

The education of breathing

– Mark Wigley, Dean, Graduate School of Architecture, Planning and Preservation, Columbia University

The Graduate School of Architecture, Planning and Preservation at Columbia University is a dense, vibrant laboratory, devoted to all dimensions of the built environment. It is a school in which the lights are never turned off; its future is always refreshingly unclear. Students do not come to Columbia to say they went there; they come to work on the future itself and, in a sense, they never leave. The school blurs professional education and advanced research to open up the field to new potentials and responsibilities. The basic model is one of parallel processing; multiple layers of independent experiments between students, teachers, labs, other schools and the profession explore key questions. The most extreme research findings feed the most basic training, and the freshest insights feed the latest research. The basic currency is always ideas, and the frame of reference for those ideas is always global.

While new forms of expertise are constantly being developed within the school's individual programmes, a key set of experimental labs devoted to cross-programme questions gathers together some of these emergent trajectories and concentrates them on a series of applied research projects, publications and events. Each lab takes on a set of partnerships with other units of the university, and with colleagues outside of it, in projects that could not be achieved without such collaborations. Considerable emphasis is placed on the findings, but also on the ongoing debates addressed by the research, and the new forms of research these debates will provoke. The set of interlinked labs constitutes a formidable machine for incubating and accelerating the latest thinking on the built environment, and communicating it in their own publications. Students and faculty often end up feeling that their home base is in a lab, rather than a programme. At the beginning of each semester, it is delightfully

Joseph Brennan, Migratory Species Research Outpost, Boreal Forest, Canada. The Color Studio (tutors: Leslie Gill, Mike Jacobs), Graduate School of Architecture, Planning and Preservation, Columbia University, 2013

unclear which groups of students, teachers, programmes or labs will most captivate the school community of around a thousand people, where, like a condensed version of New York, ideas ripple virally through the ecology. Espresso is the only constant.

The GSAPP is not a school with a revered library, but rather one inside a library. The designer (whether architect, urban planner, historic preservationist or developer) is understood as a public intellectual, crafting forms as thought and thoughts as forms. The mode of communicating these thoughts and forms constantly evolves. The most influential designers are those who identify new modes of operation that reposition and empower the figure of the designer. Publications are the major vehicle for this redefinition, fostering the invention of new sites, clients, forms of expertise and understandings of cities.

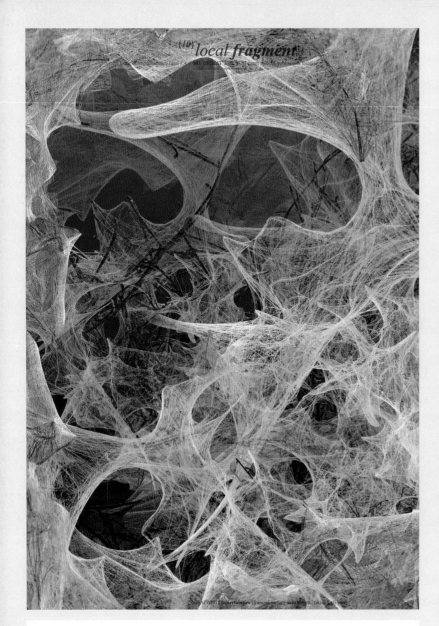

Pablo Costa Fraiz and Matt Miller, 'No heimat for you' (too late to refugee in your homeland), Santa Cruz del Sur, Cuba. Nostalgia Paradigms/5 Scenari-(n)-certainties, The Battle of Impermanency, Opus 5.4 (tutor: François Roche), Graduate School of Architecture, Planning and Preservation, Columbia University, 2012

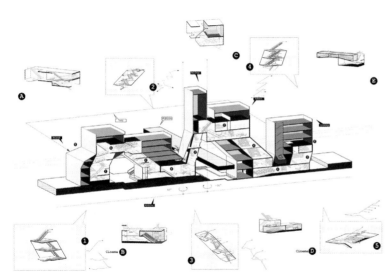

Jiaqi Xu, Jiayuan Liu, Chen Zheng, Cesar J. Langa, Five or One: Rethinking of the Kissing Towers, the Highline between 27th and 28th Streets and 10th and 11th Avenues, New York. The Dictionary of Received Ideas (tutor: Enrique Walker), Graduate School of Architecture, Planning and Preservation, Columbia University, 2013

The school's mission is to maximize professional and intellectual strength, as well as to test experimental forms of architectural communication. It is dedicated to broadening the range and increasing the intensity of architectural discourse, launching unique publications, provisional networks, video streams, television, radio and webcasts. It operates as a kind of training camp and energy source for incubating new channels for conversations and debate about architecture that last decades.

If the university is a sophisticated stupidity-reduction machine, then the GSAPP is an evolution in architectural intelligence, building on the openness to uncertainty implied in studio culture. The heart of the field is premised on a sense of mystery, a deep curiosity about the status of buildings. The ability of the architect to embrace doubt and synthesize seemingly incompatible forms of information becomes the school's guiding principle. Having assembled more books, drawings, scholars, countries, programmes, labs, global platforms, events and publications than can be found anywhere else on the planet, the GSAPP

Shih-Ning Chou, Hudson Yard Seaplane/Ferry Transfer Hub, between West 30th and 34th Streets, crossing over West Side Highway, Hudson River, New York. What if ... FLOATING New York – Post Assembly Fabrication for Expanding an Over-expanded City (tutor: Laurie Hawkinson), Graduate School of Architecture, Planning and Preservation, Columbia University, 2013

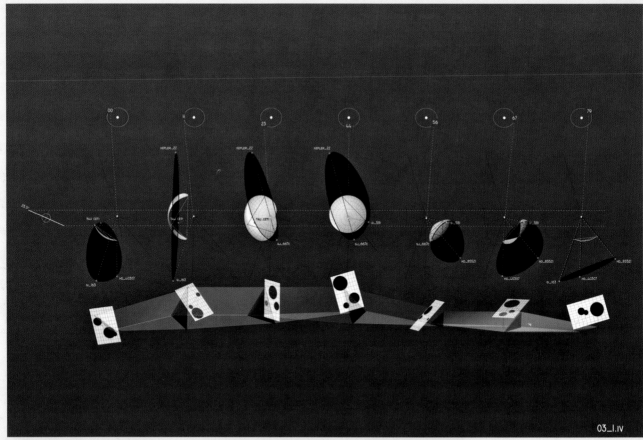

03_I.IV

left
Yvonne-Demitra
Konstantinidis, Shifting
Ground, The Meadowlands,
New Jersey. Architecture in
the Altered Landscape (tutor:
Marc Tsurumaki), Graduate
School of Architecture,
Planning and Preservation,
Columbia University, 2012

opposite, top
Ray Wang, The Fugue –
A Relay Station, Low Earth
Orbit. Space Studio 7: Health
Stations in LEO (tutor:
Michael Morris), Graduate
School of Architecture,
Planning and Preservation,
Columbia University, 2013

is finally able to embrace the instability of our collective knowledge about buildings – seemingly the most stable cultural objects, if not the very symbols of security and stability. Those who know the most are the most aware of what they do not yet know. The school is always thirsty, fostering batteries of experiments to move knowledge and practice along, and to activate ever-wider networks to broadcast its thoughts, and listen to those of others, in new ways. Cultivating new modes of listening and sharing has become an urgent task.

To go beyond the normal limits of a school is to embrace an open-source model of architectural education, a network of partners working in a global array of incubators, exchanging mutations to redefine and reactivate the architect in contemporary society. The visible boundary of the school is clear, even monumental, reflected in the self-confident symmetries of McKim, Mead & White's neoclassical design for Avery Hall (1911). But its intellectual boundary is unclear, multiple and mobile. Passionately devoted to productive mutations in architecture, the GSAPP's interior is woven out of ever-moving students and faculty. Its boundaries are porous. Like any organism, the school breathes, alternating between absorbing part of the outside world for analysis and reflection, and taking its inside world outside for engagement and feedback. The rhythm of this breathing defines everything about it.

In the end, the pleasure of being part of the school is the pleasure of constantly having someone else's drawing, project, policy, essay,

right
Geoff Bell and Rong Zhao,
Cubicit, East Harlem,
New York. Room + Body,
City + Eye (tutor: Charles
Eldred), Graduate School
of Architecture, Planning
and Preservation, Columbia
University, 2012

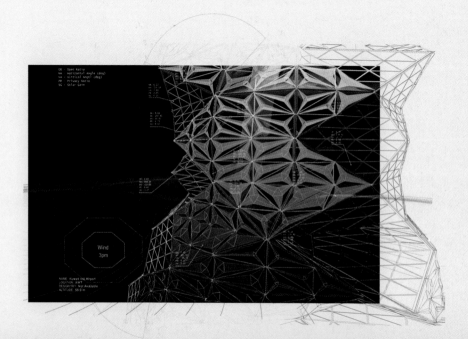

lecture, model, exhibition, film, material study, dissertation, book, concept, tweet or question make one pause and demand more from oneself, and from the field. The GSAPP is essentially an invitation to go further, faster, wider and deeper. It crafts a momentary hesitation in a world that cannot wait, when doubt rushes in and the most beautiful work is crafted.

Margarita Calero and Alfonso Simelio, Sound and Interpolations, Déserts, Metaxourgio, Athens, Greece. Architectonics of Music, Music as a Field of Time (tutors: Steven Holl, Dimitra Tsachrelia), Graduate School of Architecture, Planning and Preservation, Columbia University, 2013

The art and science of design at the Cooper Union

– Anthony Vidler, Professor and former Dean, Irwin S. Chanin School of Architecture, The Cooper Union for the Advancement of Science and Art

The distinctive nature of the Irwin S. Chanin School of Architecture at the Cooper Union in New York has from the start been influenced by its beginnings. Founded by inventor, philanthropist and educator Peter Cooper in 1859, the school was dedicated to preparing disadvantaged students for careers in architecture, art and engineering. Based on the idea of teaching through example, it was endowed 'for the purpose of establishing a public institution … for the advancement of science, art, philosophy and letters, for procuring and maintaining scientific and historical collections, collections of chemical and philosophical apparatus, mechanical and artistic models, books, drawings, pictures and statues, and for cultivating other means of instruction.'

For much of its existence, the school provided free evening courses in applied science, social and political sciences and other branches of knowledge for those without means. It also provided instruction in the design arts for women, all in the context of a polytechnic school along the lines of those in Europe. These initial programmes contained the seeds of the Cooper Union's current structure of three professional schools of architecture, art and engineering, with outreach programmes for high school students and continuing education and other public programmes. The school was the first private, higher-education institution in the US to admit students based exclusively on merit, prohibiting discrimination based on race, gender, religion or national origin; to provide a free education to every admitted student (before free public education at the college preparatory level was public policy);

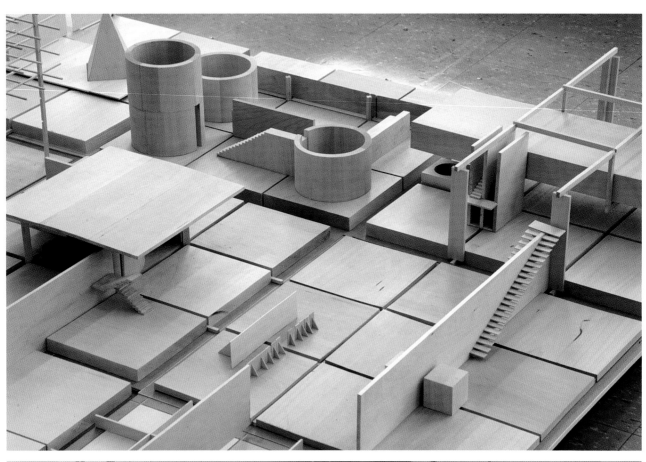

Given the 'Field' – In Regard to the Four Ideals. Architectonics (tutors: Lebbeus Woods, Diane Lewis, Aida Miron, Uri Wegman), Irwin S. Chanin School of Architecture, Cooper Union for the Advancement of Science and Art, 2012

Drawing Us Out: Drawing in the Woods (for Lebbeus), OMI International Arts Center, Ghent, New York. Architectonics (tutors: David Gersten, Aida Miron, Uri Wegman), Irwin S. Chanin School of Architecture, Cooper Union for the Advancement of Science and Art, 2013

and to offer a free reading room open to all of the city's residents – the forerunner of the public library.

The school's charter placed an emphasis on 'practical' education, to extend and develop contemporary knowledge in a democratic fashion, encouraging independence and innovation in thought. By 1907 it had grown to over 2,500 students (with 3,000 on the waiting list) taking full-time and evening courses in science, chemistry, engineering, art, stenography, typewriting, telegraphy, elocution, oratory and debate. Later, in response to the changing contexts of education and the workforce, the institution also introduced free 'training for professionals', with immigrants and the working classes remaining the primary beneficiaries. Today, the Cooper Union is still a full-scholarship college and has become one of the most highly selective educational institutions in the country, while maintaining its democratic admissions policy.

When the Cooper Union first opened, the structure of the original building closely followed Peter Cooper's educational philosophy. The original five-storey building was designed by Fred A. Petersen in the Renaissance Revival style, with studios and classrooms above a ground-floor arched arcade of shops, open to the public. In 1890, Leopold Eidlitz added studio skylights and additional storeys. The tallest building in New York at the time, this first 'skyscraper' was also the first building to be designed with a rolled-iron I-beam infrastructure, and the first to house an elevator shaft, top to bottom, although the passenger car for such a shaft had not yet been developed. In 1974, John Hejduk, the first Dean of the School of Architecture, designed a major alteration of the Foundation Building, aligning the programme of the interior with the pedagogy of the three professional schools, while leaving the exterior largely intact.

The Cooper Union's new academic building, designed by Thom Mayne of Morphosis Architects and completed in 2009, examines once again the relationships between the school's academic programmes, its place in the city and continued response to changing educational needs, through a significant work of architecture. The questions currently confronting the School of Architecture are deeply imbricated with its history, with an emphasis on a tradition of drawing that owes its inception to the first free classes, and also in the continuing reference to, and attempts to follow, the social democratic ideals of Peter Cooper himself, who believed that education at the Cooper Union should be

Sustainable Design, students investigate these issues at all scales, using their skills and knowledge to recognize the fragile contract between human settlement and the environment, urbanization and suburbanization, as seen in the light of what artist and sociologist John McHale, researching with Buckminster Fuller in the late 1960s, termed 'the ecological context' in his book of the same title, published in 1971.

The first-year studios, while introducing newcomers to the formal, arterial and programmatic principles of architectonics, operate as research laboratories in form and space, with students working in groups to investigate the parameters of visual perception, light, orientation, habitation and structure. The second year explores the ramifications of advanced topological design in creative three-dimensional exercises, often playing with the three-dimensional extrusion of the classic 'Nine-Square-Grid' problem, originally drawn by John Hejduk in 1954 while at the University of Texas (Hejduk later joined the faculty of the Cooper Union in 1964). In the second semester, the complex implications of

Door Project. Design II
(tutors: Guido Zuliani,
Katerina Kourkoula, James
Lowder), Irwin S. Chanin
School of Architecture,
Cooper Union for the
Advancement of Science
and Art, 2013

inside/outside are studied, sometimes by considering the problem of entry with intricately designed 'doors' that reveal all the exciting (and problematic) possibilities of the interstitial space of passage through a wall – the first step into a space from outside.

The comprehensive third-year studio, immersed in the analysis of interrelations between the components of architecture – from legal regulations and structure, to building and environmental technologies – considers the problems of a small institution on a real site in New York, first through an exploration of the precedents and then in a collaborative design programme, often with a 'real' client from the public or private realm. One such programme was for an elementary school in Harlem, with community participation, which entered the students into a creative field of social, educational and spatial relations. The fourth year begins with a large-scale study of the suburban environment, and brings together the insights of landscape architecture, urban renewal and ecological analysis to propose various responses to the continuing problems of suburbia. The year continues with proposals

Towards the Definition of Space III: Redefining the Relative. Design II (tutors: Pablo Lorenzo-Eiroa, Katerina Kourkoula, James Lowder), Irwin S. Chanin School of Architecture, Cooper Union for the Advancement of Science and Art, 2012

for institutional and urban spaces in Manhattan, based on the historical and archaeological 'memories' encapsulated within the selected sites.

The capstone fifth-year thesis, a whole-year research and design studio, allows each student to identify a problem field – local or global – with the potential to benefit from architectural intervention at different scales. Studies range from the challenge of declining agricultural production and aquifer exhaustion in the US Midwest, the construction of 'memory theatres' in the context of Australia's chequered history with its minority populations and the crisis of the world's growing 'informal' cities, to the potential of landscape ideas to transform urban reformulation, research into new materials and spatial techniques for going beyond orthodox geometrical design and finding ways through drawing in which philosophical thought might be explored in its three-dimensional implications. Finally, the post-professional graduate studio researches the structure and form of urban regions in order to draw out their environmental and programmatic potentials, followed by a study of large-scale landscapes and their possibilities as architectures of nature, culminating in a thesis project that is both written and designed.

Over the last decade or so, the school has remained firm in its commitment to its long tradition of design, but at the same time has transformed it in ways that allow it to confront the challenges of twenty-first-century architecture and urbanism. The need to think both globally and locally, the knowledge required of architects to practise in diverse contexts and cultures, the skills to master new technologies of

The Critical Moment: Architecture in the Expanded Field. Master of Architecture II Thesis (tutors: Diana Agrest, Lydia Xynogala), Irwin S. Chanin School of Architecture, Cooper Union for the Advancement of Science and Art, 2013

representation and construction, the changing nature of professional practice and, above all, the critical rethinking of the discipline – all these considerations and more have been folded into the curriculum. Far from static, it is a curriculum that continues its development, under the guidance of faculty and students, as a comprehensive and rigorous course of professional study.

Perhaps the most important of these new initiatives is the now flourishing post-professional M.Arch 2 programme. As part of this three-semester design research course, a select number of post-professional students from around the world engage in a common investigation into urban and natural contexts, while studying research techniques and taking part in seminars throughout the school. In a second initiative, over the last two years the Institute for Sustainable Design has emphasized our essential role in the growing environmental crisis, and become established as a centre of debate, lectures and exhibitions for engaging the most pressing environmental challenges of our time.

Wot got left out

– Ben Nicholson, Associate Professor,
School of the Art Institute of Chicago

A tidal wave of prescribed niceties is now intertwined with the passing on of architectural thought from one generation to the next. Thirty years ago, architecture schools worked with loosely defined curricula, from which the ebb and flow of thought could change direction at the drop of a hat. There now stands in its place the pedagogical contract, a document that mirrors the accreditation process and stands firm against a small army of litigious students who want to make damned sure that they get what they pay for in writing. The curriculum has been replaced by the contract.

Neo-realist pedagogues have entered the fray, and decry open-ended musing over the long memory and wide generosity of Architecture (with a capital 'A'). The new classroom espouses back-to-basics 'nuts-and-boltism', little more than a brand of spatial internationalism, albeit curvaceous, which touts big-box capitalism for the trading of trinkets, packaging health and education, or attending to the spiritual entertainment industrial complex. Baroque Modernism in the service of capitalism lives on. Over the past few years, student projects that deal with all the stuff left out of the moneyed stream have been lampooned by nut-and-boltists as being irrelevant and a waste of taxpayers' money. The last redoubt of ethicist architectural educators are ridiculed for having nothing to do with architecture and being little more than a big w***-off. Who are these teachers and tutors, who cannot conform to the current needs of the industry? Why are they questioning the very things that need to get done?

It is like this. The first page of the morning newspaper deals with collapsed states, usually associated with black gold, blood diamonds or blue scandal. Page two goes on to describe the feel-good perils of disturbing the natural order impacted by the political order mentioned on page one. Page three … let's us forget about that for a minute and get on to page somewhere else. There we find a host of home-decorating tips

Rosalia Covarrubias, Juan Deleon, Lee Kelly, Minh Nguyen and Lori Obeyesekere, The New Harmony Cave: A digitally fabricated reinterpretation of F. Kiesler's *Grotto for Meditation*, University of Houston, Texas. Kiesler Studio (tutors: Ben Nicholson, Andrew Vranas, Joe Meppelink), College of Architecture, University of Houston, 2008

Ben Nicholson, Drawing the Vesica Piscis with Samburu warriors, using spears and animal-gut, rite of passage to Mutumia Ngatha, Sasaab, Samburu Land, Kenya, 2012

Ben Nicholson, Cordelia Rose and M. D. Rose, Shuffle Labyrinth, Committed to Memory and Walked in the Dust, Whitewater Mesa Labyrinths, Glenwood, New Mexico, 2013

Saori Hisano, Geometric Construction of an Ellipse, Montrose Beach, Chicago. Master's thesis class (tutor: Ben Nicholson), College of Architecture, Illinois Institute of Technology, 2005

and where to go at the weekend. A lot has been left out. Now let us turn on the telly and do a little binge-viewing on Netflix, sitting on the couch all day, and rip through a year-long serial in twenty-four hours. What is up with all the doom-and-gloom shows, zombies pretending to give content to a plain-in-sight societal meltdown that does not need the zombies to remain relevant?

On the one hand, 'edu-topia' is asking us to build up an imaginary world that is good for the 1 per cent, while the 99 per cent languish in the dungeons of circumstance. On the other, educators and educatees are brewing up visions of apocalyptic landscapes they consider to be the precursors of the inevitable EOTWAWKI (end of the world as we know it). It is fine to sit and watch Syria being torn to shreds on the nine o'clock news, but doing something architecturally relevant for it is nuts. So what is a kid to do in the best and worst of times? Thank God, Charles Dickens found the words for the perilous situation that we still find ourselves in. We live, study and work in the parallel worlds of the 'haves' and 'have nots', and studying architecture at such a time is hazardous. We no longer know for whom we build.

In the good old days the educational mantra dealt with the space of paradox, but how do we deal with the space of unadulterated hypocrisy, the kind we are confronted with on a daily basis? I mean, how in all conscience can one design an immaculate wooden boathouse on the Thames, while half the residents of the globe live on $2 a day? What kind of education could possibly prepare us for the hypocrisies that are necessary to take on board simply to get through to 5pm without going crazy? Over the past decade, I have found it increasingly difficult to advocate a cheery-cheeked positivism that caters to the 1 per cent. The benchmark for one of the architecture classes I teach on geometry and labyrinths is that the course could be useful for the student who may one day find him- or herself incarcerated in a 'supermax' prison. What could you do all day in a 2 × 4m (7 × 13 ft) cell that would be meaningful? There is the space of 'liberty and freedom', and then there is the space of 'enclosure and reduction'. So what kind of space can we carry in our minds that would enable us to wander in both these worlds, released of all constraint, and be perfectly happy?

I have always been impressed by the Muslim Hajji, who goes to Mecca clad in two pieces of white cloth, the same two pieces for rich and poor alike. For a few hours each year, all the world's Hajjis appear in exactly the same trappings. Of course, we all know that the oily-rich slink back to their padded Meccas overlooking the Ka'aba to put their worlds to rights after the day's events, but surely something happens when you rub shoulders with your fellow human beings in a sea of similar swathes of cotton.

What is the spatial equivalent of that in architecture? That thing, whatever it is, is worth teaching. There, in the imagination, all is possible, irrespective of circumstance. In this construct of the mind, there is no need for a brick in hand or a trowel of mortar. Instead, the body's feet shuffle in the dust and imprints of the first architectural plan that is learned, carried in the head and replicated the world over. The only tools needed are a few sticks and a length of twine, vine or catgut. If these are not available, then a hand-span with a couple of fingers to act as compass points are perfectly adequate to build dreams in the sand. Everything else tends to get in the way. That kind of architectural education would out nut-and-bolt nut-and-boltism any day of the week.

Kristina Alford, The XXXXSisters House, The Old Dam, New Harmony, Indiana Anarchitecture Antedeluvian option design studio (tutors: Ben Nicholson, Taylor Lowe), College of Architecture, Art and Planning, Cornell University, 2012

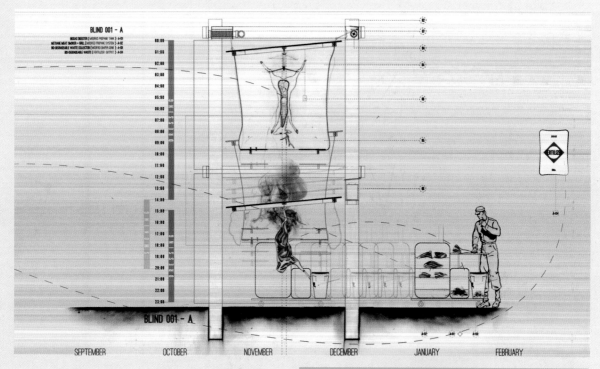

Erin Pellegrino, SFC
Quartermain's House and
Home, The Old Dam, New
Harmony, Indiana
Anarchitecture Antedeluvian
option design studio (tutors:
Ben Nicholson, Taylor Lowe),
College of Architecture,
Art and Planning, Cornell
University, 2012

Emily Wright, Keeler Avenue
Regeneration Project, Chicago
Thesis studio (tutors:
Ben Nicholson, Frances
Whitehead), Department
of Architecture, Interior
Architecture and Designed
Objects, School of the Art
Institute of Chicago, 2013

An experimental history, a history of the experiment: 1964–2013

– Neil Denari, Professor, Department of Architecture and Urban Design, University of California, Los Angeles

No one needs to be reminded of the events that occurred in 1960s America, and how they shaped the cultural politics of universities during that most tumultuousness of times. Against a backdrop of racial prejudice and dismay at cultural hegemony, student protests challenged the power of authority and condemned the control of public space itself. These sorts of conflicts brought about positive change with the establishment of new centres for research into the design of our physical environments. In 1964, the Department of Architecture and Urban Design was founded at the University of California, Los Angeles, with a mission to research and develop ideas for the future of architecture and urbanism.

Quick to take advantage of this new platform was a group of British critics that included Reyner Banham, who visited in 1965 to lecture and discuss the incipient pedagogy of the school. Banham's early immersion in Los Angeles would ultimately lead to the book *Los Angeles: The Architecture of Four Ecologies* (1971). This admiration for the city's sprawling, uncontrolled landscapes was perhaps the first assessment of Los Angeles as an imperfect utopia. Archigram member Warren Chalk followed as a guest professor in 1967, with Peter Cook (pp. 22–31) and Ron Herron visiting over the next two years. Seeing something in LA that reminded them of their speculations on the image of the 'technopolis', this 'British Invasion' helped move both school and city into a prominent position as a centre of innovation, a status UCLA has held onto ever since.

Jonathan Louie, Lilit Ustayan and Chi Zhang, A Continuous Environment, Westwood, California. SUPRASTUDIO GEO_GRAPHICS (tutor: Neil Denari), Department of Architecture and Urban Design, University of California, Los Angeles, 2012

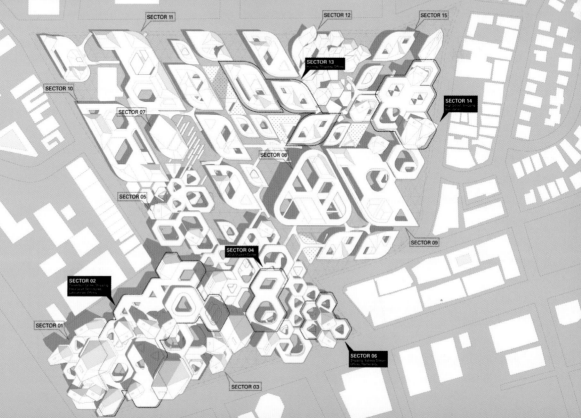

Robotics in architecture

– Greg Lynn, Professor, Department of Architecture and Urban Design, University of California, Los Angeles

Our environments have become ever more mobile, with increasing sensing and processing capability leading to greater intelligence in design. The next generation of designers will be trained to engage and imagine the potential of dynamic, deformable environments with the situational awareness to adapt and transform smartly. In an effort to reduce the real-estate footprint, as well as the energy footprint, of buildings, transformable structures are inevitable. The next frontier in architectural innovation is not shape and complexity, but rather spectacular motion.

Connecting research to professional practice, SUPRASTUDIO investigates the pressing issues of contemporary architecture and urbanism and its deployment at the city scale. Because California has the largest concentration of high-tech industries in the world and is a global centre for entertainment and animation, SUPRASTUDIO looks into the future to how architecture can express these entertainment industries in spatial and cultural building terms by integrating large-scale media and robotics to animate cities, buildings and spaces; and through the use of narrative and immersive approaches to the design of environments that are the material expression of Southern California popular cultures.

Technology Transfer (2010–11) explored how the subject of robotics is already integrated into architecture, and how it might be rethought by designers to focus on social and cultural interaction, and experience over multi-functionality, flexibility or efficiency. Instead of replacing existing functions with robotics, the students looked at design innovations that could bring a new animated sensibility and liveliness to spaces and places. The research culminated in a comprehensive design project that integrated motion elements into the architectural design of a freestanding building proposal in an urban context.

Sarah Hearne, Gateway, Orlando. Technology Transfer SUPRASTUDIO (tutors: Greg Lynn, Stephen Deters), Department of Architecture and Urban Design, University of California, Los Angeles, 2009–10

Dumĕne Comploi, Epcot,
Orlando. Technology Transfer
SUPRASTUDIO (tutors:
Greg Lynn, Stephen Deters),
Department of Architecture
and Urban Design, University
of California, Los Angeles,
2009–10

animating architectural design that would have multiple technical consequences for resolution and realization, as well as profoundly transforming the language of design and spatial interaction.

Masses in Motion (2012–13) explored the impact of robotics on architecture, not in terms of fabrication and assembly of buildings, but in the literal movement of rooms, façades, vertical transportation, furniture and equipment. The studio combined a small percentage of literal moving rooms or elements with the phenomenal movement of spatial composition and environments. It began with a 'pop-up' structure defined by the individual students, in which the spectacle of motion, along with the logistics of a movable, deployable, freestanding structure, engaged the themes of motion. A larger, second project was

Sarah Hearne, Gateway, Orlando. Technology Transfer SUPRASTUDIO (tutors: Greg Lynn, Stephen Deters), Department of Architecture and Urban Design, University of California, Los Angeles, 2009–10

designed for a permanent circus performance theatre, where robotic movement was not only limited to the stages, but was also part of the lobby, seating, restaurant, civic or theatre environment.

The project began with a visit to several Cirque du Soleil theatres in Las Vegas and an analysis of various theatres in Hollywood. The final design topic was the redesign and rethinking of the Omni Hotel, located in the cultural district of Grand Avenue in downtown Los Angeles. Concepts of motion and movement were defined by each of the students to help rethink the lobby experience for visitors and guests, the hotel experience, the landscape of pools and outdoor spaces and the urban address of the hotel, to Olive Street, Grand Avenue, the Museum of Contemporary Art, the Broad Art Foundation, Walt Disney Concert Hall, Angels Flight, and the surrounding California Plaza landscape. Eric Cheong, design director for Ace Hotels, met with the students to discuss contemporary hospitality thinking and how it connected with the students' ideas about motion and robotics.

SUPRASTUDIO aims to prepare students for issues that will face practice in the next decade, as well as giving them exposure to the vanguard of creative clients who are shaping cultural experience (such as Cirque du Soleil and Ace Hotels). The topic of robotics is already integrated into the UCLA curriculum, as well as at other schools, and is now less and less a topic for innovation. SUPRASTUDIO Masses in Motion, however, has shifted the focus from how robotics can make things to how it can move things, or help to redesign those parts of a building that already move with a new intelligence or new design opportunities.

David Stamatis, Tri-fly Theater, Urban Circus, Las Vegas. Masses in Motion SUPRASTUDIO (tutors: Greg Lynn, Julia Koerner), Department of Architecture and Urban Design, University of California, Los Angeles, 2012–13

What is SCI-Arc?

– Eric Owen Moss, Director,
Southern California Institute of Architecture

In 1972 the Southern California Institute of Architecture, or SCI-Arc, opened its warehouse doors in Santa Monica, California, to a small group of emancipated faculty and students, most of whom had rejected the prevailing institutional models of the time in favour of a more freeform intersection of teachers and learners, a patient critique of the old idioms and an aggressive pursuit of the promise of an ever-renewable pedagogy. In the beginning, SCI-Arc was a curiosity. Its advent was a surprise, from nothing to something, and something worth nothing. In a sense, it was a kinetic institution. Its institutional personality was historically introverted. We shared our experiments, imagination and priorities with those around the world who admired our endeavour, valued our perspective and supported our arguments. We were a closed unit of friends and colleagues. Our collective personality was hermetic.

Dale Strong, Who Goes and Who Stays. Graduate thesis (tutor: Andrew Zago), Southern California Institute of Architecture, 2012

For an institution to make a place for itself in the world, to remodel history's chronology, it has to force aside what went before – out of date, out of the way. In a psychotherapeutic sense, this act of intervention, or invention, is ipso facto an act of aggression, a fight for the survival of a new definition of meaning. Initially, that new definition is precarious, its fragility is precious. The pedagogical lineage that preceded SCI-Arc belonged to a number of established institutions around the globe, which propounded an established ideological form and form-language for architecture. Over a period of years, the school interrogated both, and made both different. The definition of a plausible educational venue with the capacity to overturn the discourse in architecture was altered and the form of the form-language was reformed: SCI-Arc did that.

The aspiration to determine new pedagogy was never an aspiration to formulate doctrine. It was innocent, perhaps naive, less self-conscious at first – a shared instinct that the imaginative future of architecture is not a destination, but a way of thinking critically, independently testing

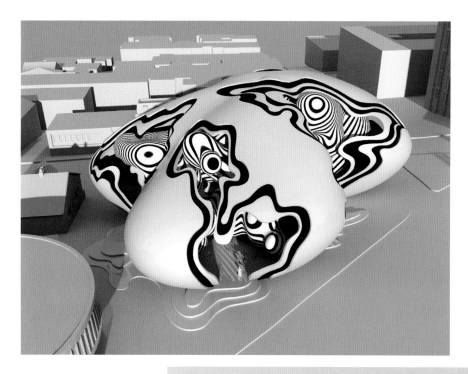

Ashley Shoulder, InsideOut,
West Hollywood, California.
M.Arch 2 (tutor: Tom
Wiscombe), Southern
California Institute of
Architecture, 2012

Ben Warwas, Field So Good.
Graduate thesis (tutor:
Florencia Pita), Southern
California Institute of
Architecture, 2012

prospects that, in retrospect, represent a chronology of provisional paradigms, at first fragile, then established, later decayed, and finally replaced. The pursuit of the fragile – conception in process – is intact today. Contemporary forms of fabrication, including digital and robotic technology, actively shape the current state of material culture at SCI-Arc. Graduate students in the Robot House are researching new forms of fabrication, such as freeform, gravity-less 3D-printing. New technologies present them with the potential to engage with materials in alternative ways. In many cases, tools are presented as faster ways of essentially doing the same thing. The jump from experimental to plausible has become shortened.

Digital tools have created a new plateau such that even the most complicated fractal shape can be reduced to a mathematical conception. The freest, most intuitive shape to be constructed requires an antithetical spirit, enormous rigour. The computer might or might not give you the first, but it certainly guarantees the second. This explains why the odd instinct is built more often now; the computer rationalizes the instinct, making it technically plausible. The first step was the advent of software that allowed us to conceive in a precise way what was previously very difficult to represent. But now that the software is available, the goal is not to deliver what it initially allowed; rather, it is to find a way to contradict its original intention. What SCI-Arc is supportive of is an inventive minority and how that minority applies the new tools, as opposed to how they are more generally applied.

When architecture is teachable and learnable, it is simultaneously repetitive and redundant. Students and faculty are perpetually in search of what the rules do not rule on, but this does not mean that SCI-Arc will warrant such discoveries. Discovery is an aspiration. Imagination in architecture should exceed the rules and tools of the contemporary discourse. This is the critical intellectual mindset. There is also the issue of radical idea versus the image of a radical idea. Whether something is genuinely radical is so only if it has not been done, or is difficult to do, or the results are uncertain, which is different from reproducing years later what the profession learned to do in former times. The struggle to implement and to understand new work, as a valued act of architectural conduct, is very different from repeating a learned image. Now we notice many buildings that are carrying forward the image of what is supposed to be radical, but it is now a learned response, as opposed to a discovered one. And the question is whether the digital process facilitates this 'living up to an image'.

New tools are conceived to implement the architectural surprise we cannot yet draw or construct. The advent of new tools allows us to do what before we could only imagine. The tools in turn become obligatory means to produce a predictable result. And a surprise is no longer a surprise. The repertoire of CNC modelling, BIM, the Rhino menu, and so on supplant the repertoire of the parallel rule and the triangle. Self-congratulations are in order on our mastery of a new technical pro forma. But dissatisfaction is the impetus to new architecture. The provisional paradigm is the sole credo of the radical architect; it is an allegiance to non-allegiance. It insists that any design hypothesis is intrinsically fragile. It understands its advocacy, strengths and limitations, so the next time that previously insisted-upon pro forma is replaced with a model that interrogates what was previously prized.

SCI-Arc is the institute of the provisional paradigm, and when the provisional paradigm threatens to become a permanent allegiance – and it inevitably does – we begin again. The school has little or no interest in the academic rivalries that so often fractionalize the discourse. It is never 'our guys' versus 'your guys', but simply an enduring pursuit of that changing model of the discourse, wherever it leads. Those who join this debate, whether they belong to Los Angeles or to other venues, come to SCI-Arc regularly to discuss the prospects for architecture's future. Here is the paradox: SCI-Arc is a school with no pedagogy, but if the intellectual disputation mechanism is in working order. Individual characters – faculty or students – are encouraged to imagine the next pedagogy, which becomes the next attempt at homogeneity, which the next generation will, in turn, overturn.

SCI-Arc began as a race with a moving finish line. It is still running, and the finish line is still in motion.

opposite
Xiaofeng Mei, A Sensitive City, Japan. Graduate thesis (tutors: Florencia Pita, Tom Wiscombe), Southern California Institute of Architecture, 2012

left
Stefano Passeri and Johannes
Beck, Fused Volumes, Massive
Joints, Nervous Edge,
West Hollywood, California.
M.Arch 2 (tutor: Tom
Wiscombe), Southern
California Institute of
Architecture, 2012

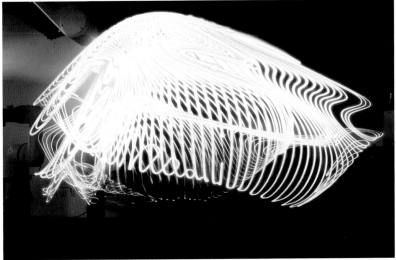

right
Robbie Crabtree and
Byungmo Kang, Real-time.
M.Arch 2 (tutor: Peter Testa),
Southern California Institute
of Architecture, 2011

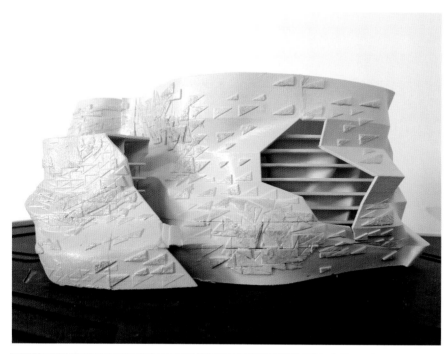

Jiarui Liu, Massing Air Flow, Tianjin, China. Graduate thesis (tutor: Marcelo Spina), Southern California Institute of Architecture, 2012

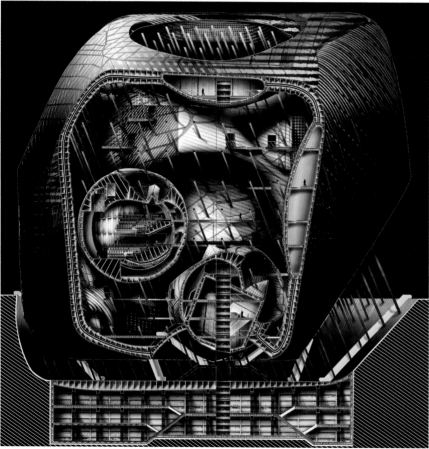

Daniel Karas, The New Painterly. M.Arch 2 (tutor: Andrew Atwood), Southern California Institute of Architecture, 2013

Sara Gaskari, Vogueing:
Dancing with the Self.
Graduate thesis (tutor: Coy
Howard), Southern California
Institute of Architecture, 2012

Elizabeth von Hasseln and
Kyle von Hasseln, Phantom
Geometry. Graduate thesis
(tutors: Peter Testa, Devyn
Weiser), Southern California
Institute of Architecture, 2012

Pretentious and incoherent thoughts on architecture – right now

– Hernan Diaz Alonso, Graduate Programs Chair, Southern California Institute of Architecture

I believe … whatever doesn't kill you simply makes you … stranger.

— The Joker, in *The Dark Knight*, 2008

First let me be clear: the present is always better than the past. Over the last twenty years or so, the digital explosion has brought about a major transformation in architecture, in terms of aesthetics and form, which can be seen as reminiscent of child's play – immediate and born of and curiosity, but at the same time absolutely serious and committed. This is a good thing in times of confusion. At first, one has to believe blindly in the tools, which then become techniques. As the genre evolves further, some choose to reinforce the canon, and others, including myself and others at SCI-Arc, choose to contaminate it. Such evolution is rejected, producing a critical reactionary antidote. To advance an intellectual agenda, issues sometimes need to be detached from any traditional practicality or application, and evolve instead as a species on their own terms.

Architects aspire to be original, and if we think in more contaminated, grotesque ways, we can be more open in our pursuit of a pure state of architecture. No compromise. Proud of the work and the commitment to uselessness, in the sense that true innovation and progress often come when the work focuses on itself, without being bothered with practical deployment. Architecture is a discipline in which

Ivan Bernal, Familiar Primitives, El Malécon, La Habana, Havana. Graduate thesis (tutor: Hernan Diaz Alonso), Southern California Institute of Architecture, 2011

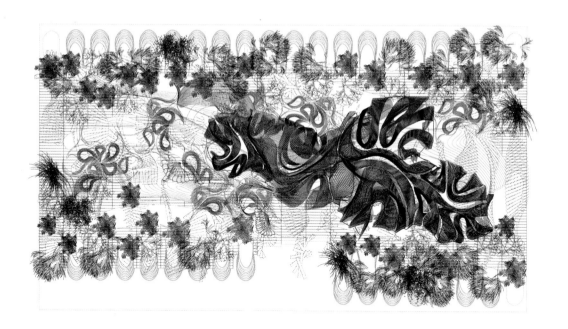

above
Keyla Hernandez and Jason
Orbe-Smith, Bundle House,
Hollywood, Los Angeles.
Vertical Studio (tutor: Hernan
Diaz Alonso), Southern
California Institute of
Architecture, 2012

left
Edward Kim, Exquisite
Heartbreak Hotel, Manhattan,
New York. Graduate thesis
(tutor: Hernan Diaz Alonso),
Southern California Institute
of Architecture, 2009

one cannot get away with not understanding and knowing its history. Though this is perhaps also true in other disciplines, it is particularly evident in architecture as our own work or that of our students often has similarities with work that has been produced before. It is thus much better to have history and precedent in one's repertoire than to not. At the same time, overplaying this risks revisiting some of the nightmares of Postmodernism; architects are always revolving in their own crap.

Architecture is much like a game in which it is necessary to keep moving towards the finish line. In this I am all for excess; it is good to take an idea to the extreme and then say, 'Forget history, let's do that.' Or, 'Forget contemporary technology, let's look into this.' It is always better to be black or white, rather than keeping a balance. A big part of the recent transformation in architecture has been aesthetics. The idea of aesthetics mutates the tradition of composition and order, acting as an agent to study the paradigm shift towards formal excesses, as opposed to the ubiquitous platform of types. If types are traditionally viewed as categories of standardization and symbolic expressions of form, then formal mutation/rituals/techno-romanticism are the malleable entities in constant metamorphosis. As such, adaptation and mutation represent the main characteristics of current discourse.

A shifting aesthetics paradigm – butchery, grotesque, etc. – requires a lineage in order to be acknowledged as such. Indeed, a type also needs a lineage, but a mutant sense of aesthetics has more freedom because it can mutate. A type can change, but it cannot mutate; it can be combined or renewed, but it will always be a type. The most relevant project needs to be constantly updated. It needs to conduct an extensive trip into the new logics of contamination, and address issues of structural and cultural instability, to radicalize architecture's agenda of aesthetics of form with both artificial and natural interaction.

If, traditionally, design was derived from expertise in form and proportion, 'mess aesthetic' design is an advanced state, or evolution, of that tradition: it cannot escape it. Dynamic topology/ecology, then, becomes a tool that pertains in large degree to the highest control of the manipulations of those formal strategies. Where traditional architecture needed to determine the degree to which a particular project had achieved its beauty, these topologies explore the emergent aesthetics as material methods: the structure as a reversed mechanism of a more traditional beauty, and the material as a will to anguish, or to create a more appalling encounter with the work. Rooting this aesthetics design paradigm within the confines of architecture's aim for proportion and beauty, the ugly and the horrific of a new kind of structural organization based on excess allow us to escape the traditional and instead create a spatial model of shocking presence that can produce lust and arouse.

Despite the fascination with current technologies, architecture is and should remain an existential, humanist and artistic problem. And in order to be all that, it cannot be only certain things. This is why we use scripts, robots or whatever is available to find new possibilities to corrupt or contaminate these systems. In any event, we are not interested in reclaiming a kind of religious, paralysing canon, in which any technological apparatus will eventually be replaced with another. The construction of a discourse is a crucial aspect of any pedagogical or cultural endeavour – it is why we should never abandon the strangeness; we need to remain curious, channelling different ways of seeing. Contaminated aesthetics is a body of work that is vital, necessary – and, yes, useless.

There is beauty in mess, contamination, putrefaction, all of which must be approached with passion. How can something be moved forward if there is no confrontation? We need to strive for the equilibrium necessary to create the perfect ideal of imagination, innovation and originality. We should believe in the integrity of the pursuit – and the obsessions. In the end, the sole purpose of architecture is to imagine and challenge the culture of the discipline from every possible angle.

Keyla Hernandez and Jason Orbe-Smith, Bundle House, Hollywood, Los Angeles. Vertical Studio (tutor: Hernan Diaz Alonso), Southern California Institute of Architecture, 2012

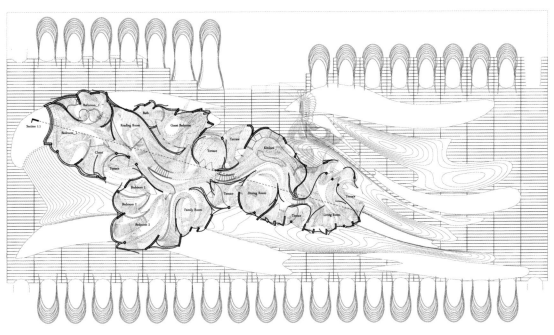

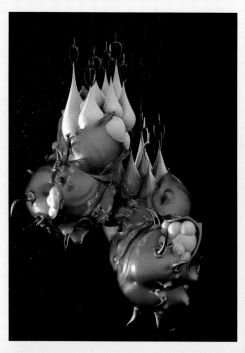

Hernan Diaz Alonso/
Xefirotarch, MONSTER,
MONSTROSITY,
MONSTROUS LAMP,
Los Angeles, 2011

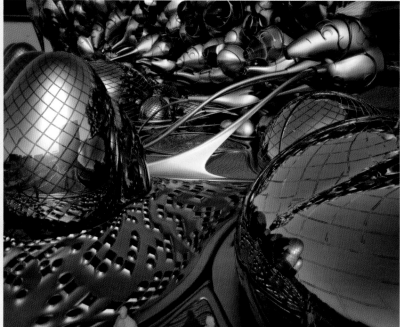

Hernan Diaz Alonso/
Xefirotarch, Helsinki Library
Competition, Helsinki, 2012

Hernan Diaz Alonso/
Xefirotarch, TBA 2.0,
Patagonia, Argentina, 2011

Building the Berlage: Notes on a continuing educational project

— Salomon Frausto, Head of Education, Berlage Center for Advanced Studies in Architecture and Urban Design, Delft University of Technology

The renaissance of urban investigation and research over the past two decades, and the emergence of digital processes and technologies, has subjected architectural education to unprecedented transformations – some related to changes within professional practice and to theoretical discourse, and others to reforms (such as the Bologna Declaration) and the increase of higher-degree programmes. This, together with today's increasingly globalized, rapidly evolving cross-cultural field of architectural practice, has left many architects unprepared for what they encounter when they start their careers.

It is tempting to view architects as members of a cosmopolitan culture that transcends national boundaries and identities, where drawings, technologies, clients and even work forces flow easily between continents and cultures. Yet architects must still confront the sometimes intractable characteristics of local conditions. Construction industries vary from country to country; regionally specific legal frameworks and regulations greatly impact the built environment; and value systems, from social norms to understandings of public and private space, remain strongly bound to cultural identity.

How can architects practise within the clash between cosmopolitanism and localism? What are the design strategies and research approaches that can mediate between global and local conditions? How can designers engage with local mores and trades? Do practitioners who operate internationally have an ethical duty to transfer new skills to local architects? These questions underscore

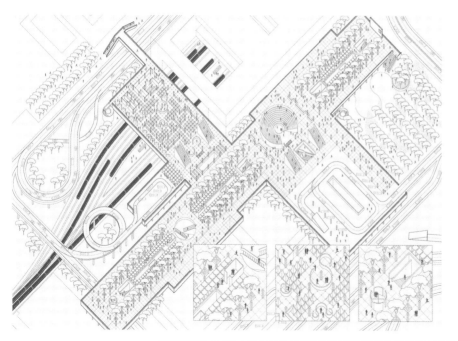

left and below
Like Tao, A Square for One Million: Linking Border Checkpoint, Train Station and Bus Stop, Luohu, Shenzhen, China. Fence, Trade, Desire, Happiness: Shenzhen from Necessity to Destination (tutors: Sanne van den Breemer, Don Murphy), The Berlage, 2013

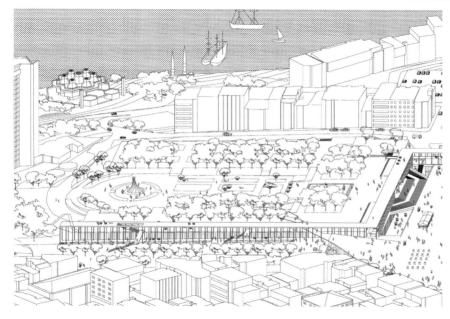

left
Congxiao Liu, Colonnade, Istanbul. Taksim Square, the Animist City (tutors: Ido Avissar, Marcus Kempers), The Berlage, 2013

the new reality not only of architectural practice, but also, more importantly, of architectural education.

Ever since its beginnings in 1990, in Aldo van Eyck's restored orphanage in Amsterdam, the Berlage has met these challenges by expanding the range of education architects receive and redefining the methods, instruments and approaches of research and design practice. The establishment of the Berlage was the result of a collaboration between the Dutch Minister for Welfare, Health and Culture and a number of prominent architects, including Herman Hertzberger, the school's first Dean, and Carel Webber, to create an international study programme for architects, landscape architects and urban designers, marking a profound political commitment to the built environment.

It is this vision and support for a centre for disciplinary excellence, the promotion of architecture in the service of culture at large, and the involvement of prominent and innovative practitioners, that led to the birth of the Berlage as we know it today. In the first prospectus, outlining the intentions of the Berlage Institute (as it was known until 2012), Hertzberger wrote:

> [The Berlage] should not be seen as a school in the narrow sense of the word – somewhere that mainly concentrates on teaching – but more as an 'atelier', a workshop for project education. Participants will work both individually and collectively in small groups. Intensity of design is mainly the fruit of great individual concentration, but discussions within this international environment can add considerably to its depth.

Hertzberger set about establishing the Berlage's worldwide reputation as a place for discussion and research by creating a unique and intimate school that was counter to the large architecture schools in Delft and Eindhoven. Following a government mandate to create a study programme that focused on excellence, he invited internationally renowned practitioners and scholars to teach at the school, including architectural historian Kenneth Frampton; Steven Holl, a practitioner just beginning his career at the time; and the educator and practitioner Elia Zenghelis, who still occasionally teaches workshops and gives lectures. The aim was to bring to the Netherlands a range of personalities and perspectives to advance disciplinary conversations, while also building on the rich tradition of Dutch modern architecture by focusing on societal concerns related to the built environment.

In 1995, after a tumultuous period of financial uncertainty, Wiel Arets became the school's second Dean. Along with overseeing a move to Marnixstraat in Amsterdam, one of his first official acts was to change the Berlage's byline from a 'school' to a 'laboratory' of architecture. This simple change marked a shift from a predominantly educational institution to a place of radical experimentation that focused on research, anticipating what would become the dominant model for architecture schools in the twenty-first century. This new focus grew under the core educational team of Raoul Bunschoten, Vedran Mimica, Roemer van Toorn, Bart Lootsma and Elia Zenghelis, each of whom developed a research perspective within a shared framework.

For Arets and his team, 'research' was thought of more in terms of the development of spatial interventions or speculative, risk-taking scenarios. He extended the disciplinary conversation to the US, and Stan Allen, Elizabeth Diller, Hani Rashid (pp. 288–94) and Greg Lynn (pp. 248–55), among many others, made the trip to the Netherlands throughout Arets' seven-year deanship, often crossing paths with locals including Ben van Berkel and Winy Maas. During this time the Berlage relocated to Rotterdam, a hub for architects and designers, establishing a home there for the next twelve years. Arets also introduced the opportunity to perform doctoral research in conjunction with the Delft University of Technology. This 'progressive research', as it was dubbed by Van Toorn, aimed to assess theoretically processes in society and their related architectural strategies and concepts to discover new modes of architectural practice.

Alejandro Zaera-Polo became the third Dean in 2002, and, critical of the speculative, research-based approaches in the curriculum, restructured the Berlage's activities to emphasize the connection of research to professional practice. He positioned the school to use 'reality' as a field of inquiry, and had students confront directly the transformative processes of the built environment and contemporary culture. For Zaera-Polo, reality provided a framework to give students a degree of friction and accountability for their studies. Also deeply influenced by the American scene, he continued to invite a renowned roster of scholars and practitioners, including Peter Eisenman, Jeffrey

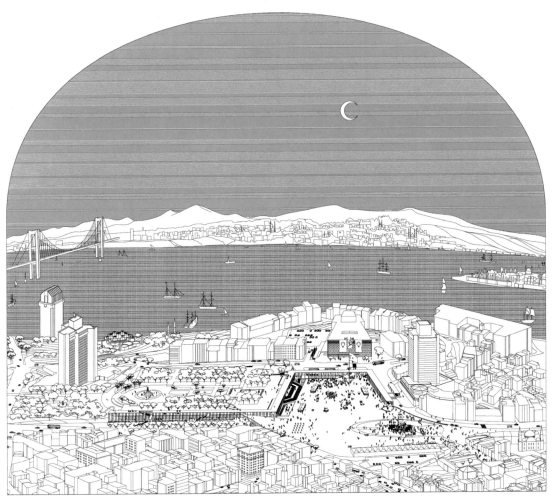

Congxiao Liu, Colonnade, Istanbul. Taksim Square, the Animist City (tutors: Ido Avissar, Marcus Kempers), The Berlage, 2013

Kipnis and Sylvia Lavin, to be part of a rotating team of teachers and lecturers, as well as supporting emerging figures such as Pier Vittorio Aureli, Penelope Dean and Peter Trummer.

Zaera-Polo based the curriculum around three research studios: two in the first year, and an in-depth studio in the second year. The first-year studios involved ongoing real-world projects, in which students studied topics such as data manipulation, cultural analysis and technology and typological analysis, allowing them to engage in real conditions by applying professional techniques and approaches. In the second year, which was organized with their input, students focused on the relationship between new production technologies and typologies, and participated in one of two research trajectories. The first investigated the use of generative algorithms and time-based models to establish new connections across architectural and urban scales, while the second explored new and existing large- and small-scale planning techniques in relation to actual planning and development situations.

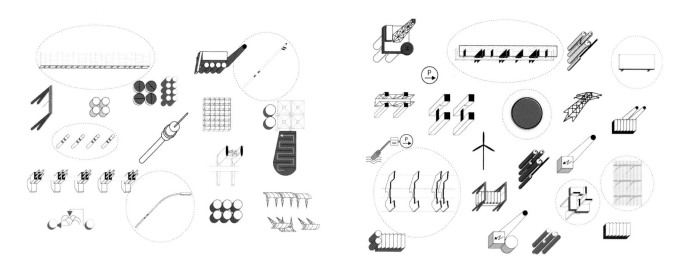

After finishing his five-year tenure, Zaera-Polo, together with the supervisory board, made the decision to increase the Berlage's institutional profile towards more research-orientated modes. A consequence of this was the rethinking of the institutional organization. In 2007, a new leadership structure was established, based around a research board. The first of these, with a term of three years, included Zaera-Polo, Ben van Berkel, Robert E. Somol and Elia Zenghelis; the second (2011–12) consisted of Jean-Louis Cohen and Nanne de Ru. Both boards were responsible for identifying new research trajectories and connecting their individual networks. In addition, board members engaged in one or more components of the programme: leading masterclasses, teaching studios and participating in presentations and other public events. Daily leadership was delegated to Vedran Mimica, who supervised the core staff, Pier Vittorio Aureli, Joachim Declerck, Martino Tattara, Roemer van Toorn, Peter Trummer and myself.

After several years of dormancy, the doctoral programme was revitalized in 2009 with a new three-year PhD programme entitled 'The City as a Project', supervised by Pier Vittorio Aureli and devoted to the study of how a city's form is theorized, represented and projected. Numerous other initiatives were launched, including a two-year design and research project on innovative housing proposals in Turkey; curating the third International Architecture Biennale Rotterdam; and a three-part research project on the creation of new knowledge spaces,

Ulrich Gradenegger, Parallel Deltaworks: The Territorial Boulevard of the Delta Metropolis, The Netherlands. The Delta: An Architecture for Four Ecologies (tutors: Kersten Geers, David van Severen), The Berlage, 2011

completed in collaboration with workplace services company Steelcase. But with the changing political landscape in the Netherlands and the global financial crisis, funding for cultural initiatives and institutions began to be radically cut in 2011, and after twenty-two successful years, in 2012 all governmental funding for the Berlage ceased.

Seeing an opportunity to continue and expand the school's tradition and reputation, the Faculty of Architecture and the Built Environment at Delft University of Technology took over responsibility. Continuing its original mission, the renamed Berlage Center for Advanced Studies in Architecture and Design developed a new educational programme that complements the existing faculty degree programmes, while at the same time keeping its innovative and distinct character. The Berlage's new three-term, eighteen-month programme focuses intensively on how architects and urban designers practise in a globalized world, concentrating on the complex development of the built environment within different physical and intellectual contexts.

Students develop specific tools, instruments and approaches, which allow them to act across cultural borders. Along with their tutors, they are asked to bring the experience of their local conditions to the programme to discuss and evaluate the work within a broader framework. At the same time, students take part in discussions with public authorities and private entities to learn about reality-based conditions and projects, expanding their knowledge of international practices, cultural institutions and universities. They also interact with an interdisciplinary team of research organizations, corporations, property developers and municipal planners, as well as scholars and professionals, giving them the opportunity to actively listen and react to various perspectives.

The result is a high degree of responsiveness to contemporary developments, around which, each year, the curriculum is organized according to defined themes. The idea is that operative research and design knowledge is more likely to emerge from direct engagement in analysing, projecting and transforming the built environment. The attention to real structures and processes, from social and cultural determinants to managerial and policy-related issues, is a trigger for innovative critical thinking and practice. Students start to place design-related concerns at the point of encounter between supra-disciplinary

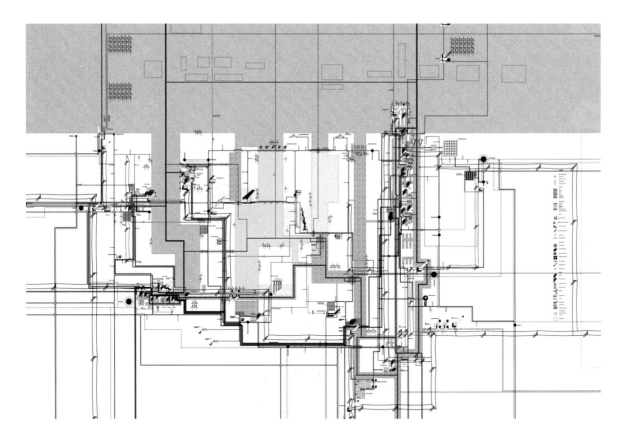

knowledge (economy, sociology, ecology) and sub-disciplinary
knowledge (planning, organization, representation, typology).

In the first term, 'Cultures, Methods and Instruments', students
are introduced to methods of advanced critical thinking and research,
historical and contemporary design instruments, and emerging
digital technologies and platforms. They engage in a broad range
of tools and topics, examining the relationship between architectural
thought and practice within different cultures and contexts. Intelligent
communication is developed as a tool for learning, research and design,
exploring how experimental mediums may frame academic work
for engagement with a broader public audience.

In the second term, 'Societies, Environments, and Economies',
students focus on societal, environmental and economic determinants
related to contemporary architecture and urban design, building on
the knowledge gained in the previous term. Within select architectural
and urban contexts, they develop advanced research methods, design
tools and theoretical approaches. In the third term, students culminate
their education by producing an individual research- and design-based
thesis project under a defined thematic framework, in which they are
encouraged to reflect, speculate and develop alternative models

Ulrich Gradenegger, Parallel
Deltaworks: The Territorial
Boulevard of the Delta
Metropolis, The Netherlands.
The Delta: An Architecture
for Four Ecologies (tutors:
Kersten Geers, David van
Severen), The Berlage, 2011

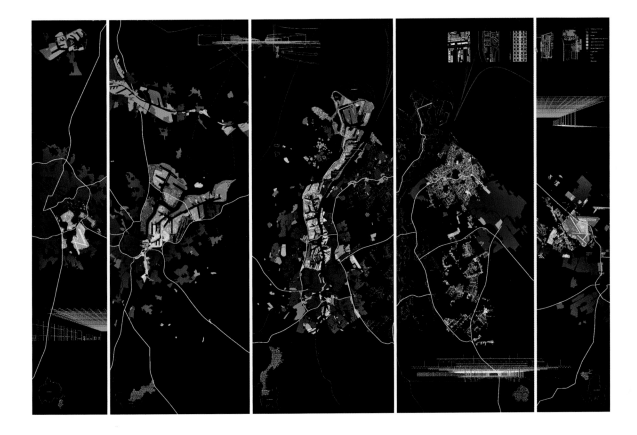

Sarah Nichols, The Gleaners: Additional Objects for a Very Crowded Table, Rotterdam. The Delta: An Architecture for Four Ecologies, The Berlage, 2011

and new insights into today's architectural and urban challenges, positioning themselves at the intersection of theory and practice.

The success of this educational model is strongly dependent on the Berlage's experimental setting, in which students work with an international teaching team composed of leading and emerging practitioners and scholars to foster collaboration and communication. Students learn to place themselves within a spectrum of global architectural practices and theories, allowing them to formulate a theoretical framework of their own. While the perspectives, practices and processes shaping the twenty-first-century built environment are ever more multifaceted and complex, the challenge for architectural education is much the same as it was in 1990: to equip the next generation of architects with a dynamic toolbox from which to construct alternative realities.

The mission of the Berlage, therefore, also remains the same: to provide students with conflicting viewpoints, differences of opinion, and contrasting stylistic and intellectual approaches in order to get them to think differently about the built environment.

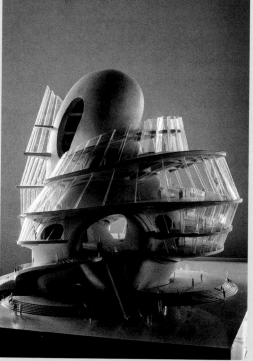

below
Martina Lesjak, Confluent
S(c)en(t)sations, Grasse,
France. Diploma thesis, Studio
Lynn, University of Applied
Arts Vienna, 2012

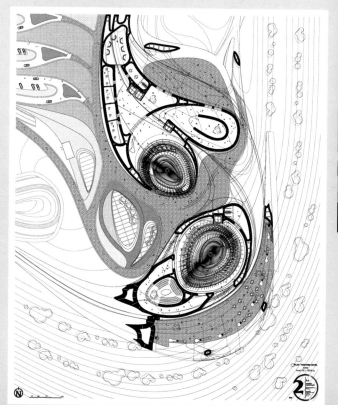

above
Sim Tuksam, Dim Sum
(A Vertical Restaurant),
Hong Kong. Diploma thesis,
Studio Lynn, University of
Applied Arts Vienna, 2013

opposite, top
Sebastian Kaus, Jules Verne
Foundation for Submarines
and Deep Sea Robotics,
Le Havre, France. Diploma
thesis, Studio Lynn, University
of Applied Arts Vienna, 2011

inscribe themselves into the discipline of architecture as a cultural
practice. The technical departments of structural design, energy design
and building construction provide platforms for integrating vision and
implementation. Technology, therefore, has the dual nature of being
both an inspiration and a reality check. A new experimental laboratory
for model-making probes emerging paradigms in printing and robotics;
here, students are not only taught to understand and use these new
technologies, but also encouraged to challenge them.

The architecture department is organized around the notion
of 'strategy', which implies anticipating things to come and making
decisions as to how to stay on top of them. As such, it respects
programme, but at the same time cultivates students as part of a
common cultural effort. Students learn to reread programme by deciding
what are relevant data for the problems at hand. They are taught how to
materially execute their proposals using state-of-the-art technologies
and production methods, but are made aware that architecture is a social
endeavour that must communicate with different audiences and serve
different interests. Strategy operates in a liquid field, where the roles of
stakeholders are constantly being revised. A successful and responsible
school must identify what ways the profession is transforming, and the
legitimate attitudes towards these developments.

right
Martina Lesjak, Confluent
S(c)en(t)sations, Grasse,
France. Diploma thesis, Studio
Lynn, University of Applied
Arts Vienna, 2012

To strengthen its profile as an advanced architectural institution, the school revised its curriculum from a five-year diploma to a three-year M.Arch programme. The majority of its graduates wish to become practising architects. Because of the requirement to have three years' experience in an architectural practice before legally qualifying as an architect, most go on to work in offices, but many self-organize into shared practices, starting out with small-scale jobs and slowly acquiring a portfolio. A growing number of graduates go into research and embark on PhDs. Students at the school are required to finish six projects in three years, embracing all of the knowledge on offer. Project 5 is a preparation for Project 6: the thesis. Of the studio leaders, Zaha Hadid is based in London, Greg Lynn in Los Angeles and Hani Rashid in New York, while Klaus Bollinger shares his time between Frankfurt and Vienna. Teaching is in English, and students come from all over the world. There is also an international series: the Sliver Lectures.

In 2005, the Institute of Architecture introduced the Urban Strategies Postgraduate Programme, a three-semester MSc.

above
Hessamedin Fana and Kaveh Najafian Razavi, Future Observatory, Gobi Desert, China. Deep Futures Expo: Prototypes for a Future City, Studio_Hani Rashid, University of Applied Arts Vienna, 2013

opposite
Sille Pihlak, HyperveloCITY Cultural Cluster, downtown Los Angeles. Diploma thesis, Studio_Hani Rashid, University of Applied Arts Vienna, 2012

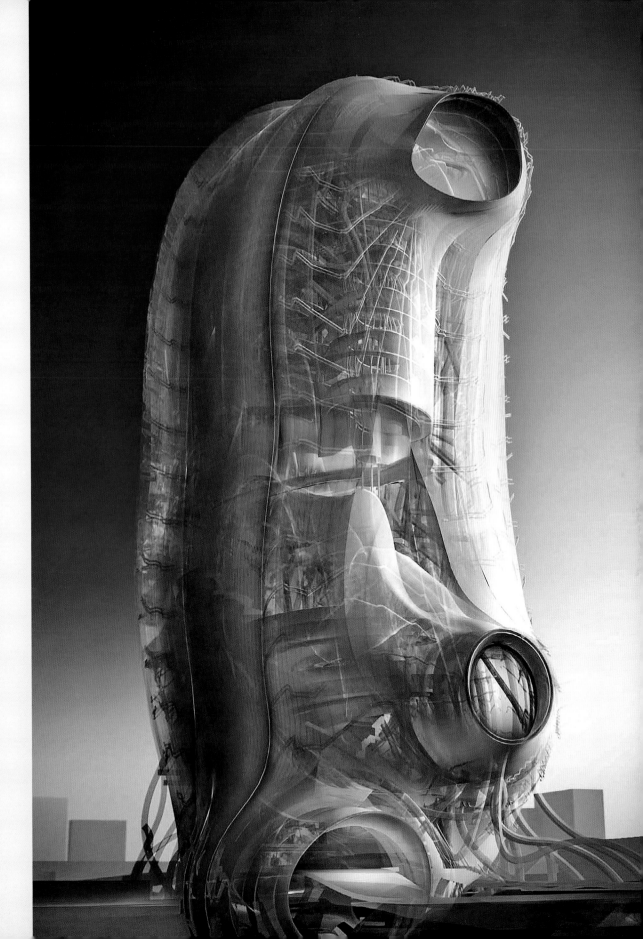

The two courses are 'Urban Technique', headed by Reiner Zettl, and 'Excessive', led by Hernan Diaz Alonso (pp. 264–70). The former deals with comprehensive urban models in a domain where urban and architectural logics overlap, as an ongoing research programme that covers various European cities in close collaboration with local institutions. The second focuses on the conditions for new sensibilities that affect existing architectural types, opening the door for new urban logics and atmospheres.

Kristina Rypáková, Blurred Hyphen, Central Station, Vienna. Diploma thesis, Studio_Hani Rashid, University of Applied Arts Vienna, 2012–13

Daniel Bolojan and Daniel
Zakharyan, Ubiquitous
Urbanism. Ubiquitous
Urbanism: Studio Zaha Hadid,
University of Applied Arts
Vienna, 2012

Martine Nicolay and Birgit
Schmidt, The Naked City.
Urban Laboratory London:
Studio Zaha Hadid, University
of Applied Arts Vienna, 2008

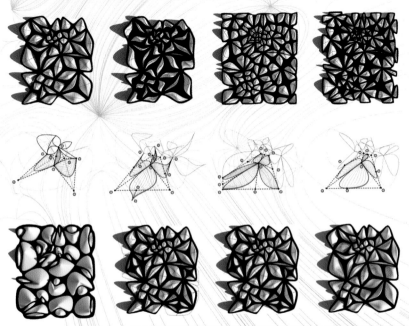

The question of questioning

– Hani Rashid, Director, Studio_Hani Rashid, University of Applied Arts Vienna

The studio programme under my leadership at the University of Applied Arts Vienna focuses primarily on students mastering conceptual spatial thinking, particularly while utilizing digital tools in all aspects of architectural creation, from design to fabrication. The studio critique and discourse looks at architecture as an object-driven pursuit, while also being an art and science discipline impacted by environmental, phenomenological, utilitarian and technological forces at play. For the most part, our experiments deal with the wide spectrum of spatiality in all of its guises, but particularly as defined by atmospheric and unexpected experiences and readings.

Andrea Sachse, Re:Trace Memory, Cologne, Germany. Diploma thesis, Studio_Hani Rashid, University of Applied Arts Vienna, 2012–13

The mandate for each student project, whether carried out individually or in small groups, is to uncover new, forward-thinking ideas that marry form, programme and being. Students are encouraged to consider all aspects of form- and space-making, and there is a large emphasis on model-making (digital and analogue), animation, graphics, rendering and theory. The work is linked by the students' shared explorations of 'engineered space' in a search for 'elegance', such as we might find in objects subjected to speed and movement, or the results of natural forces, time and environment. Coupled with 'induced interferences', such as atmospheric flux and optical distortion, this can create ambiguous architectural outcomes that hover between eloquent artistic expression and intelligent problem-solving.

Christoph Pehnelt, Urban Extraction, La Spezia, Italy. Diploma thesis, Studio_Hani Rashid, University of Applied Arts Vienna, 2012–13

Each project absorbs and responds to an important thematic – that of the city. Notions of urbanism and city space contextualize the projects, allowing them to operate within a larger and more pertinent conceptual and theoretical framework. When asked to engage with notions of the city and spatiality in this way, more powerful outcomes are realized. The results are often landscape-like, linking analogous structures and formal

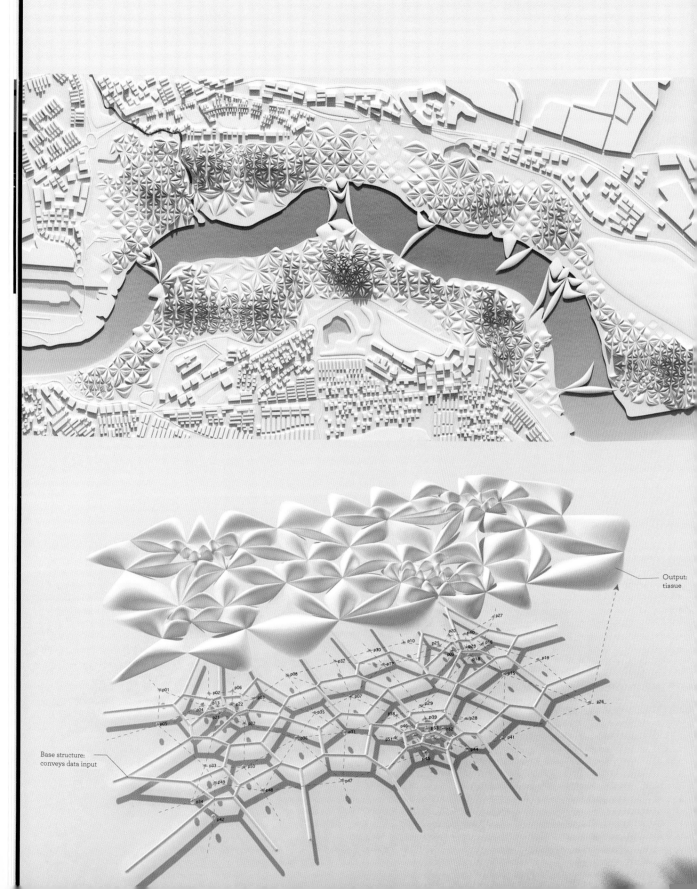

Output: tissue

Base structure: conveys data input

Kings, Queens and Broadways: Two projects for a new University of Applied Arts Vienna

– Wolfgang Tschapeller, Wolfgang Tschapeller ZT GmBH

In 2009, fellow tutor Titusz Tarnai and myself, together with our students, embarked on a quest for a new building at the University of Applied Arts. This took the form of a workshop, during which we attempted to identify how to best work together in a way that would allow all ten participants to maintain their independence during a joint project. We did not want a homogeneous building, but rather a multifaceted palimpsest of different subjective, autobiographical circumstances. We decided in favour of a cinematic project, in which ten animated sequences were inscribed on the building's rectangular format like a blurred and layered 'exquisite corpse'. The project was given the title 'Ten Ingredients for a New University of Applied Arts', and later 'School of Ten Atmospheres'. Each of the ten atmospheres represented a layer of the new school in a description that was not yet conceptualized, with each an elusive event.

A second version in 2012 was the winning entry in an international competition. The brief was not to create a new building, but to expand the existing Ferstel and Schwanzer-Wörle buildings in a way that would create more space for research and education. The driving force of the design was found by studying the history of the existing buildings. On 5 July 1957, we discovered, a meeting took place at the Austrian Ministry

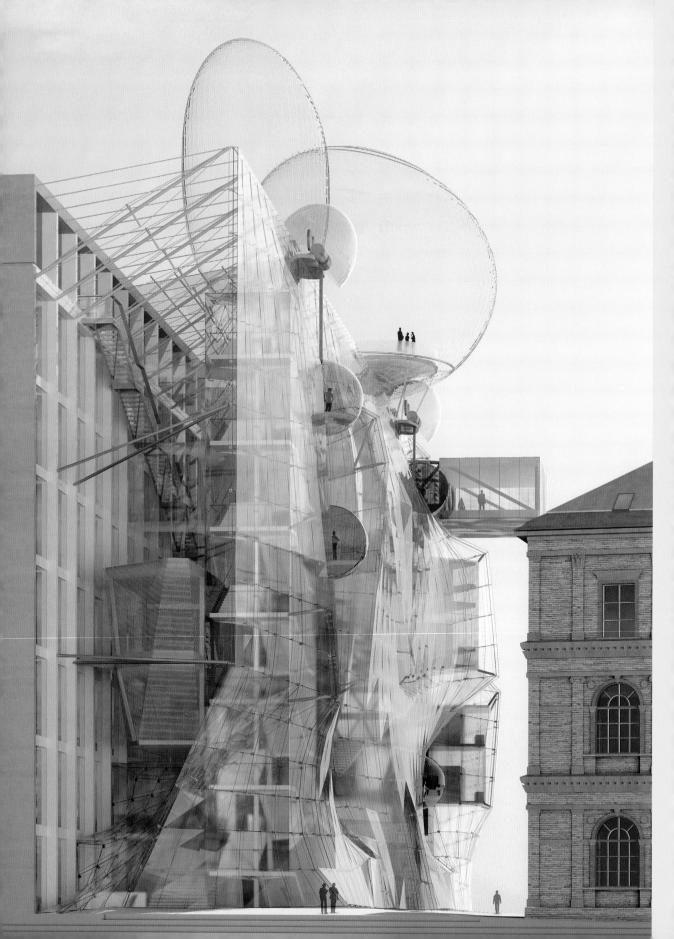

of Commerce in Vienna, during which the architect of the University of Applied Arts, Ceno Kosak, demanded that the architects of the new building, Karl Schwanzer and Eugen Wörle, make certain improvements. Kosak submitted a comprehensive and critical statement the following year, in which he demanded greater room depths and the elimination of an unnecessary central corridor.

Kosak demonstrated how he envisioned this implementation in a schematic drawing. The number (twenty-one) and length (3.9m, or 13 ft) of the axes would remain the same, but the two central rows of supports would be replaced by a single line within the central axis, which would open up the structure and introduce greater permeability, lightness and better utilization of the volume. Whether deliberate or not, Kosak's intervention exhibited a more progressive approach than Schwanzer and Wörle, along with Max Fellerer, had originally intended. Kosak's move was extremely interesting for us, as we were also seeking more space in the university's existing buildings, just as he had done fifty-four

Wolfgang Tschapeller ZT GmbH, New University of Applied Arts Vienna, 2012–

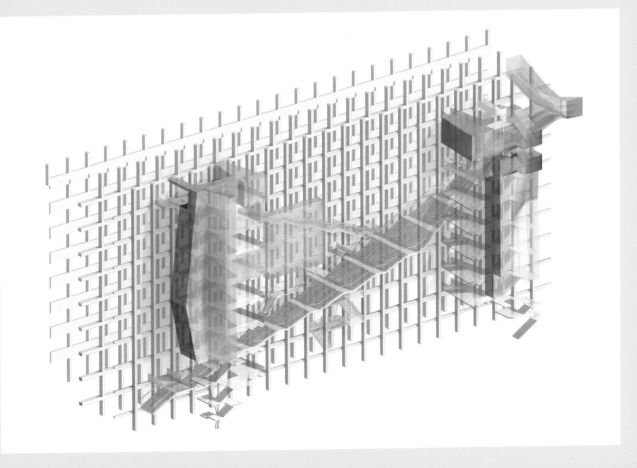

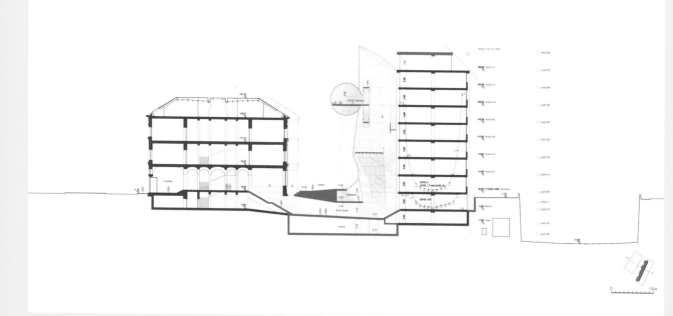

Wolfgang Tschapeller ZT
GmBH, New University of
Applied Arts Vienna, 2012–

years earlier. By eliminating the corridor, the space became a productive surface. This was not just an economic measure; it was much more far-reaching in that it disposed of the circulation areas as an architectural topos, turning a three-aisled building into a two-aisled one.

In 2012, we were sitting around the drafting table, as Wörle, Schwanzer and Kosak had done in 1958, and continuing their game. But we wanted to branch out from their ideas, and move the circulation areas that remained: removing the staircases and lift cores and freeing up the entire space for studios, workshops and laboratories. This provided usable floor space that already existed, and meant the circulation areas could be built somewhere else. Thus both brief and project changed: it was not usable floor space that needed to be added, but rather circulation-serving elements, or 'figures'. In addition to the necessary figures of the 'King' and 'Queen' (the lift and fire escape), a proposed third figure – the 'Broadway' – runs diagonally across the building grid. This spatial element engages the seventeen different studios of the school in dialogue; the disciplines are no longer separated.

The new figures – 'King', 'Queen' and 'Broadway' – are not set on the ground, but are structurally suspended from the now-empty framework of the Schwanzer-Wörle building. Combined with the surrounding membrane, a tension structure stretching between the floor and roof of the building transfers forces into this empty framework. The standing grid and hanging network of cables opens up a tension between the emptied building shelf and the play of figures. The project represents yet another change in attitude in the planning history of the building – no longer shifting and editing its structural grid, but instead creating a new relationship of forces, establishing new dependencies and adjusting zones of interaction, while simultaneously allowing the different construction components to engage with each other.

Here, we are participating in the history of revisions, erasures, extractions and additions, reaching back into the past, as if in a science-fiction film, to change the future – to move ahead.

Wolfgang Tschapeller ZT
GmbH, New University of
Applied Arts Vienna, 2012–

Towards new aesthetics and new culture: Architecture and landscape programmes at Peking University

– Kongjian Yu, Dean, School of Landscape Architecture, College of Architecture and Landscape Architecture, Peking University

Design disciplines at Peking University have a long and complex history. In 1928 the Beijing University School of Arts established its Department of Architecture, whose teachers had backgrounds in the French Beaux-Arts system; nineteen years later the department merged with the School of Engineering at PKU, marking the beginning of architectural education at the university. In 1952, as part of the national adjustment of universities, the Department of Architecture moved once again, to Tsinghua University, turning PKU into a pure research university for science and humanities, while Tsinghua became an institute of engineering and technology.

For the next forty-five years, the architecture and design disciplines were missing from PKU, and it was not until 1997, with the arrival of a leading faculty member from the US, that the Centre for Landscape Architecture and Planning established landscape architecture as a new profession in China. Defined as an 'art of survival', rather than one of ornamental craft, the landscape programme was initially located within the Department of Geography, but by 2003 had grown into an independent institute, the Graduate School of Landscape Architecture. The Centre of Architecture, established in 2000, also recruited US-

the slice alternative

A site of ten square kilometers was selected to test the possibilities of new urban development patterns based on EI. Three alternatives are proposed: the SLICE, GRID and WATER TOWN.

The slice alternative let the ecological services from the regional EI delivered through corridors and penetrate into the urban fabric just like vegetable layers in a sandwich.

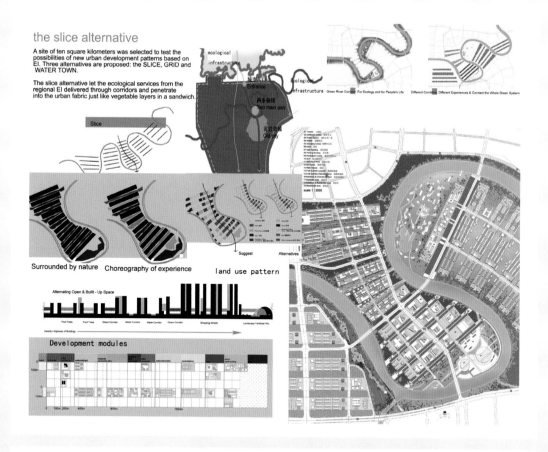

Surrounded by nature   Choreography of experience

land use pattern

Development modules

The grid alternative

Use a grid system of green in steady of roads to deliver the ecological services into the urban fabric

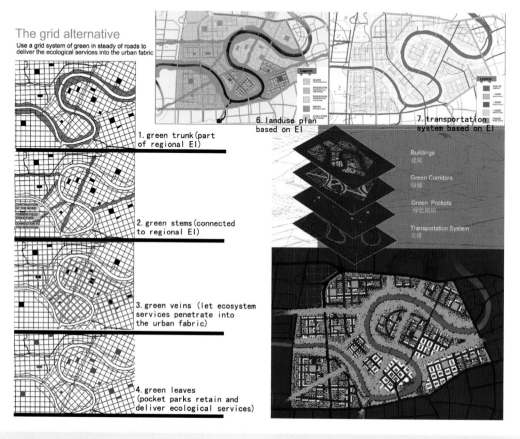

1. green trunk (part of regional EI)

2. green stems (connected to regional EI)

3. green veins (let ecosystem services penetrate into the urban fabric)

4. green leaves (pocket parks retain and deliver ecological services)

6. landuse plan based on EI

7. transportation system based on EI

Buildings 建筑

Green Corridors 绿廊

Green Pockets 绿色斑块

Transportation System 交通

Zhang Lei, Fang Wanli, Li
Chun Bo, Pei Dan, Huang
Gang, Wang Xiaoxio, Liu
Hailong, Li Wei, Jiang
Bing, Zong Zhisheng, Liu
Ming, Guo Linyun, Wang
Jiangwu, Zuu Qiang and Yang
Jiangni, Site-specific Urban
Development Alternatives
Based on Ecological
Infrastructure, Taizhou City,
Zhejiang Province, China.
Ecology-based Urban Design
Studio (tutors: Han Xili,
Antje Stockman, Li Dihua),
College of Architecture and
Landscape Architecture,
Peking University, 2003

educated faculty to restore the study of architecture. In 2010, the architecture and landscape architecture programmes merged to become the College of Architecture and Landscape Architecture.

CALA, as it is known, is now a graduate college with around two hundred students currently enrolled, including ten doctoral candidates. Though the history of the design discipline at PKU is long, its spirit remains young, and it is this youthful mindset that enables the programme to be devoted to innovation and exploration, passionate about learning and continually striving for constant improvement. Peking University was founded in 1898 during the Hundred Days' Reform, and the university was tasked with the mission of saving the country. In the same way, CALA was established to meet the challenges of contemporary China. Today, its mission is to meet four main challenges: unparalleled urbanization; human–land relationships; globalization and cultural identity; and finally, new ethics, new aesthetics and new life.

Unparalleled urbanization

With more than ten million new city-dwellers each year, it is estimated that within the next two decades 60 to 70 per cent of China's population will be living in cities. And with hundreds of new cities springing up throughout China, the countryside is experiencing unprecedented change. Such transformations have contributed to the importance of restoring the landscape, creating homes and establishing new systems of living. Design disciplines, therefore, need to be redefined. The task for us is to educate the new generation of designers who will be responsible for planning and designing the livable, beautiful cities of the future, for a country with an ever-increasing population (now 1.3 billion).

Human–land relationships

The pressures on human–land relationships, including the shortage of resources and environmental change, are also unprecedented. China has 20 per cent of the world's population, but only 8 per cent of its fresh water and 9 per cent of its farmland. Overdevelopment over the course of 5,000 years, and particularly intensive urban, infrastructural and industrial development in the past three decades, are having a serious impact on the landscape. How can the polluted soil that accounts for 10 per cent of the national territory, or the polluted water that accounts 75

Li Hailong, Wang Sisi, Xi Xuesong, Xu Man, Cheng Yin, Li Jin, Wang Shuang, Wang Meng and Li Yiran, The Ecological Security Pattern at the National Scale: China. National Ecological Security Pattern Planning Studio (tutors: Kongjian Yu, Li Dihua), College of Architecture and Landscape Architecture, Peking University, 2007–10

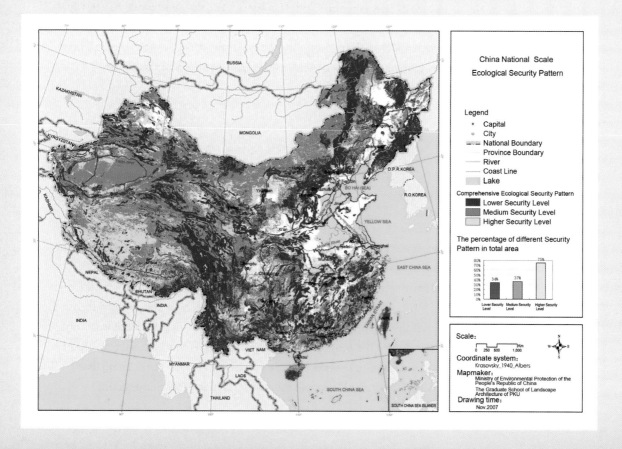

Implications of architectural education: Yesterday, today and tomorrow

- Li Xiaodong, Chair Professor, School of Architecture, Tsinghua University

Unlike Western countries, architectural education has a very short history in China, as architecture had never been seen as a discipline that required formal training. As with most other crafts, masters passed their knowledge of the art of building down the generations. But after the fall of the Qing dynasty in 1912, the emergence of a newly reformed economy forced a rethink of the country's educational structure. The turbulent political environment of the years that followed led to an unusual modernization process of both architecture and architectural education in China.

In the first phase of this reform, during the 1920s and '30s, many architecture students were sent to the US, where they were educated in the American Beaux-Arts system. Upon returning to China, they imparted their education in their own practice and teachings, encouraging widespread local acceptance of the Beaux-Arts ethos. Two figures who were instrumental in defining contemporary Chinese architectural education, Liang Sicheng and his wife Lin Huiyin, came from this background. After graduating from the University of Pennsylvania, they travelled across Europe to study its buildings, both historic and modern, and upon returning to China in 1928, they established Northeast University in Shenyang. Three years later, the growing threat of war from Japan forced the school to close. In the 1940s as the Chinese consultant for the design of the new UN Headquarters in New York, Liang saw the work of Oscar Niemeyer and Le Corbusier. After this encounter,

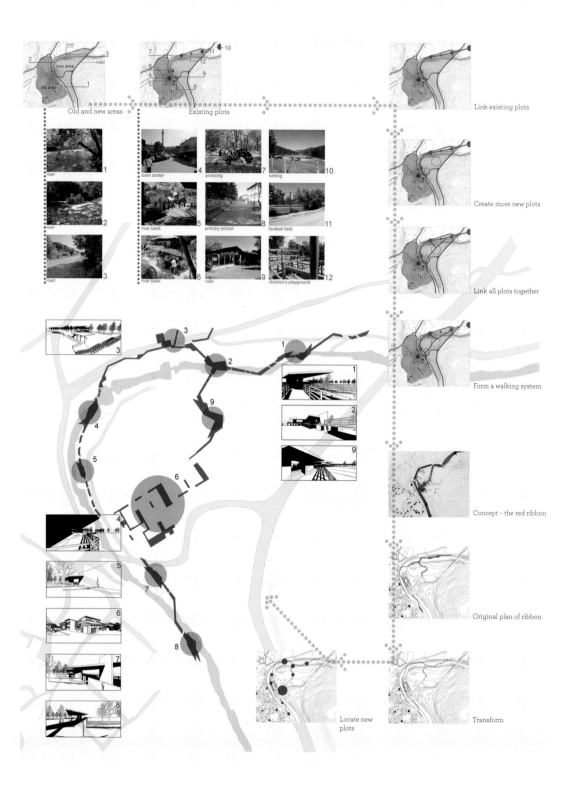

Old and new areas

Existing plots

Link existing plots

river
river
road

town center   picnicing   karting

river bank   primary school   football field

river bank   cafe   children's playground

Create more new plots

Link all plots together

Form a walking system

Concept – the red ribbon

Original plan of ribbon

Locate new plots

Transform

Liu Min and Wang Chong, Red Ribbon, Misi, Bursa, Turkey. School of Architecture, Tsinghua University, 2010

he began to propose the adoption of a 'physical environment' in place of the narrow definition of architecture as merely buildings, where humanity, technology and the arts would be integrated.

Such holistic design thinking was reflected in Liang's ideas for the new School of Architecture at Tsinghua University, which he founded in 1946 with an emphasis on social science, history and practical training in a conscious reflection of the Beaux-Arts tradition. But the ideologies of the school and the university have evolved over the years alongside wider changes in Chinese society. While the school was initially based on Liang's theories of physical environment, new models of integrated urbanization have been necessary since the further opening up of China in the 1980s. The school's co-founder, Wu Liangyong, developed his own theories on urban regeneration, architecture and the sciences of the human habitat. Concerned with nesting architecture within the wider development of cities and their respective regions, these theories are now the guiding principles of the school's curriculum.

Today, the school focuses on contributing to the integral processes that shape our living environment. Design tasks are treated as part of their respective environments, as the social, cultural and economic significance of architecture and architectural education becomes increasingly prominent in the development of larger regions. Continuing the lineage of such thinking and the link between craft and theory, the university combines critical academic learning with real-world issues that are emerging as a result of rapid urbanization. In contrast to much of contemporary architectural education, which can be highly formal or highly abstract, students are concerned with real projects and interventions. Within this process, the school is strengthening its identity as a pioneer of innovation, advanced research and design excellence. It attracts individuals who want to contribute, students and faculty who take into account the needs of contemporary society and set standards for others to build upon.

As part of a university-wide initiative, the aim of the School of Architecture is to engage in international dialogue by introducing joint studios and publications, as well as dual-degree tracks and a dedicated international programme. Design theory based on 'reflexive regionalism' continues to integrate a critical understanding of local conditions within a global, multidisciplinary network environment. This international profile works as a bridge between cultures within which various styles coexist and local achievements are shared. Through this programme, the discipline of architecture goes beyond the mere construction of objects to educating critical designers who think globally, act locally, and make a difference for the benefit of all.

The extraordinary scale and speed of urbanization in China mean that the example the country sets will have an impact on the living environments of people across the globe. At Tsinghua University, we are ready to take on this responsibility. Our current architecture curriculum includes a wide range of topics that will shape the future of Chinese living environments and human habitats in a global context. Within this framework, four main topics are proposed: ecological design, highlighted through such projects as the Solar Decathlon; urbanization and the development of sustainable cities; rural urbanization, sustainable development of the countryside and its areas for food production; and reflexive regionalism.

opposite
Wang Gutian, Infiltration, Beijing. School of Architecture, Tsinghua University, 2012

on p. 320
Liu Min and Wang Chong, Red Ribbon, Misi, Bursa, Turkey. School of Architecture, Tsinghua University, 2010

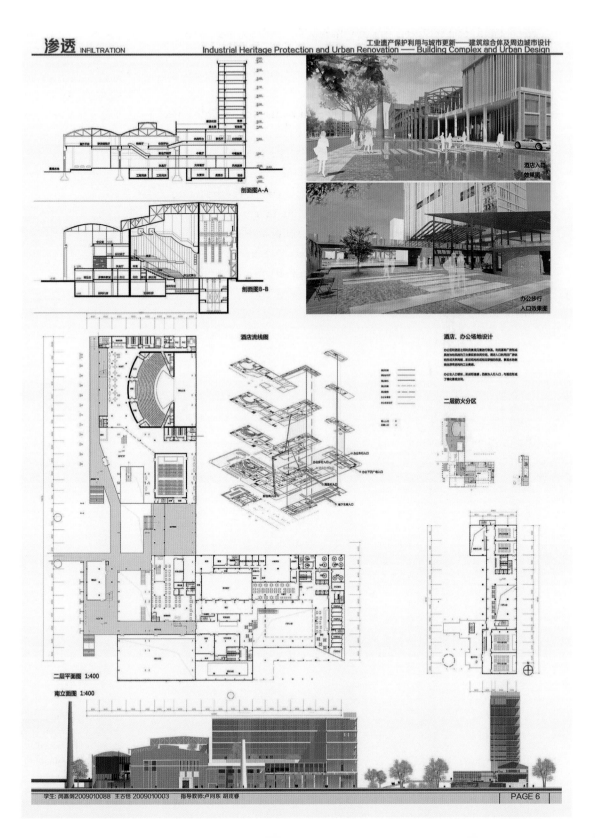

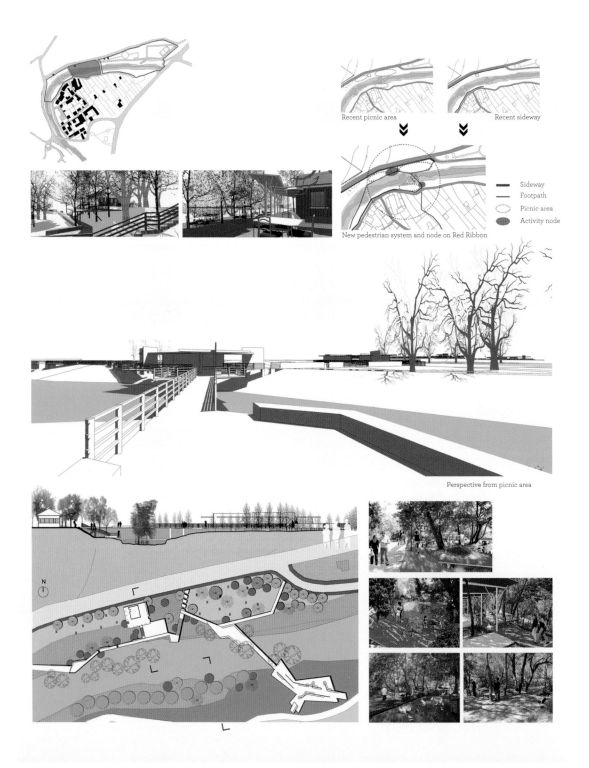

Recent picnic area

Recent sideway

New pedestrian system and node on Red Ribbon

Sideway
Footpath
Picnic area
Activity node

Perspective from picnic area

Sharp Centre for Design, Ontario College of Art and Design

– Will Alsop, founder, ALL Design

I have always played with architecture in a similar manner to artists playing with art. The act of fiddling is a preparation for things that might come in the future, but is relevant even if nothing happens. We absorb things through experience and doing, which is why cultural evolution is fundamentally piracy. The only thing that can take you, if you are lucky, beyond an assimilation of the known is playing, so when asked to design a school of art and design, where does one start?

I had to play, and encourage others to play. The evolution of a project, in many ways, *is* the project. The version of the building actually built is less important. I stated that I had no agenda, and that I would work with the students, staff and neighbours to explore what 'might be' in a creative way. Everyone is invited to write, draw, paint and talk with the express intention of making a noise through playing. The building had to come from an enjoyable process, because I knew that whatever was built, success could only come out of fun. To understand this, just look at the death machines of glass that we call hospitals. No joy, no fun; all risk, all death. (Note, too, how our architectural critics and journalists have connived in creating a world of dangerous boredom with the excuse of dealing with anxiety measures. Irresponsible!)

My workshops produced a lot of paper and ideas (noise). I have often done this, and have met many types, but essentially there are two types: Type A – 'Hey! I want to enjoy and contribute'; and Type B – 'I have a right to demand what I want and you have to listen. People with other views that don't align with mine can go and f*** themselves.'

Alsop Architects, Sharp
Centre for Design, Ontario
College of Art and Design,
Toronto, 2004

Out of these sessions came an idea that the building should not be
on the site originally intended for it, because the site could become
an extension of the existing park and make a valuable link between
McCaul Street and verdant pastures.

Question: Where could the building be?

Answer: Flying over the existing building, as well as the park.

The height was determined by the condominium-block roof (nine
storeys) in order to protect their views of said park. We would build a
flying box. Through the process we also learned that the internal space
should be robust, flexible, under-designed, friendly and cosy. I think
we suspected all of that, but the site change was still out of the blue.

A flying box

In my private playtime I had been hanging objects in space. From
this exercise, I learned that the simpler the object, the more effective
the experience. I knew that a simple rectilinear form, hung by piano
wire, created a void in space that was almost a negative. I admit that
I did have a preconception, but only after the process had suggested
'something' in the air. Hoisted on my own preconception – fair cop.

The building has now been standing for nearly ten years and has
been very successful. People enjoy using it, and the neighbours like it
very much. It increased the number of students applying to study at the
OCAD by 300 per cent in one year, and increased tourist numbers to
downtown Toronto by 2.9 per cent. It is a loved building, and because
of that, in part, the students are happy.

Having built it, we learn from it. For example, it is possible to leave
existing buildings, even if from an architectural point of view they are
indifferent. This has huge implications if we seriously consider the
advantages of evolutionism. People live with an altered familiarity.

Because the building is ultra-functional and yet looks unusual,
it works on many different levels. Students of art and architecture, and
people in general, are attracted to and want to feel part of what is new
and fresh. We created a place that inspires and has nothing to do with
context or many other normal architectural considerations. The world
of education should inspire through example, and I think the users
respond to the building in a very positive way.

I am proud of it.

Alsop Architects, Sharp
Centre for Design, Ontario
College of Art and Design,
Toronto, 2004

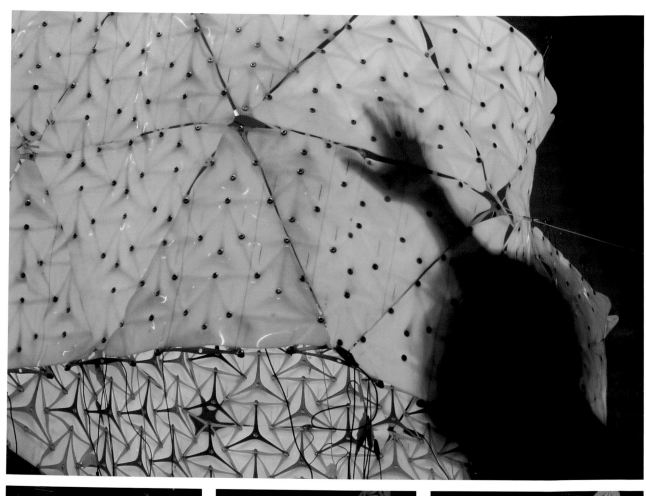

Chin Koi Khoo, Morphing
Architecture with Responsive
Material Systems. Spatial
Information Architecture
Laboratory, RMIT University,
2013

Dermoid III, exhibited as part
of the *Convergence* exhibition,
Design Hub, RMIT University.
Spatial Information
Architecture Laboratory,
RMIT University; and Berlin
University of the Arts, 2013

NOTES

40 Alvin's AA: A panorama
Peter L. Wilson

1. 'A Homage to Alvin', in Robin Middleton, ed., *Architectural Associations: The Idea of the City* (London, 1996), p. 225.
2. Alvin Boyarsky, introduction, in *Themes 4: People in Architecture* (London, 1983), p. 6.
3. Dalibor Vesely, in *Themes 4: People in Architecture,* p. 7.
4. Peter Cook, '2013 Gold Medal: Discriminating Shapes', *Architecture AU* (March/April 2013):78.

50 Architectural anti-realism: The AA School in 2013
Brett Steele

1. Anaïs Nin, *Henry and June: From A Journal of Love: The Unexpurgated Diary of Anaïs Nin, 1931–1932* (Boston, Massachusetts, 1986), p. 354.
2. Mark Rakatansky, 'Fabricators', in *Tectonic Acts of Desire and Doubt* (London, 2012), p. 12.
3. Jean Cocteau, *The Difficulty of Being* (1947; Brooklyn, New York, 2013), p. 12.
4. For an extended discussion about the perils and potentials of contemporary architectural pedagogies, see Brett Steele, 'The Key Project of the Architectural School Today is the Making of Audiences, Not Architects', in *Log* 28: *Stocktaking* (Summer 2013):87–98.
5. Thomas Hardy, *Tess of the D'Urbervilles* (1891; London, 2003), p. 49.
6. J. G. Ballard, *Cocaine Nights* (1996; London, 2012), p. 192.

92 Convergence: Architecture as integrated spatial design
Nic Clear

1. Vitruvius, *Ten Books on Architecture*, trans. Morris Hickey Morgan (Project Gutenberg, 2006), gutenberg.org/files/20239/20239-h/29239-h.htm.
2. Edgar Dale, *Audiovisual Methods in Teaching* (New York, 1969).
3. Keiichi Matsuda, *Augmented(hyper)Reality: Domestic Robocop* (2010); keiichimatsuda.com; Kibwe Tavares, *Robots of Brixton* (2011); factoryfifteen.com.

102 Design animated: Unit 15
Nic Clear

1. Paul Virilio, *The Aesthetics of Disappearance*, trans. Philip Beitchman (New York, 1991), p. 65.
2. Nic Clear, 'Drawing Time', in 'Drawing Architecture', special issue, *Architectural Design* 275 (September/October 2013):70–9.
3. Darko Suvin, 'On the Poetics and History of the Science Fiction Genre', in *College English* 34:3 (December 1972):372–82.
4. Nic Clear, 'Architecture', in Rob Latham, ed., *Oxford Handbook of Science Fiction* (Oxford, 2014).
5. Fredric Jameson, *Postmodernism: The Cultural Logic of Late Capitalism* (Durham, North Carolina, 1991).
6. Fredric Jameson, *Archaeologies of the Future: The Desire Called Utopia and Other Science Fictions* (London and New York, 2005).

109 A user's guide to the anthropocene (a short passage through a brief moment in time)
Simon Herron

1. Dr Carl Sagan of Cornell University chaired the NASA contents committee for the Golden Record phonographic disc of sounds, images and writings from earth on board Voyager 1. This was later chronicled in Sagan's *Murmurs of Earth: The Voyager Interstellar Record* (1978).
2. See Paul Crutzen and Eugene F. Stoermer, 'The Anthropocene', in *International Geosphere-Biosphere Programme: A Study of Global Change of the International Council for Science* 41 (May 2000):17. The thesis is currently awaiting the ruling of the International Subcommission on Stratigraphic Classification.
3. Buckminster Fuller, 'The Year 2000', in '2000+', special issue, *Architectural Design* (February 1967):60–3. The article was a freely edited version of a lecture given at San Jose State College, California, in 1966.
4. Economist Nikolai Kondratiev, founder and director of the Institute of Conjecture, Moscow (1920–8), developed a theory of economic long cycles that provoked, or were provoked by, technological change and social upheavals: K1 (1780–1830), steam, clothing; K2 (1830–80), rail and steel, mass transport; K3 (1880–1930), electricity and chemical mass production; K4 (1930–70), cars, petrochemicals, individual mobility; K5 (1970–2010), information and communications technology.
5. Reyner Banham, 'The Man-Mauled Desert', in Richard Misrach, *Desert Cantos* (Albuquerque, New Mexico, 1987).
6. A facsimile of the original newsletter was produced by the Centre for Land Use Interpretation, which also produces *The Nevada Test Site: A Guide to America's Nuclear Proving Ground (1996)*.
7. The film was produced in collaboration with the National Paint Varnish and Lacquer Association, under the umbrella of the National Clean Up-Paint Up-Fix Up Bureau, with the cooperation and support of the Federal Civil Defense Administration.
8. See Tom Vanderbilt, *Survival City: Adventures Amongst the Ruins of Atomic America* (Princeton, New Jersey, 2002).
9. Herman Kahn, 'Some Possible Sizes and Shapes of Thermonuclear War', in *Thinking About the Unthinkable* (New York, 1962).
10. See Julia Brown, ed., *Michael Heizer: Sculpture in Reverse* (Los Angeles, 1984).
11. Nancy Holt, ed., *The Writings of Robert Smithson* (New York, 1979).
12. Adam Roberts, *Yellow Blue Tibia* (London, 2010). The original source is unclear, but H. G. Wells interviewed Lenin in 1920, documented in Wells's book *Russia in the Shadows* (1921).

128 Working the realities of landscape
Ed Wall

1. Elizabeth Meyer, 'Site Citations', in Carol Burns and Andrea Kahn, *Site Matters* (New York, 2005), p. 94.
2. Henri Lefebvre, *The Production of Space* (Oxford, 1991), p. 189.
3. James Corner, *Recovering Landscape: Essays in Contemporary Landscape Architecture* (New York, 1999).
4. Greater London Authority, *All London Green Grid Supplementary Planning Guidance*, March 2012; london.gov.uk/priorities/environment/greening-

london/improving-londons-parks-green-spaces/ all-london-green-grid; *East London Green Grid*, February 2008; legacy.london.gov.uk/mayor/ strategies/sds/docs/spg-east-lon-green-grid-08. pdf.

5. Peter Beard, 'Slack Nature and Working Wild', in Greater London Authority, *East London Green Grid Primer*, November 2006; legacy.london.gov. uk/mayor/auu/docs/elgg-primer.pdf.

6. James Corner, 'Terra Fluxus', in Charles Waldheim, ed., *The Landscape Urbanism Reader* (New York, 2006), p. 31.

7. Beard, op cit, pp. 6–7.

8. Field Operations, et al, *Fresh Kills Park: Lifescape*, The City of New York and New York City Department of City Planning, 2006; nyc.gov/ html/dcp/pdf/fkl/dmp.pdf.

9. Guy Nordenson, Catherine Seavitt and Adam Yarinsky, *On the Water: Palisade Bay* (Ostfildern, Germany, 2010); Guy Nordenson and Catherine Seavitt, 'High Stakes: Soft Infrastructure for the Rising Seas', in Barry Bergdoll, ed., *Rising Currents* (New York, 2011), p. 46.

10. Lefebvre, op cit.

11. Corner, *Recovering Landscape*, op cit, p. 158.

145 The imaginarium of urban futures
C. J. Lim

1. David Crystal, 'Moving Words', BBC; bbc.co.uk/ worldservice/learningenglish/movingwords.

2. Charles Jencks, *The Architecture of the Jumping Universe* (London, 1997).

3. Robert Hughes, *The Shock of the New: Art and the Century of Change* (New York, 1980).

4. J. G. Ballard, 'Kaleidoscope' (1987), in *Science Fiction Writers*, audio CD (London, 2011).

154 Audacious encounters
Nigel Coates

1. Italo Calvino, *Invisible Cities*, trans. W. Weaver (London, 1974); first published as *Le città invisibili* (Turin, 1972), p 164.

2. Catrina Beevor, Martin Benson, Nigel Coates, Peter Fleissig, Christina Norton, Robert Mull, Mark Prizeman, Melanie Sainsbury, Carlos Villanueva.

3. Brian Hatton, 'Configuring Mercurius: Capriccio', in Nigel Coates, *ArkAlbion and Six Other Projects* (London, 1984), p. 4.

4. Mark Prizeman and Carlos Villanueva formed their own practices; Robert Mull became Dean of Architecture and Fine Art at London Metropolitan University; Christina Norton formed Fluid Architects; Peter Thomas and Cathi du Toit founded 51% Studios; Amanda Levete was a founding partner of Future Systems and is now principal of AL_A.

5. Payam Sharifi became an artist and philosopher; three graduates formed the AOC architectural design and research agency; Finn Williams formed Common Office; Vincent Lacarova runs the planning department at Croydon; Carl Turner founded his own practice; Aberrant Architecture set themselves up as a cultural architectural project; Charlie Luxton became an architecture presenter for Channel 4; Will Hunter is deputy editor of *Architectural Review*; and Oliver Wainwright is architectural editor of the *Guardian newspaper*.

6. Isabel Allen, Peter Buchanan, Nigel Coates, Niall Hobhouse, Tom Holbrook, Crispin Kelly, Lewis Kinneir, Niall McLaughlin, Deborah Saunt, James Soane, Will Hunter.

166 School of thought
Mark Morris

1. Alexander Caragonne, *The Texas Rangers: Notes from an Architectural Underground* (Cambridge, Massachusetts, 1995), p. 17.

2. Caragonne's use of the word 'Shinto' focuses on its characteristic pluralism and lack of singular dogma.

3. Rowe's influence on American architectural education is reviewed in the university's Faculty Memorial Statement: 'His presence at Cornell over more than three decades has directly inspired hundreds of architects, and through them, indirectly inspired thousands of other architects, and unaccountable numbers of individuals who have wandered, with eyes and minds, through the prodigious spaces engendered by Colin's scions. No one has built more for as many.' Jerry Wells and Val Warke, *Colin Frederick Rowe*, faculty

memorial statement (1999); ecommons.library. cornell.edu/bitstream/1813/17882/1/Colin_ Frederick_Rowe_1999.pdf.

4. Kazys Varnelis, 'The Education of the Innocent Eye', in *Journal of Architectural Education* (May 1998):212.

5. Herbert Muschamp, 'Colin Rowe, Architecture Professor, Dies at 79', in *The New York Times*, 8 November 1999, p. B10.

6. Vanessa Quirk, 'The 100 Largest Architecture Firms in the World', 11 February 2013; archdaily. com/the-100-largest-architecture-firms-in-the-world. In 2012 *Building Design* published a list of the 'most admired' architecture firms (Foster + Partners, Renzo Piano Building Workshop, Herzog & de Meuron, Gensler, Rogers Stirk Harbour & Partners and Zaha Hadid Architects) as part of its more extensive survey of the world's largest offices.

7. Meghan Casserly, 'The Secret Power of the Generalist and How They Will Rule the World', *Forbes Online*, 10 July 2012; forbes.com/sites/ meghancasserly/2012/07/10/the-secret-power-of-the-generalist-and-how-theyll-rule-the-future.

8. US studios dominate the curriculum, yet they are more mutable than UK studios in terms of 'culture'. Most of their design faculty do not teach the same studios over and over again, but shift around as a matter of routine, and many advanced studios are taught by guest critics or noted architects teamed with faculty as one-off studio offerings. In the UK, however, studio units are often wedded to specific faculty and driven by their pedagogical and research outlook. Saying which unit you are in says quite a bit about your academic life and preoccupations. The physical space of US studios is generally subdivided into sections or classes, but many programmes (including Harvard, UCLA and Cornell) feature collective spaces intended to foster cross-studio dialogue. Studio culture is not created in any particular studio section, but held as the sum of all studios in the collective space. It is only partially moulded during classroom hours; much of studio life is nurtured during late-night sessions to meet deadlines, sustained by food, music and gossip. The identity of any given UK school is more federated, more down to the units and their leadership, and less about the physical space of a studio or its nocturnal goings-on.

9. Marina Warner, BBC2, 1987.

183 BLENDscapes: In support of a new era of transdisciplinary exchange in architecture
Evan Douglis

1. Mae Jemison, 'Teach Arts and Sciences Together', TED (2002); ted.com/talks/mae_jemison_on_ teaching_arts_and_sciences_together.html.

2. Anna Dyson; case.rpi.edu.

326 Making a difference: Embedding academic research in practice
Mark Burry

1. See Horst Rittel and Melvin Webber, 'Dilemmas in a General Theory of Planning', in *Policy Sciences* 4 (1973):155–69; repr. in Nigel Cross, ed., *Developments in Design Methodology* (Chichester, 1984), pp. 135–44.

2. Leon van Schaik continues to develop and lead this innovative research stream, core to the school's philosophy. Together with the current Dean, Richard Blythe, he has evolved the Graduate Research Conference into the international Practice Research Symposium, a leading partner in the EU Framework 7 'Marie Curie' ITN-funded PhD project.

5. Australian research funding and the recently introduced Excellence in Australian Research (aspects of which are modelled closely on the UK's equivalent Research Assessment Exercise) are highly orientated to discrete disciplines identified as FORs (fields of research, or disciplines).

BIBLIO-GRAPHY

Ballard, J. G., *Cocaine Nights* (1996; London, 2012).

————, 'Kaleidoscope' (1987), in *Science Fiction Writers*, audio CD (London, 2011).

Banham, Reyner, 'The Man-Mauled Desert', in Richard Misrach, *Desert Cantos* (Albuquerque, New Mexico, 1987).

Beard, Peter, 'Slack Nature and Working Wild', *East London Green Grid Primer*, Greater London Authority, November 2006; legacy.london.gov.uk/mayor/auu/green-grid.jsp.

Bellamy, Edward, *Looking Backward: 2000–1887* (New York, 1888).

Boyarsky, Alvin, introduction, in *Themes 4: People in Architecture* (London, 1983).

Brown, Julia, ed., *Michael Heizer: Sculpture in Reverse* (Los Angeles, 1984).

Bryant, Peter, *Red Alert* (1958).

Calvino, Italo, *Invisible Cities*, trans. W. Weaver (London, 1974); first published as *Le città invisibili* (Turin, 1972).

Caragonne, Alexander, *The Texas Rangers: Notes from an Architectural Underground* (Cambridge, Massachusetts, 1995).

Casserly, Meghan, 'The Secret Power of the Generalist and How They Will Rule the World', *Forbes Online*, 10 July 2012: forbes.com/sites/meghancasserly/2012/07/10/the-secret-power-of-the-generalist-and-how-theyll-rule-the-future.

Clear, Nic, 'Architecture', in Rob Latham, ed., *Oxford Handbook of Science Fiction* (Oxford, 2014).

————, 'Drawing Time', in 'Drawing Architecture', special issue, *Architectural Design* 275 (September/October 2013):70–9.

Cocteau, Jean, *The Difficulty of Being* (1947; Brooklyn, New York, 2013).

Cook, Peter, '2013 Gold Medal: Discriminating Shapes', in *Architecture AU* (March/April 2013).

Corner, James, *Recovering Landscape: Essays in Contemporary Landscape Architecture* (New York, 1999).

————, 'Terra Fluxus', in Charles Waldheim, ed., *The Landscape Urbanism Reader* (New York, 2006).

Crutzen, Paul, and Eugene F. Stoermer, 'The Anthropocene', in *International Geosphere–Biosphere Programme: A Study of Global Change of the International Council for Science* 41 (May 2000):17.

Crystal, David, 'Moving Words', BBC; bbc.co.uk/worldservice/learningenglish/movingwords.

Dale, Edgar, *Audiovisual Methods in Teaching* (New York, 1969).

Dyson, Anna, case.rpi.edu/CASE.html.

Field Operations, et al, *Fresh Kills Park: Lifescape*, The City of New York and New York City Department of City Planning, 2006; nyc.gov/html/dcp/pdf/fkl/dmp.pdf.

Fuller, Buckminster, 'The Year 2000', in '2000+', special issue, *Architectural Design* (February 1967):60–3.

Greater London Authority, *All London Green Grid Supplementary Planning Guidance*, March 2012; london.gov.uk/priorities/planning/publications/all-london-green-grid-spg.

————, *East London Green Grid*, February 2008; legacy.london.gov.uk/mayor/strategies/sds/docs/spg-east-lon-green-grid-08.pdf.

Hardy, Thomas, *Tess of the D'Urbervilles* (1891; London, 2003), p. 49.

Hatton, Brian, 'Configuring Mercurius: Capriccio', in Nigel Coates, *ArkAlbion and Six Other Projects* (London, 1984).

Holt, Nancy, ed., *The Writings of Robert Smithson* (New York, 1979).

Hughes, Robert, *The Shock of the New: Art and the Century of Change* (New York, 1980).

Jameson, Fredric, *Archaeologies of the Future: The Desire Called Utopia and Other Science Fictions* (London and New York, 2005).

————, *Postmodernism: The Cultural Logic of Late Capitalism* (Durham, North Carolina, 1991).

Jemison, Mae, 'Teach Arts and Sciences Together', TED (2002); ted.com/talks/mae_jemison_on_teaching_arts_and_sciences_together.html.

Jencks, Charles, *The Architecture of the Jumping Universe* (London, 1997).

Kahn, Herman, 'Some Possible Sizes and Shapes of Thermonuclear War', in *Thinking About the Unthinkable* (New York, 1962).

Kapfinger, Otto, and Matthias Boeckl, *Abgelehnt, nicht ausgeführt. Die Bau- und Projektgeschichte der Hochschule für Angewandte Kunst in Wien 1873–1993* (Vienna, 1993).

Lefebvre, Henri, *The Production of Space* (Oxford, 1991).

McHale, John, *The Ecological Context* (New York, 1971).

Matsuda, Keiichi, *Augmented(hyper)Reality: Domestic Robocop* (2010); keiichimatsuda.com.

Melly, George, *Paris and the Surrealists* (London, 1991).

Meyer, Elizabeth, 'Site Citations', in Carol Burns and Andrea Kahn, *Site Matters* (New York, 2005).

Middleton, Robin, ed., 'A Homage to Alvin', in *Architectural Associations: The Idea of the City* (Cambridge, Massachusetts, 1996).

Muschamp, Herbert, 'Colin Rowe, Architecture Professor, Dies at 79', in *The New York Times*, 8 November 1999, p. B10.

Nin, Anaïs, *Fire: From 'A Journal of Love' the Unexpurgated Diary of Anaïs Nin, 1934–1937* (Boston, Massachusetts, 1996).

Nordenson, Guy, and Catherine Seavitt, 'High Stakes: Soft Infrastructure for the Rising Seas', in Barry Bergdoll, ed., *Rising Currents* (New York, 2011).

Nordenson, Guy, Catherine Seavitt and Adam Yarinsky, *On the Water: Palisade Bay* (Ostfildern, Germany, 2010).

Quirk, Vanessa, 'The 100 Largest Architecture Firms in the World', 11 February 2013: archdaily.com/the-100-largest-architecture-firms-in-the-world.

Rakatansky, Mark, 'Fabricators', in *Tectonic Acts of Desire and Doubt* (London, 2012).

Rittel, Horst, and Melvin Webber, 'Dilemmas in a General Theory of Planning', in *Policy Sciences* 4 (1973):155–69; repr. in Nigel Cross, ed., *Developments in Design Methodology* (Chichester, 1984).

Roberts, Adam, *Yellow Blue Tibia* (London, 2010).

Rowe, Frederick, *The Architecture of Good Intentions* (1994).

————, *The Mathematics of the Ideal Villa and Other Essays* (1976).

Rowe, Frederick, and Alexander Caragonne, eds, *As I Was Saying* (1996).

Rowe, Frederick, and Fred Koetter, *Collage City* (1978).

Sagan, Carl, *Murmurs of Earth: The Voyager Interstellar Record* (1978).

Steele, Brett, 'The Key Project of the Architectural School Today is the Making of Audiences, Not Architects', in *Log* 28: *Stocktaking* (Summer 2013):87–98.

Suvin, Darko, 'On the Poetics and History of the Science Fiction Genre', in *College English* 34:3 (December 1972):372–82.

Tavares, Kibwe, *Robots of Brixton* (2011); factoryfifteen.com.

————, *Jonah* (2013); film4.com/reviews/2013/jonah.

'Top Five Most Admired Architecture Firms', *Building Design* (2012).

Vanderbilt, Tom, *Survival City: Adventures Amongst the Ruins of Atomic America* (Princeton, New Jersey, 2002).

Varnelis, Kazys, 'The Education of the Innocent Eye', in *Journal of Architectural Education* (May 1998):212.

Vesely, Dalibor, in *Themes 4: People in Architecture* (London, 1983).

Virilio, Paul, *The Aesthetics of Disappearance*, trans. Philip Beitchman (New York, 1991).

Vitruvius, *Ten Books on Architecture*, trans. Morris Hickey Morgan (Project Gutenberg, 2006), gutenberg.org/files/20239/20239-h/29239-h.htm

Wells, H. G., *Russia in the Shadows* (New York, 1921).

Wells, Jerry, and Val Warke, *Colin Frederick Rowe*, faculty memorial statement (1999); ecommons. library.cornell.edu/bitstream/1813/17882/1/Colin_ Frederick_Rowe_1999.pdf.

BIOGRAPHIES

Mike Aling is Design Coordinator of the Diploma in Architecture programme at the Department of Architecture and Landscape, University of Greenwich, where he co-runs the Diploma/MSc Unit 15 with Nic Clear and Simon Withers. He is also a member of the university's AVATAR group, and is coordinator of AVATAR publications. Aling previously worked for a number of architecture practices across London.

Will Alsop is a prominent architect whose practice, ALL Design, is an international operation guided by the principle that architecture is a vehicle for and symbol of social change and renewal. The iconic Glenwood Power Plant in Yonkers, New York, and the Sharp Centre for Design, Ontario College of Art and Design (p. 321) are just two of many designs that have established Alsop as a visionary in his field.

Klaus Bollinger is Dean of the Institute of Architecture at the University of Applied Arts Vienna. He previously taught at Dortmund University, and studied civil engineering at the Technical University Darmstadt. In 1983, with Manfred Grohmann, he established the architectural practice Bollinger + Grohmann, with offices in Frankfurt, Berlin, Vienna, Paris, Oslo and Melbourne.

Mark Burry is a practising architect, and has published internationally on the life and work of Antoni Gaudí. He has been Senior Architect at Sagrada Família, Barcelona, since 1979, and was the Founding Director of the Spatial Information Architecture Laboratory, a transdisciplinary research environment dedicated to contemporary spatial design activity. Burry is Director of the Design Research Institute, RMIT University.

Nic Clear is Head of the Department of Architecture and Landscape, University of Greenwich, where he teaches Unit 15, which specializes in the use of film and animation to generate and represent architectural spaces. He was guest-editor of the *AD* issue *Architectures of the Near Future* (2009), and has contributed to the *Oxford Handbook of Science Fiction*.

Nigel Coates is an architect, designer and educator. He trained and taught at the Architectural Association School of Architecture and founded the avant-garde NATO group in 1983. His experimental work has been shown at the Venice Architecture Biennale, Tate Modern and the Milan Triennale. His books include *Guide to Ecstacity* (2003) and *Narrative Architecture* (2012). Coates was head of the Department of Architecture, Royal College of Art (1995–2011), and is currently RCA Professor Emeritus. In 2012 he received the Annie Spink Award for excellence in architectural education.

Sir Peter Cook is a notable architect, lecturer and author. He is a founder of Archigram, and a former director of the Institute of Contemporary Arts, London and professor of the Bartlett School of Architecture, University College London. He is a Commandeur de l'Ordre des Arts et des Lettres of the French Republic, and a Senior Fellow of the Royal College of Art. He has professorships at the Royal Academy of Art and the Hochschule fur Bildende Kunste (Städelschule), Frankfurt. In 2007, Cook was knighted for his services to architecture and teaching. He currently practices with Gavin Robotham as CRAB Studio.

Neil Denari is Principal of Neil M Denari Architects and a Professor in the Department of Architecture and Urban Design, University of California, Los Angeles. Among his many awards are the AIA Gold Medal 2011 and a Fellowship from the United States Artists organization in 2009. In 2012, NMDA completed HL23 in New York, and won first prize in the Keelung Harbour Service Building competition.

Hernan Diaz Alonso is principal and founder of the Los Angeles-based design practice, Xefirotarch. He was Distinguished Professor of Architecture and Graduate Thesis Coordinator at Southern California Institute of Architecture, before becoming Graduate Programs Chair in 2010. He has taught at Columbia University and the University of Applied Arts Vienna. Alonso was Louis I. Kahn Visiting Assistant Professor of Architectural Design, Yale University, 2010; Educator of the Year, American Institute of Architects, 2012; and Eero Saarinen Professor of Architectural Design, Yale, 2015. His work is in the

permanent collections of the Museum of Modern Art, New York; San Francisco Museum of Modern Art; Museum of Applied Arts, Vienna; and the Art Institute of Chicago.

Evan Douglis is Dean of the School of Architecture, Rensselaer Polytechnic Institute. Prior to this, he was Chair of the undergraduate department at the School of Architecture, Pratt Institute; Assistant Professor and Director of the Architecture Galleries, Columbia University; and visiting instructor at the Cooper Union. Douglis's awards include an NYFA fellowship, a 'Design Vanguard' profile by *Architectural Record*, the FEIDAD Design Merit Award, ACADIA Award for Emerging Digital Practice and a Presidential Citation from the Cooper Union.

Salomon Frausto is Head of Education at the Berlage Center for Advanced Studies in Architecture and Urban Design, Delft University of Technology. He coordinated the public and scholarly programmes of the Temple Hoyne Buell Center for the Study of American Architecture, Columbia University, 2001–7. Frausto was co-editor of *Architourism: Authentic, Exotic, Escapist, Spectacular* (2005) and editor of *The Berlage Survey of the Culture, Education and Practice of Architecture and Urbanism* (2011), produced to mark the Berlage's twentieth anniversary.

Mark Garcia is Senior Lecturer at the Department of Architecture and Landscape, University of Greenwich. He previously worked for Branson Coates Architecture and Skidmore, Owings & Merrill, and has held academic posts at St Antony's College, Oxford University, and the Department of Architecture, Royal College of Art, where he was Head of Research. He was guest-editor of the *AD* issues *Architextiles* (2006), *Patterns of Architecture* (2009) and *Future Details of Architecture* (2014) and editor of *The Diagrams of Architecture* (2010). He is currently researching the forthcoming book *Diagrams of Architecture II*.

Zaha Hadid, founder of Zaha Hadid Architects, is currently Professor at the University of Applied Arts Vienna, and Visiting Professor at Yale University. She completed her first building, the Vitra Fire Station, Germany, in 1993. Among her high-profile projects are the Aquatics Centre for the 2012 London Olympics; and the Guangzhou Opera House, China. Hadid won the RIBA Stirling Prize in 2010 and 2011, for the MAXXI National Museum of XXI Century Arts, Rome, and the Evelyn Grace Academy, London. In 2012, Hadid was made a Dame Commander of the Order of the British Empire.

Heneghan Peng Architects (Róisín Heneghan and Shih-Fu Peng) are designing the new building for the Department of Architecture and Landscape and Library, University of Greenwich. Both Heneghan and Peng teach, most recently at Yale University. The work of the practice was the subject of the Irish Pavilion at the 2012 Venice Biennale. Projects by the team were also selected for the 1999 Architectural League's Young Architects (New York) and shortlisted for the 2013 RIBA Stirling Prize.

Simon Herron is Academic Leader in Architecture at the Department of Architecture and Landscape, University of Greenwich. He is a tutor (with Susanne Isa) of Unit 16, formerly based at the Bartlett School of Architecture, University College London. He trained at the Architectural Association and the Städelschule. Frankfurt, and has lectured and taught at the University of Westminster, SCI-Arc and the AA. He was formerly a partner of Herron Associates, and is currently Principal Registrar of the Ron Herron Archive. Herron is a member of the AVATAR research group.

Susanne Isa is Year One Coordinator and Senior Admissions Tutor, and Postgraduate Design Studio Tutor of Unit 16, Department of Architecture and Landscape, University of Greenwich, which she formed in 1999 with Simon Herron at the Bartlett School of Architecture, University College London. She has also taught at the University of Westminster and SCI-Arc. She previously worked for Nicholas Grimshaw & Partners and Herron Associates. Built works include a collaboration with Allford Hall Monaghan Morris and Studio Myerscough for the British Council.

Perry Kulper is an architect and Associate Professor of Architecture at the University of Michigan. After receiving his M.Arch from Columbia University,

he worked in the offices of Eisenman/Robertson, Robert A. M. Stern and Venturi, Rauch & Scott Brown. Kulper taught at SCI-Arc for seventeen years, and held visiting teaching positions at the University of Pennsylvania and Arizona State University.

C. J. Lim is Professor of Architecture and Urbanism and Vice-Dean at the Bartlett School of Architecture, University College London, and is the founder of Studio 8 Architects, which designed the award-winning 'Smartcities' for the Chinese and Korean governments. Lim is the recipient of the Royal Academy's Grand Architecture Prize. His books include *Smartcities + Eco-Warriors* (2010), *Short Stories: London in Two-and-a-Half Dimensions* (2011) and *Food City* (2014).

Greg Lynn has taught in the Department of Architecture and Urban Design at the University of California, Los Angeles since 1996. His studio Greg Lynn FORM was an innovator in redefining the medium of design with digital technology and pioneered the fabrication and manufacture of complex functional and ergonomic forms using CNC machinery. Lynn's work is in the permanent collections of the Canadian Centre for Architecture; the Museum of Modern Art, New York; San Francisco Museum of Modern Art and the Museum of Contemporary Art Chicago.

Mark Morris teaches history, theory and design at the Department of Architecture, Cornell University, where he has served as Director of Graduate Studies and is now Thesis Coordinator. He studied architecture at Ohio State University and the London Consortium (University of London, Architectural Association, Tate Galleries and the Institute of Contemporary Arts). His essays have featured in *Domus*, *Critical Quarterly*, *Cabinet*, *Log* and *Frieze*. He is the author of *Models: Architecture and the Miniature* (2006) and *Automatic Architecture: Designs from the Fourth Dimension* (2006). Morris received an AIA medal for excellence in the study of architecture, and the RIBA Trust award.

Eric Owen Moss has been Director at SCI-Arc since 2002, having first taught at the school in 1974. He has held chairs at Yale and Harvard universities, and appointments at the University of Applied Arts Vienna and the Royal Danish Academy of Fine Arts. He received M.Arch from Harvard and the University of California, Berkeley, and founded Eric Owen Moss Architects in 1973. Moss was the recipient of the Arnold Brunner Memorial Prize, American Academy of Arts and Letters (2007) and the RIBA Jencks Award (2011).

Mohsen Mostafavi is Dean and Alexander and Victoria Wiley Professor of Design at the Harvard Graduate School of Design. He has taught at Cornell, Pennsylvania and Cambridge universities, and the Städelschule, Frankfurt. He is on the steering committee of the Aga Khan Award for Architecture and the board of the Van Alen Institute, and has served on the design committees of the London Development Agency and the RIBA Gold Medal. Publications include *Ecological Urbanism* (2010), *In the Life of Cities* (2012) and *Instigations: Engaging Architecture, Landscape and the City* (2012).

Ben Nicholson is Associate Professor at the School of the Art Institute of Chicago. He was educated at the Architectural Association, Cooper Union and Cranbrook, and has guest-taught at SCI-Arc and Edinburgh, Michigan, Houston and Cornell universities. He has exhibited at the Venice Biennale, Canadian Centre for Architecture and Whitney Museum of American Art. Publications include *Appliance House* (1990), *Thinking the Unthinkable House* (1997), *The World, Who Wants It?* (2002) and the forthcoming *Modern Architecture, Landscape, and Preservation in New Harmony*.

Hani Rashid, along with partner Lise Anne Couture, formed the architectural practice Asymptote in 1989. He has taught at numerous institutions, including Harvard Graduate School of Design, Princeton University and Columbia University. He is currently Director of the Studio_Hani Rashid M.Arch programme at the University of Applied Arts Vienna. In 2004, he co-represented the USA at the 9th Venice Biennale. Rashid is currently President and CEO of the Kiesler Foundation, Vienna.

Jesse Reiser received his B.Arch from the Cooper Union, and M.Arch from the Cranbrook Academy of Art. In 1985 he was appointed a fellow of the American Academy in Rome. He is currently a professor of architecture at Princeton University. Together with Nanako Umemoto, Reiser created RUR Architecture. In 2012, the duo received the USA Booth Fellowship for Architecture and Design from United States Artists.

Patrik Schumacher has been with Zaha Hadid Architects since 1988, where he is Company Director and Senior Designer. He has been a project partner on projects including the MAXXI National Museum of XXI Century Arts; the BMW Central Building; and the Guangzhou Opera House. He has taught at various schools in the US, UK and Europe, and is co-director of the Design Research Laboratory at the Architectural Association School of Architecture. He has co-taught postgraduate option studios with Hadid at the University of Illinois, Columbia University, Harvard Graduate School of Design and currently at the University of Applied Arts Vienna.

Bob Sheil is Director of the Bartlett School of Architecture, University College London, where he runs Unit 23 with Kate Davies and Emmanuel Vercruysse, and directs the Protoarchitecture Lab. Sheil is a founding partner of Sixteen*(Makers), whose experimental building (55/02) won a RIBA award in 2010. He has guest-edited three issues of *AD – Design Through Making* (2005); *Protoarchitecture* (2008); and *High Definition: Zero Tolerance in Design and Production* (2014) – and edited *55/02: A Sixteen*(Makers) Project Monograph* (2012). In 2011 he co-founded and co-chaired the Fabricate conference at UCL.

Michael Sorkin is Principal of Michael Sorkin Studio, and Distinguished Professor of Architecture and Director of the Graduate Program in Urban Design, City College of New York. He is founder of Terreform, a non-profit institution dedicated to research into sustainable urbanism, and the Institute for Urban Design. He has taught at the Academy of Fine Arts Vienna, the Cooper Union, Yale, Columbia, Pennsylvania and Harvard universities, SCI-Arc, Aarhus, and other schools. He has written and edited many books on architecture and urbanism, and is the architecture critic for *The Nation*. Sorkin is a Fellow of the American Academy of Arts and Sciences, and won a National Design Award in 2013.

Neil Spiller is Hawksmoor Chair of Architecture and Landscape and Deputy Pro Vice Chancellor at the University of Greenwich. Prior to this he was Vice Dean and Graduate Director of Design at the Bartlett School of Architecture, University College London. He has guest-edited several issues of *AD*, including *Architects in Cyberspace I* (1995) and *II* (1998), *Reflexive Architecture* (2002), *Protocell Architecture* (2010) and *Drawing Architecture* (2013). His books include *Digital Dreams: Architecture and the New Alchemic Technologies* (1998), *Cyberreader: Critical Writings of the Digital Era* (2002), *Visionary Architecture: Blueprints of the Modern Imagination* (2007) and *Digital Architecture Now* (2008).

Brett Steele is Director of the Architectural Association School of Architecture. Current projects include multi-year masterplans expanding the school's historic location in Bedford Square, London and rural campus in Hooke Park, Dorset. Since 2005, he has hired 150 new teachers from Europe, Asia and the Americas, who now teach at the London campus, alongside 100 teachers in the worldwide visiting school. Initiatives at the AA have included the launch of the Digital Prototyping Lab, full-time MSc and MPhil graduate courses, and a PhD by Design programme.

Wolfgang Tschapeller founded his architectural firm Wolfgang Tschapeller in 2007; a second office in Belgrade opened in 2012. Among his major projects are the University of Applied Arts Vienna; the BVA 1, 2 and 3 series; European Cultural Centre, Aachen; Centre for Promotion of Science, Belgrade; an administrative building for the municipal authority, Murau, Austria; and St Joseph House, Austria. Tschapeller has exhibited work at the Venice Biennale, and since 2012 has been the head of the Institute of Art and Architecture, Academy of Fine Arts Vienna.

Nanako Umemoto graduated from the Cooper Union, following studies at the School of Urban Design, Osaka University of Art. She has lectured and taught at various institutions throughout the US,

Europe and Asia, and is currently a Visiting Professor at the University of Pennsylvania. She is a partner, with Jesse Reiser, in the firm RUR Architecture.

Anthony Vidler is a critic and historian of modern architecture. He graduated from Cambridge University, and received his PhD from the Technical University of Delft. He was Professor and Chair of the Doctoral Program at the School of Architecture, Princeton University (1965–92), Chair of the Art History Department, UCLA (1993–2001), and Dean of the School of Architecture, Cooper Union (2001–13). During 2013–14, he was Visiting Professor of Humanities and Art and Architectural History, Brown University. Among Vidler's many publications include *Histories of the Immediate Present* (2008), *James Frazer Stirling* (2010) and *The Scenes of the Street* (2011).

Ed Wall is a landscape architect, and the Academic Leader for Landscape at the Department of Architecture and Landscape, University of Greenwich. Wall has written articles for *Landscape* and *Topos*, and co-authored, with Tim Waterman, *Basics Landscape Architecture: Urban Design* (2009). He is the founding director of Project Studio, a platform for design and research collaborations. Since 2008 Wall has been a Visiting Professor at the Polytechnic University of Milan.

Mark Wigley is the Dean of the Graduate School of Architecture, Planning and Preservation, Columbia University. He is the author of *The Architecture of Deconstruction: Derrida's Haunt* (1993); *White Walls, Designer Dresses: The Fashioning of Modern Architecture* (1995); and *Constant's New Babylon: The Hyper-Architecture of Desire* (1998), and co-edited *The Activist Drawing: Retracing Situationist Architectures from Constant's New Babylon to Beyond* (2001). He has curated exhibitions at the Museum of Modern Art, New York, the Canadian Centre for Architecture and the Witte de With Museum, Rotterdam. Wigley received both his B.Arch (1979) and his PhD (1987) from the University of Auckland, New Zealand.

Peter L. Wilson is partner at Bolles + Wilson, established in 1980 with partner Julia Bolles-Wilson.

He served as a unit master at the Architectural Association (1978-88) and guest professor at the Accademia di Architettura di Mendrisio (2006-9). Current projects include the City Library, Münster; Luxor Theatre, Rotterdam; Suzuki House, Tokyo; and the National Library, Luxembourg. In 2013 Bolles + Wilson was awarded the Australian Institute of Architects Gold Medal.

Li Xiaodong is a practising architect, educator and researcher. He is a graduate of Tsinghua University, and received his PhD from Delft University of Technology. Among his many awards are the AR Award for Emerging Architecture (2009) and the Aga Khan Award for Architecture (2010). He received the tutor's prize from RIBA (2000) and Society of American Registered Architects (2001), and in 2012 was awarded an AIA Honorary Fellowship. Xiaodong is currently Chair Professor of the School of Architecture, Tsinghua University.

Kongjian Yu received his PhD from Harvard Graduate School of Design, where he is currently a Visiting Professor. He is the founder and Dean of the School of Landscape Architecture, College of Architecture and Landscape Architecture, Peking University. The work of his landscape architecture and urbanism firm Turenscape has won numerous international awards, and was the subject of *Designed Ecologies: The Landscape Architecture of Kongjian Yu* (2012). Yu served on the Master Jury for the Aga Kahn Architecture Award in 2010, and the Super Jury for the 2011 World Architecture Festival.

Reiner Zettl is an art historian, and Associate Professor at the University of Applied Arts and the Academy of Fine Arts Vienna. He was co-curator of the *Design Now: Austria* exhibition (1998-2002), and curator of *Rock Over Barock: 7+2 Young and Beautiful*, Kunsthaus Mürzzuschlag (2004) and *Stadt = Form Raum Netz*, Austrian Pavilion, Venice Biennale (2006).

DIRECTORY

Mike Aling | pp. 67–72
Department of Architecture and Landscape,
University of Greenwich
Old Royal Naval College, Park Row, London SE10 9LS, UK
gre.ac.uk

Will Alsop | pp. 321–5
ALL Design
33 Parkgate Road, London SW11 4NP, UK
9–10 St Andrew's Square, Edinburgh EH2 2AF, UK
14/05 Creative Concept Building, 388 Xinhua Road,
Yu Zhong District, Chongqing 400010, China
all-worldwide.com

Klaus Bollinger | pp. 281–7
Institute of Architecture, University of Applied Arts Vienna,
Oskar Kokoschka Platz 2, 1010 Vienna, Austria
dieangewandte.at
bollinger-grohmann.com

Mark Burry | pp. 326–35
Spatial Information Architecture Laboratory,
RMIT University, GPO Box 2476,
Melbourne, Victoria 3001, Australia
sial.rmit.edu.au

Nic Clear | pp. 60–6, 92–101, 102–8
Department of Architecture and Landscape,
University of Greenwich
Old Royal Naval College, Park Row, London SE10 9LS, UK
gre.ac.uk

Nigel Coates | pp. 154–65
Royal College of Art (Professor Emeritus)
Kensington Gore, London SW7 2EU
rca.ac.uk
nigelcoates.com

Sir Peter Cook | pp. 22–31
Bartlett School of Architecture, University College London
Gower Street, London WC1E 6BT, UK
bartlett.ucl.ac.uk
CRAB Studio
50a Rosebery Avenue, London EC1R 4RP, UK
crab-studio.com

Neil Denari | pp. 242–7
Department of Architecture and Urban Design,
University of California, Los Angeles
1317 Perloff Hall, Box 951467,
Los Angeles, California 90095, USA
aud.ucla.edu
denari.co

Hernan Diaz Alonso | pp. 264–70
Southern California Institute of Architecture
960 East 3rd Street, Los Angeles, California 90013, USA
sciarc.edu
xefirotarch.com

Evan Douglis | pp. 183–9
Rensselaer Polytechnic Institute
110 8th Street, Troy, New York 12180, USA
rpi.edu
evandouglis.com

Salomon Frausto | pp. 271–80
Berlage Center for Advanced Studies in Architecture
and Urban Design, Delft University of Technology
Julianalaan 134, 2628 Delft, Netherlands
theberlage.nl

Mark Garcia | pp. 67–72
Department of Architecture and Landscape,
University of Greenwich
Old Royal Naval College, Park Row, London SE10 9LS, UK
gre.ac.uk

Zaha Hadid | pp. 295–300
Zaha Hadid Architects
10 Bowling Green Lane, London EC1R 0BQ, UK
zaha-hadid.com

Heneghan Peng Architects | pp. 73–7
Róisín Heneghan and Shih-Fu Peng
14-16 Lord Edward Street, Dublin 2, Ireland
Waldemarstraße 37a, 10999 Berlin, Germany
hparc.com

Simon Herron | pp. 109–20, 121–7
Department of Architecture and Landscape,
University of Greenwich
Old Royal Naval College, Park Row, London SE10 9LS, UK
gre.ac.uk

Susanne Isa | pp. 121–7
Department of Architecture and Landscape,
University of Greenwich
Old Royal Naval College, Park Row, London SE10 9LS, UK
gre.ac.uk

Perry Kulper | pp. 205–11
Taubman College, University of Michigan,
2000 Bonisteel Boulevard, Ann Arbor, Michigan 48109, USA
taubmancollege.umich.edu

C. J. Lim | pp. 145–53
Bartlett School of Architecture, University College London,
Gower Street, London WC1E 6BT, UK
bartlett.ucl.ac.uk
cjlim-studio8.com

Greg Lynn | pp. 248–55
Department of Architecture and Urban Design,
University of California, Los Angeles
1317 Perloff Hall, Box 951467,
Los Angeles, California 90095, USA
aud.ucla.edu
glform.com

Mark Morris | pp. 166–76
Department of Architecture, Art and Planning,
Cornell University
155 East Sibley Hall, Ithaca, New York 14850, USA
aap.cornell.edu

Eric Owen Moss | pp. 256–63
Southern California Institute of Architecture
960 East 3rd Street, Los Angeles, California 90013, USA
sciarc.edu
ericowenmoss.com

Mohsen Mostafavi | pp. 190–9
Graduate School of Design, Harvard University
48 Quincy Street, Cambridge, Massachusetts 02138, USA
gsd.harvard.edu

Ben Nicholson | pp. 236–41
School of the Art Institute of Chicago
36 S. Wabash Avenue, Chicago, Illinois 60603, USA
saic.edu

OMA | pp. 177–82, 200–4
Headquarters: Heer Bokelweg 149, 3032 Rotterdam,
Netherlands (with offices in China, USA and Qatar)
oma.com

Hani Rashid | pp. 288–94
Institute of Architecture, University of Applied Arts Vienna,
Oskar Kokoschka Platz 2, 1010 Vienna, Austria
dieangewandte.at
asymptote.net

Jesse Reiser | pp. 212–19
Reiser + Umemoto/RUR Architecture
118 East 59th Street, #402, New York, New York 10022, USA
reiser-umemoto.com

Patrik Schumacher | pp. 295–300
Zaha Hadid Architects
10 Bowling Green Lane, London EC1R 0BQ, UK
zaha-hadid.com

Bob Sheil | pp. 138–44
Bartlett School of Architecture, University College London
Gower Street, London WC1E 6BT, UK
bartlett.ucl.ac.uk

Michael Sorkin | pp. 32–9
City College of New York
160 Convent Avenue, New York, New York 10031, USA
sorkinstudio.com

Neil Spiller | pp. 10–21, 78–85, 86–91
Department of Architecture and Landscape,
University of Greenwich
Old Royal Naval College, Park Row, London SE10 9LS, UK
gre.ac.uk
neilspiller.com

Brett Steele | pp. 50–9
School of Architecture, Architectural Association
36 Bedford Square, London WC1B 3ES, UK
brettsteele.net

Wolfgang Tschapeller | pp. 301–6
University of Applied Arts Vienna, Institute of Architecture
Oskar Kokoschka Platz 2, 1010 Vienna, Austria
dieangewandte.at
tschapeller.com

Nanako Umemoto | pp. 212–19
Reiser + Umemoto/RUR Architecture
118 East 59th Street, #402, New York, New York 10022, USA
reiser-umemoto.com

Anthony Vidler | pp. 227–35
Cooper Union
30 Cooper Square, New York, New York 10003, USA
cooper.edu

Ed Wall | pp. 128–37
Department of Architecture and Landscape,
University of Greenwich
Old Royal Naval College, Park Row, London SE10 9LS, UK
gre.ac.uk
onehundredprojects.com

Mark Wigley | pp. 220–6
Graduate School of Architecture, Planning and
Preservation, Columbia University
1172 Amsterdam Avenue, New York, New York 10027, USA
arch.columbia.edu

Peter L. Wilson | pp. 40–9
Bolles + Wilson
Hafenweg 16, 48155 Münster, Germany
bolles-wilson.com

Li Xiaodong | pp. 315–20
School of Architecture, Tsinghua University
Beijing 100084, China
arch.tsinghua.edu.cn
lixiaodong.net

Kongjian Yu | pp. 307–14
Peking University
No. 5 Yiheyuan Road, Haidian District,
Beijing 100871, China
pku.edu.cn
turenscape.com

Reiner Zettl | pp. 281–7
Institute of Architecture, University of Applied Arts Vienna,
Oskar Kokoschka Platz 2, 1010 Vienna, Austria
dieangewandte.at
bollinger-grohmann.com

PICTURE CREDITS

11 Krisztian Csémy, Jasmina Frincic, Jakub Klaska and Studio Hadid Vienna; 16, 17 Tobias Titz; 18 Qing Wen Li/courtesy of SCI-Arc; 25, 26, 29 Peter Cook; 30 CRAB Studio: Peter Cook and Gavin Robotham; 41 © Ban Shubber and Architectural Association, School of Architecture; 42 © Nigel Westbrook and Architectural Association, School of Architecture; 43 © Kathryn Findlay and Architectural Association, School of Architecture; 44 © Jee Seng Heng and Architectural Association, School of Architecture; 47 © Mark Prizeman and Architectural Association, School of Architecture; 48 © Peter St John and Architectural Association, School of Architecture; 51 (top) © Oliver Pershav and Architectural Association, School of Architecture; 51 (bottom left) © William Gowland and Architectural Association, School of Architecture; 51 (bottom right) © Soonil Kim and Architectural Association, School of Architecture; 55 (left) © Antoine Vaxelaire and Architectural Association, School of Architecture; 55 (right) © Chris Johnson and Architectural Association, School of Architecture; 56 © Yvonne Weng and Architectural Association, School of Architecture; 61 Petya Nikolova, University of Greenwich; 63 (top) Daniel Meredith, University of Greenwich; 63 (bottom) Georg Arnoudov, University of Greenwich; 64 Razna Begum, University of Greenwich; 65 Prince Yemoh, University of Greenwich; 66 (left) Mohammed Abd Rahman, University of Greenwich; 66 (right) William Lamburn, University of Greenwich; 69, 70, 72 Mike Aling and Mark Garcia; 75-7 © Heneghan Peng Architects; 87 Christopher McCurtin, Mount Analogue, Unit 19/AVATAR, School of Architecture, Design and Construction, University of Greenwich, London, 2012-13; 88 Neal Tanna; 90, 91 William Lamburn; 93 Jonathan Gales; 95 Vipin Dhunnoo; 96, 107 (bottom) Chris Kelly; 98 Kibwe Tavares; 104 (top) Rich Bevan; 104 (bottom) Paul Nicholls, Factory Fifteen; 105 Dan Farmer; 111 (left) NASA; 111 (right), 112 (middle and bottom), 115, 116 Susanne Isa; 119, 125 (top) Joerg Majer; 122 (top), 124 Adam Bell; 122 (bottom) Adis Dobardzic; 125 (bottom left), 125 (bottom right) Kevin Yu Bai; 126 (top left) Sarah Primarolo; 126 (top right) Meor Haris Kamarul Bahrin; 126 (bottom) Mike Dean; 127 Luke Chandresinghe; 129 Courtesy of Guy Nordenson and Associates, Catherine Seavitt Studio and Architecture Research Office; 130-1 © Imray Laurie Norie & Wilson Ltd; 132 © Greater London Authority; 134 West 8 Urban Design & Landscape Architecture; 135 Project Studio with Ed Wall and Aaron Carpenter; 136 Project Studio with Ed Wall, Joe Sanders and Harry Bix; 139 Emma-Kate Matthews; 140 (top) Maria Knutsson-Hall; 140 (middle and bottom) Misha Smith; 142 © Tom Svilians; 143 (middle) Tamsin Hanke, 2013; 143 (bottom) © Ollie Palmer, 2011; 144, 150, 151 Ned Scott; 148, 149 Martin Tang; 147 C. J. Lim; 152 (left) Steven McCloy; 152 (right), 153 Thandi Loewenson; 157-9, 163 courtesy Nigel Coates Archive;

161 (top) Nicola Koller; 161 (bottom) Tomas Klassnik; 162 Mark Prizeman; 164-5 courtesy of Haiwei Xie; 166-76 courtesy of Dino Paxenos / Modern50.com; 179, 180, 201-4 Philippe Ruault; 184, 189 Evan Douglis Studio; 187 Michael Moran/OTTO; 191 (top) J. Arthur Liu; 191 (bottom) J. Arthur Liu; 192 (top) Yarinda Bunnag and Mark Rukamathu; 192 (bottom) James Leng; 195 (top) Nicholas Potts and Peter Zuroweste; 195 (bottom) Jeremy Roc Jih; 206 (top) Paul Holmquist; 206 (bottom) Brian Foster; 209 (top) You Ling Lim; 209 (middle) Sen Liu; 209 (bottom) Vittorio Lovato; 210 Chi Song; 211 Perry Kulper; 213 Reiser and Unemoto; 214 (top and bottom) Reiser and Unemoto/RUR Architecture; 221 Joseph Brennan/GSAPP; 222 (top) Pablo Costa Fraiz and Matt Miller/GSAPP; 222 (bottom) Jiaqi Xu, Jiayuan Liu, Chen Zheng and Cesar J. Langa/GSAPP; 223 Shih-Ning Chou/GSAPP; 224 (top) Ray Wang/GSAPP; 224 (bottom) Yvonne-Demitra Konstantinidis/GSAPP; 225 Geoff Bell and Rong Zhao/GSAPP; 226 Margarita Calero and Alfonso Simelio/GSAPP; 228-34 courtesy The Irwin S. Chanin School of Architecture Archive, The Cooper Union; photos: Pat McElnea; 237, 239 Ben Nicholson; 240 Kristina Alford; 241 (top) Erin Pellegrino; 241 (bottom) Emily Wright; 245 Fuk Man Mui; 246 (top) James Janke; 246 (bottom) Lillian Zeinalzadegan, Yuichi Tada; 247 Yuna Kubota; 249, 253 Sarah Hearne; 250 Celene Lehrer; 251 Hongkai Li; 255 David Stamatis; 257 Dale Strong/courtesy of SCI-Arc; 258 (top) Ashley Shoulder/courtesy of SCI-Arc; 258 (bottom) Ben Warwas/courtesy of SCI-Arc; 261 (top) Stefano Passeri and Johannes Beck/courtesy of SCI-Arc; 261 (middle) Robbie Crabtree and Byungmo Kang/courtesy of SCI-Arc; 261 (bottom) Xiaofeng Mei/courtesy of SCI-Arc; 262 (top) Jiarui Liu/courtesy of SCI/Arc; 262 (bottom) Daniel Karas/courtesy of SCI/Arc; 263 (top) Sara Gaskari/courtesy of SCI/Arc; 263 (bottom) Kyle von Hasseln and Elizabeth von Hasseln/courtesy of SCI/Arc; 272-80 TU Delft/The Berlage Archive; 282 (top) Sebastian Kaus; 282 (middle) Sim Tuksam; 282 (bottom), 283 Martina Lesjak; 289 (bottom) © 2013 Christoph Pehnelt/Urban Extraction; 290 (top) Stefan Ritzer, Daniel Prost; 290 (middle) Kyle Branchesi, Abraham Fung, Hulda Gudjonsdottir; 290 (bottom) © Ralph S. Steenblik 2012; 292 (left), 293 Reiner Zettl; 292 (right) Ursula Trost; 294 Sille Pihlak; 296 Simon Aglas, Lorenz Krisai, Stephan Ritzer and Studio Hadid Vienna; 298 Christoph Hermann and Studio Hadid Vienna; 299 Gilles Greis, Nicolay Ivanov, Irina-Elena Preda and Studio Hadid Vienna; 300 Martine Nicolay, Birgit Schmidt and Studio Hadid Vienna; 302-6 © 2013 Wolfgang Tschapeller ZT GmBH; 308-14 Kogjian Yu; 322-5 2004 © Richard Johnson; 327 courtesy RMIT Gallery, photo: Mark Ashkanasy 2013; 328, 329 John Gollings; 330-3 Prof. Mark Burry, RMIT University, Melbourne, Australia; 334 Chin Koi Khoo